JERUSALEM
—— DC ——
{DAVID'S CAPITAL}

#1 *NEW YORK TIMES* BESTSELLING AUTHOR

MIKE EVANS

JERUSALEM
—— DC ——

{DAVID'S CAPITAL}

TimeWorthy
BOOKS

P.O. Box 30000, Phoenix, AZ 85046

This book is dedicated to
Governor Mike Huckabee,

my dear friend, lover of Jerusalem
and the Jewish people.

PREFACE

n 1967, Jerusalem changed dramatically from a divided city barred from applauding its Jewish heritage to a reunited city whose inhabitants were joyfully remembering its past and reveling in its future.

Jerusalem! The very name evokes a stirring in the heart and soul. It has been called by many names: City of God; City of David; Zion, the City of the Great King; Ariel (Lion of God); Moriah (chosen of the Lord), but only one name has resonated down through the centuries— Jerusalem! David's capital!

A world map drawn in 1581 has Jerusalem at its very center with what were the then-known continents of the world surrounding it. It resembles a ship's propeller with the shaft in the center being Jerusalem. Another analogy is of Jerusalem as the navel of the earth. Why? According to Midrash Tanchuma, *Qedoshim*:

> As the navel is set in the centre of the human body, so is the land of Israel the navel of the world. . . situated in the centre of the world, and Jerusalem in the centre

of the land of Israel, and the sanctuary in the centre of Jerusalem, and the holy place in the centre of the sanctuary, and the ark in the centre of the holy place, and the foundation stone before the holy place, because from it the world was founded.[1]

Jerusalem's history can be summed up in one word—*troubled*. Lying as she does between the rival empires of Egypt to the west and south, and Syria to the north and east, both striving for dominance in the region, Israel has been repeatedly trampled by opposing armies. It has been conquered at various times by the Canaanites, Jebusites, Babylonians, Assyrians, Persians, Romans, Byzantines, Arabs, Crusaders, Ottomans, and most recently the British. While its origins are shrouded in the hazy mists of antiquity, archaeological evidence of human habitation goes back some four thousand years. Jerusalem is first mentioned in the Bible in Joshua 10:1. We read there that Adoni-Zedek was the king of Jerusalem and fought unsuccessfully against Joshua.

The Israelites first occupied Jerusalem during the days of the Judges (see Judges 1:21) but did not completely inhabit the city until 1049 BC when David wrested it from the Jebusites and declared it the capital city of the Jewish people.

In *Jerusalem, Sacred City of Mankind*, Teddy Kollek and Moshe Pearlman wrote:

The spiritual attachment of the Jews to Jerusalem has remained unbroken; it is a unique attachment. Should one doubt that statement, he would have to look long and hard to find another relationship in history where a people, even in captivity, remained so passionately attached to a city for 3,000 years.[2]

When the Jews were driven from their land at various times, wherever they found themselves in exile, they faced toward Jerusalem when praying. After Nebuchadnezzar signed a decree making it illegal to pray to anyone except him, Daniel 6:10 records:

> Now when Daniel learned that the decree had been published, he went home to his upstairs room where the windows opened toward Jerusalem. Three times a day he got down on his knees and prayed, giving thanks to his God, just as he had done before.

Historically, Jewish synagogues faced Jerusalem. When a Jew built a house, part of a wall was left unfinished symbolizing that it was only a temporary dwelling—until he could return to his permanent home, Jerusalem. Even today the traditional smashing of a glass during a wedding ceremony has its roots in the temple in Jerusalem. This act of remembering the loss of the center of Jewish festivities during the marriage feast calls Jerusalem "my highest joy" (Psalm 137:6).

When compared with the great cities of the world, Jerusalem is small. She stands alongside no great river as do London, Paris, and Rome, boasts no port, no major industries, no mineral wealth or even an adequate water supply. The city stands along no major thoroughfare connecting it to the rest of the world. Why, then, is Jerusalem the navel of the earth, the shaft that propels the world ever forward?

The answer can be found in its spiritual significance. Jerusalem is the home of two of the world's monotheistic faiths—Judaism and Christianity—and is claimed by a third—Islam. Biblical prophets decreed that from Jerusalem the Word of the Lord would go out to the world—a Word that when embraced would change the moral standards of all mankind.

The spiritual stature of Jerusalem is echoed in its physical location; it sits upon the Judean hills high above the surrounding countryside. Traveling to Jerusalem is always spoken of as "going up to Jerusalem." Those who leave the City of God are said to "go down"—in perhaps more than just the physical sense.

For the Jewish people whose cry for centuries has been, "Next year, Jerusalem," it is more than a spot on a map; it is not just a tourist Mecca where one can visit various holy sites; Jerusalem *is* the Holy City. It is the essence of all for which the Jews have hoped and prayed and cried and died. It is their God-given land:

The Lord had said to David and to his son Solomon, "In this temple and in Jerusalem, which I have chosen out of all the tribes of Israel, I will put my Name forever." (2 Kings 21:7)

Jerusalem is the *only* city God claims as His own; it is called the City of God and the Holy City in Scripture.

CHAPTER
1

You will arise and have mercy on Jerusalem—
and now is the time to pity her,
now is the time you promised to help.
For your people love every stone in her walls
and cherish even the dust in her streets.

PSALM 102:13–14 NLT

When standing on the Mount of Olives, the sweeping panorama of Jerusalem is breathtaking. The multi-towered landscape is a splendid drama written in stone, one that has received rave reviews from countless pilgrims to the Holy Land.

Seen from atop the mount are landmarks such as the ancient ruins of the City of David, the gilded cupola on the *Haram esh-Sharif*, the Dome of the Rock, and the Kidron Valley where tombstones dot the hillside beneath the crenellated walls of the ancient city. These massive stone walls with their battlements intact have proudly surveyed the sieges of countless invading armies. The parapets of these walls once sheltered archers; today, soldiers patrol them with automatic rifles.

The Olivet view entices pilgrims to descend into Jerusalem, a city of stones, and to visit the Old City with its Jewish Quarter. Stones and more stones. The building blocks are also known as Jerusalem stone—usually meaning sedimentary limestone, dolomite, and dolomitic limestone quarried from beneath the hills and mountains of Israel. As the traveler wanders through the tangled labyrinth of narrow alleyways, one can almost touch the stone walls on either side. There are stone arches above and paving stones beneath. From ancient ruins to the medieval ramparts, these streets and walls that have baked in the warmth of a million sunrises each have a story to tell.

Those most beloved by the people of Israel are the stones that rise to form the Western Wall, the holiest shrine of the Jewish faith. The fifty-foot-high wall is all that remains of the Temple Mount as it existed in the first century. The stones stacked one upon another to build this wall are so massive that it's hard to imagine how they were chiseled out and transported up the hills of Jerusalem to the sacred site.

To grasp the perspective, it is helpful to look backward across the centuries and then follow the events that have led to today's impasse in the City of David. Consider the view from the temple when the stones were newly hewn and the city of Jerusalem shone like alabaster in the morning sun. Herod the Great began rebuilding Solomon's temple in 20 BC; the project occupied the remainder of his reign.

While the fifteen-story-high temple was constructed during Herod's administration, the outer courts and walls were not fully completed until AD 64, some sixty-eight years after his death.

One day, after Jesus had been teaching in the temple precincts, He called His disciples' attention to the buildings:

> "Do you see all these things?" he asked. "Truly I tell you, not one stone here will be left on another; every one will be thrown down." (Matthew 24:2)

The words of Jesus were precisely fulfilled in AD 70 when Roman armies swept through Jerusalem and reduced Herod's magnificent temple to a pile of blackened rubble. The stones of the temple are buried in antiquity, somewhere deep beneath the Old City.

The remaining stones of the Western Wall have become a symbol of the enduring hope of the Jewish people. Even nonpracticing Jews venerate the Wall as a national monument. The plaza in front of the Western Wall can accommodate 100,000 congregants. It is the gathering place of the people of Israel, the scene of both joyous celebration and solemn memorial. For a city that has been completely destroyed twice, occupied by enemies twenty-three times, surrounded fifty-two times, and liberated forty-four times, the Wall remains a testimony of God's all-encompassing providence.

The walls of Jerusalem summon pilgrims to return again and again to that eternal city. They speak to the soul and hum with the sound of ancient songs in a minor key—songs of anguish and suffering—songs of "Rachel weeping for her children and refusing to be comforted, because they are no more." (Jeremiah 31:15)

The Western Wall is also known by some as the Wailing Wall. Worshipers who have gone there to pray over the centuries have washed those stones with rivers of tears—tears of mourning, tears of joy, tears of intercession. Visible in the cracks and crevices between the huge stones are tiny pieces of paper, crinkled and wedged in the nooks and crannies of the Wall. It is tradition to write a prayer on a slip of paper and place it among the stones. It has become a place of prayer for peoples of all nations. Once each month, caretakers of the Western Wall carefully remove the scraps of paper and ceremonially bury them.

Stand in front of those hulking stones and a spiritual connection is made with the other worshipers offering their prayers and praises to God. Reach out and touch the ancient weathered boulders. Listen to the distant sounds of the *muezzin,* the Muslim crier that heralds the Islamic call to prayer from atop Mount Moriah; it is also a reminder of the many Jews killed for daring to stand beside the Western Wall to pray to *Yahweh.* It has long been a silent witness to the sufferings of God's chosen people. If only those ancient weathered rocks could speak!

Tellingly, the very fact that the Jewish people and the nation of Israel exist today is a miracle. No other group of people has been so systematically targeted for destruction. In earlier times most Jews were exiled from their homeland, and even then were hunted and humiliated, menaced and massacred by the millions. The Jews as a people would surely not have survived were it not that the sovereign Lord of the universe had ordained their preservation.

The nations that ransacked, burned, and leveled Jerusalem while trying to annihilate the Jewish people are rife with devastation. We have only to examine history to ascertain that the remnants of those once-great empires are now only dust and ashes. Numerous nations have come against Israel from the beginning of her existence. Yet, like the Phoenix, she has risen from the ashes each time. Nebuchadnezzar conquered Jerusalem in 586 BC and was doomed to live as a beast of the field for seven terrifying years. He was restored to sanity only after he had recognized the God of the Israelites.[3] His kingdom of Babylon was conquered by Cyrus the Great.

In 332 BC, Alexander the Great captured Jerusalem. His empire fragmented after his death; the followers of Ptolemy in Egypt and then the Seleucids of Syria later ruled over Jerusalem. The Jews, horrified by the desecration of the temple under the Seleucid ruler Antiochus IV staged a revolt and regained independence under the Hasmonean dynasty. The dynasty flourished for one hundred years until Pompey established Roman rule in the city. The Holy Roman Empire collapsed after destroying the temple and leveling Jerusalem.

The British, who ruled over Palestine and Jerusalem following World War I, then boasted that the sun never set on the British Empire. Indeed, one-fifth of the world's population was under its rule. However, after turning away Jews seeking asylum in both Britain and Palestine as they fled Hitler's gas chambers, and after arming Arabs to fight against Jews in the Holy Land, the empire quickly began to disintegrate. Great Britain today is comprised of just fourteen territories, consisting of a number of islands. Gone are the days when the empire stretched from India to Canada and from Australia to Africa.

Jerusalem, however, continues to stand as a testimony to the determination and courage of the Jewish people. That God has ordained the preservation of his chosen people is written throughout the pages of the Scripture.

It was first noted in His covenant with Abraham:

> The LORD had said to Abram, "Go from your country, your people and your father's household to the land I will show you. I will make you into a great nation, and I will bless you; I will make your name great, and you will be a blessing. I will bless those who bless you, and whoever curses you I will curse; and all peoples on earth will be blessed through you." (Genesis 12:1–3)

In addition to the covenant, the Lord gave Abraham and his descendants, Isaac and Jacob, the title deed to the land of Israel.

He declared that it would perpetually be in their possession. In Genesis God again spoke:

> On the same day the LORD made a covenant with Abram, saying: "To your descendants I have given this land, from the river of Egypt to the great river, the River Euphrates—the Kenites, the Kenezzites, the Kadmonites, the Hittites, the Perizzites, the Rephaim, the Amorites, the Canaanites, the Girgashites, and the Jebusites." (Genesis 15:18–21 NKJV)

In secular terms, this would be called a royal land grant. This type of grant, common in antiquity, was always perpetual and unconditional. The king or sovereign granted parcels of his land to loyal subjects as reward for faithful service. In biblical terms, however, God is sovereign over all the earth—He created it, and there is no greater right of ownership than that—so the land is inarguably His to bequeath as He wishes.

Years after He made his original covenant with Abraham, God confirmed it. Abraham accepted the terms of the covenant by the right of circumcision:

> "As for Me, behold, My covenant is with you, and you shall be a father of many nations. No longer shall your name be called Abram, but your name shall be Abraham;

for I have made you a father of many nations. I will make you exceedingly fruitful; and I will make nations of you, and kings shall come from you. And I will establish My covenant between Me and you and your descendants after you in their generations, for an everlasting covenant, to be God to you and your descendants after you. Also I give to you and your descendants after you the land in which you are a stranger, all the land of Canaan, as an everlasting possession; and I will be their God." And God said to Abraham: "As for you, you shall keep My covenant, you and your descendants after you throughout their generations. This is My covenant which you shall keep, between Me and you and your descendants after you: Every male child among you shall be circumcised."
(Genesis 17:4–10 NKJV)

As we have seen, this covenant with Abraham has no pre-conditions or expiration date. It was given as an everlasting possession to Abraham and his descendants. Only mankind is capable of impeding the fulfillment of the contract through disobedience, but the pact can never be rescinded. Moses declared:

God is not human, that he should lie, not a human being, that he should change his mind. Does he speak and then not act? Does he promise and not fulfill? (Numbers 23:19)

To avoid any confusion or equivocation, God reconfirmed the covenant with Abraham's son, Isaac:

> For to you and your descendants I will give all these lands and will confirm the oath I swore to your father Abraham. I will make your descendants as numerous as the stars in the sky and will give them all these lands, and through your offspring all nations on earth will be blessed. (Genesis 26:3–4)

Neither did God leave out Abraham's grandson Jacob nor the generations that followed. He declared:

> I am the LORD, the God of your father Abraham and the God of Isaac. I will give you and your descendants the land on which you are lying. Your descendants will be like the dust of the earth, and you will spread out to the west and to the east, to the north and to the south. All peoples on earth will be blessed through you and your offspring. I am with you and will watch over you wherever you go, and I will bring you back to this land. I will not leave you until I have done what I have promised you. (Genesis 28:13–16)

Of what value is this ancient covenant between God and Abraham today? God remains sovereign over the land He bestowed upon Abraham and his offspring. He has never vacated the title deed nor, as some mistakenly believe, has He rescinded His covenant declaration. The land still belongs to Abraham, Isaac, Jacob, and their descendants—as numerous as the sands of the sea.

Today, the place where God made and confirmed this covenant lies in an area north of Jerusalem between Bethel and Ai. It is in the heart of the West Bank (actually Judea and Samaria) on land the United Nations has inaccurately decreed Israel occupies illegally. World leaders continue to demand that Israel forego this area for the sake of an ever-elusive peace.

In summation, the Jewish people have a God-given inalienable right to possess the land of Israel. Many have the mistaken idea that an inalienable right is one that cannot be taken from you. In reality, it means just the opposite: It is one that cannot be given away, sold, surrendered, or legally transferred to another.

The all-time bestselling book—the Bible—confirms it. Since it is an inalienable right, this means Israel's leaders do not have the authority to give away her land or convey the property to another party. The children of Israel were forbidden to sell the land permanently, even to another Jew. God instructed, "The land must not be sold permanently, because the land is mine and you reside in my land as foreigners and strangers." (Leviticus 25:23)

Giving away any of the land violates the covenant God made with Abraham, Isaac, and Jacob and places the nation of Israel outside God's covenant blessings. Likewise, the nations that are coercing Israel into giving up the land come under the curse of God.

God's sovereignty over the land of Israel extends in a special way to the city of Jerusalem. It is the only city He has ever claimed as His own. In the Scriptures it is called "the City of God" and the "Holy City." For that reason alone, Christians should be concerned about the fate of Jerusalem. If Jerusalem is dear to God's heart, it should be dear to the hearts of every Bible believer.

CHAPTER

2

Jerusalem is where he lives; Mount Zion is his home.

PSALM 76:2 NLT

In order to look forward, we must first walk back through the pages of Jerusalem's history. The city seems always to have been exceptional—almost an oddity. Back in Joshua's time, when the Israelites were battling to take the land of Canaan from its previous inhabitants and conquered Jerusalem, its name was omitted from the review of Joshua's conquests. We see later in Joshua 15:63 that the tribe of Judah was unable to rid the village of the Jebusites who controlled it. Things remained that way until roughly four hundred years later.

After King Saul's death on Mount Gilboa, David ceased to be a fugitive running for his life. When he became king something important happened: God instructed David to establish his headquarters in Hebron in the midst of his own tribe. Abner ruled over the northern tribes after Saul's death, but after his murder, the elders of Israel made a pact with David and anointed him their king. The prophet Samuel's words had come to pass, and the nation of Israel was reunited under David's leadership.

Now David needed a city from which to rule a united Israel. Jerusalem was ideally located. It stood on the border between the northern tribes and Judah and, more importantly, had never been associated with any specific tribe of Israel. It would be the capital of all the tribes and a center for the worship of *Yahweh*, to whom David was deeply devoted.

After determining that this would be the seat of government, David and his men marched to Jerusalem. The Jebusites refused to take David's challenge seriously. They had successfully held the Israelites at bay from their high perch before; why should things be different this time? David, however, succeeded where others had failed. He used a water channel to get inside the Jebusite fortifications surrounding Jerusalem. In short order, he took the city and began to consolidate his people from the new capital.

Hiram, king of Tyre, sent men and material to assist David in building a palace. David saw it all as God's favor and understood that his rule as king was blessed for the sake of His people Israel. David's success would go unchallenged, until the entry of the Philistines. They viewed David, who had been lucky in killing the giant Goliath, as just a renegade shepherd, and set out to punish this upstart. David soundly defeated them in two separate battles and sent them back to their fortresses along the southern coast.

Afterward, David mustered his troops to escort the Ark of the Covenant to the fledgling capital. This was of vital importance to him. It was *Yahweh*, the God of Abraham, Isaac, and Jacob, who had brought David through his years of shepherding, Samuel's anointing and prophecy, battling Goliath, Saul's attempts to kill him, and his years of exile. Never had God forsaken him.

The false gods of Astarte and Baal held no allure for King David. *Yahweh* was his one true God. David was so devoted that he was unashamed to let everyone know of his dedication. His wife Michal, Saul's daughter, ridiculed and scorned her husband for making a fool of himself dancing before the ark of the covenant as it was being returned to Jerusalem. David was unperturbed and informed Michal that he would gladly do that and much more. No display of heartfelt exuberance was inappropriate to the worship of this great and wonderful God who had blessed him so abundantly!

Once David had settled in Jerusalem, it became the center for worship of the God of the Hebrews. King David desired to build a temple for the Lord he loved and revered, but the prophet Nathan told David that his warlike ways had made it inappropriate for him to carry out such a task.

During his reign, although the Ark of the Covenant continued to dwell in a tent, it in no way hampered David's enthusiasm in promoting the worship of *Yahweh*. Animals were sacrificed morning and evening, and the Sabbath was rigorously observed. Even today, David's intimate relationship with his God and the worship that relationship evoked is preserved in the book of Psalms. Both Christians and Jews are deeply affected by the beauty and sense of awe of Almighty God that flow through its pages.

Jerusalem is what it is—a center of worship. No other reason can be offered for its importance. It is a mystery to be pondered at length. It sits astride a range of unremarkable hills at a narrow neck of land that joins the two largest continents on planet Earth: Asia and Africa. From ancient times great and prosperous societies flourished both north of Jerusalem in Mesopotamia, that fertile region around the Tigris and Euphrates, and south of Jerusalem around the Nile River valley. Alternatively, those great societies sought to impose their rule over each other. To do so, they had to pass through Israel—every country's doormat.

For one shining moment, all that changed when God found in David a man after His own heart. During David's reign the great tides of history that generally governed events around Jerusalem were interrupted. Neither Mesopotamia nor Egypt was active; both great centers of civilization were stagnant. During this temporary lull, David's star rose to heights unimaginable in the little backwater province he ruled. To this day, it is difficult to imagine a kingdom centered in Jerusalem that would extend almost from the Nile to the

Euphrates. But that is the land David and his son Solomon ruled in peace and prosperity.

It was a golden age unforgotten by the Jews. In the dark days during Solomon's reign, his heart began to follow the false gods of some of his many wives and concubines. The prophets of Israel comforted those who remained faithful to *Yahweh*. They announced that God would one day bring another like David, an anointed one, a Messiah who would reestablish Zion (Jerusalem). He would exalt it in the eyes of all men so that the nations, the *goyim*, would come from the four corners of the earth to acknowledge the God of Israel as the one true God of all creation—the King of Glory, *Yahweh Sabaoth*. It was to this promise alone that God's people have clung in succeeding centuries.

After Solomon's death, the kingdom split. Samaria became the kingdom of the northern tribes of Israel. All that was left to Jerusalem was the tribe of Judah. By then Jerusalem with its temple had become fixed in the hearts and minds of all true worshipers of *Yahweh* as the place to bring one's sacrifices, fulfill one's vows, and offer loud songs of praise.

This posed a problem for the northern rulers who didn't want their subjects to make pilgrimages to Jerusalem—capital of a rival kingdom. They sought to offer the people substitute places of worship with manmade gods. The worship of *Yahweh* barely survived in the north. That it did so is due to such prophets as Elijah and Elisha, who never let the fire go out. It was essentially a time of decline. In the south where the worship of *Yahweh* was still the official religion, the decline happened more slowly. It was occasionally interrupted by the fires of revival, but most kings who ruled in Jerusalem were little better than the monarchs who sat in Samaria. The worship of *Yahweh* was fading, almost irretrievably.

In 722 BC, Samaria fell to the Assyrians, and in 586—or some historians say 587 BC—Jerusalem succumbed to the Babylonians—just as Jeremiah had warned. On each occasion inhabitants of the cities were carried into exile by their captors. The sharp rebuke of exile had a cleansing effect on those who suffered it. In losing Jerusalem, they began to value it as never before. Perhaps they sang:

> Beside the rivers of Babylon, we sat and wept as we thought of Jerusalem. We put away our harps, hanging them on the branches of poplar trees. For our captors demanded a song from us. Our tormentors insisted on a joyful hymn: "Sing us one of those songs of Jerusalem!" But how can we sing the songs of the LORD while in a pagan land? If I forget you, O Jerusalem, let my right hand forget how to play the harp. May my tongue stick to the roof of my mouth if I fail to remember you, if I don't make Jerusalem my greatest joy. (Psalm 137:1–6 NLT)

Jerusalem had become much more than David's capital. Because of the temple Solomon had built there, it had become God's special dwelling place on earth. It was not that He was contained there, but in that building and its environs He had covenanted to receive the worship of His people and to hear their prayers. It was there that *Yahweh* met His people in a very special way. Although He could be praised and thanked anywhere in all the earth, Jerusalem became the only place appointed for the sacrifice of burnt offerings for the sins of the people.

Babylon fell to the Persians in 539 BC, and a year later the Persian emperor Cyrus issued a decree authorizing the rebuilding of *Yahweh's* temple in Jerusalem, after which a remnant of God's people returned to the hills of the Holy City. Their arrival was not greeted with rejoicing by those who had made the area their home during the previous fifty years. Questions of ownership and authority gave immediate cause for conflict.

It didn't help the cause when locals—some of them mixed-race Samaritans who had adopted the worship of *Yahweh*—were offended when offers of help to rebuild the temple were rebuffed. They actively opposed the work of the Jews by trying to frighten or discourage them. They sometimes bribed the Persian officials to do whatever could be done to hinder progress.

The Jews did manage to quickly erect an altar on the temple site and secure the other items needed for sacrifices and offerings that were at the heart of *Yahweh's* worship. Rebuilding the temple— a more modest structure than the one erected by Solomon—took much longer, for poverty and shortages persisted in and around Jerusalem.

The new temple was dedicated around 515 BC, under the direction of Zerubbabel the prince and Joshua the priest. Later Ezra, a priest thoroughly versed in God's Law, arrived with authorization from the Persian emperor, Artaxerxes. Ezra was chosen to take the funds to Jerusalem and do everything he could to strengthen temple worship and devotion to *Yahweh* there.

Then, as we will see in a later chapter, God sent Nehemiah to rebuild the walls that encircled Jerusalem. Nehemiah worked diligently and courageously in the face of violent resistance. He arranged for more people to live inside the city, recognizing that its puny population was insufficient to defend it.

Between Ezra and Nehemiah, the worship of *Yahweh* and the life of His people underwent change. Some would even suggest it was in this time of revival that the essential groundwork for modern Judaism was laid. These men loved and endeavored to serve the God of David. They cared greatly about His laws and sought to observe them strictly. Intermarriage with Gentiles was banned, the weekly Sabbath was honored, land reforms limited the extent to which the rich could exploit the poor, tithing was observed, and priests and Levites were properly certified and ordained for service in the temple.

The fire was still burning—certainly less intensely than in the days of David—but still aflame after it had been nearly extinguished by waves of adversity and judgment. Jerusalem was and remains the symbol of the persistence and perseverance of the Jews—led by David—to inhabit his city with the praise and worship of *Yahweh*. David is known for his worship of the Lord, and so is his city, Jerusalem. Yet today, one of the defining images of the city is an edifice dedicated to Islam.

As mentioned previously, King David, who conquered Jerusalem and made it his capital city, is described in Scripture as a man "after God's own heart." The desire of David's heart was to build a temple in Jerusalem as the dwelling place of God. Because David's kingdom was so associated with warfare and bloodshed in the conquest of Israel's enemies, the Lord would not allow David to move forward with his plans. He did, however, promise the king that his son and successor, Solomon, would fulfill the dream.

God made an unconditional promise, another "everlasting covenant" with David. This covenant assured that his line would endure forever, and that the Messiah would come from the Davidic lineage:

> The LORD became angry with Solomon because his heart had turned away from the LORD, the God of Israel, who had appeared to him twice. Although he had forbidden Solomon to follow other gods, Solomon did not keep the LORD's command. So the LORD said to Solomon,

"Since this is your attitude and you have not kept my covenant and my decrees, which I commanded you, I will most certainly tear the kingdom away from you and give it to one of your subordinates. Nevertheless, for the sake of David your father, I will not do it during your lifetime. I will tear it out of the hand of your son. Yet I will not tear the whole kingdom from him, but will give him one tribe for the sake of David my servant and for the sake of Jerusalem, which I have chosen." (1 Kings 11:9–13)

Solomon's disobedience precluded his participation in the covenant blessing, but because God had made an unconditional pact, and for the sake of Jerusalem, Solomon was not totally cut off. God is faithful to always keep His pledge. Not only did He choose Jerusalem as His city and the symbol of His intent to dwell among His people, He continued to exercise control over it. His sovereignty over Jerusalem is demonstrated in that He decreed both its destruction and rebuilding.

The Lord is "slow to anger," says Psalm 103:8. What an understatement! Decade after decade—century after century—God's heart was broken because of the repeated idolatry of the children of Israel. As He had promised Abraham, the Israelites were led out of slavery in Egypt and into the promised land. God had established them in the area promised unconditionally to Abraham, Isaac, Jacob and their descendants in the royal land grant.

Time after time the people left the worship of the one true God and followed after pagan gods from the nations surrounding them. A righteous king of the line of David would bring reform and revival, and the groves and high places where Baal, Asherah (Ishtar), and other idols were worshiped were torn down. The next king would then prove to be as wicked as the previous one, and pagan beliefs would again be accepted by God's chosen people—even that of child sacrifice. Could this have been a foreshadowing of today's child sacrifice through abortion, all in an effort to worship at the altar of self-fulfillment?

Prophet after prophet warned the people to return to God or face the consequences. Yet this "stiff-necked" people refused to obey God's commands. The Bible reveals in Jeremiah 27 that He *allowed* the Babylonian king to conquer Israel and expand his empire. Nebuchadnezzar was but a tool in God's hand because His children refused to repent of continued idolatry.

The people failed to heed Jeremiah's warning. Why? His message was one of gloom and doom; they much preferred the teachers who assured that all would be peaceful. Perhaps they were much like those to whom the apostle Paul referred when he wrote:

> For the time will come when people will not put up with sound doctrine. Instead, to suit their own desires, they will gather around them a great number of teachers to say what their itching ears want to hear. (2 Timothy 4:3)

Those in Jeremiah's day simply could not imagine that God's punishment would fall and the temple, the sanctuary where He placed His name, would be destroyed. The Israelites continued to worship, but their hearts were far from *Yahweh*. Jeremiah 7:12, 14 warned that the temple would face destruction just as the tabernacle at Shiloh had earlier:

> Go now to the place in Shiloh where I first made a dwelling for my Name, and see what I did to it because of the wickedness of my people Israel. . . . Therefore, what I did to Shiloh I will now do to the house that bears my Name, the temple you trust in, the place I gave to you and your ancestors.[3]

For forty years Jeremiah faithfully delivered God's word to the people without any sign of their repentance. From reading accounts of that time, one may assume that Nebuchadnezzar, the well-known Babylonian conqueror of the sixth century BC, simply decided one day that Israel would be a nice little piece of real estate to add to his collection. In 597 BC, he captured the city, plundered the temple, and according to historical sources carried away the king, Jehoiakim, and between 10,000 and 12,000 men. In that day, as in many Asian and Islamic cultures today, only the men were counted; therefore, the totals could easily have been as high as perhaps 48,000 Hebrew men, women, and children wrenched from their homeland and forced into slavery.[4]

Rather than returning Jehoiakim to Jerusalem as ruler, in 596 BC Nebuchadnezzar elevated the king's uncle, Zedekiah, to the throne. He rebelled against the Babylonian king, and in Jeremiah 34:2–3, the prophet delivered a warning that any attempt to defy their captors would be met with destruction:

> "Thus says the LORD, the God of Israel: Go and speak to Zedekiah king of Judah and say to him, 'Thus says the LORD: Behold, I am giving this city into the hand of the king of Babylon, and he shall burn it with fire. You shall not escape from his hand but shall surely be captured and delivered into his hand. You shall see the king of Babylon eye to eye and speak with him face to face. And you shall go to Babylon.'" (ESV)

The prophecy proved to be accurate. In 586 BC the Babylonians launched another army to put down Zedekiah's rebellion. They overran Judah, and for eighteen long months the marauders stripped the region bare and then built siege walls outside the city before attacking. A horrific famine then beset the inhabitants of Jerusalem. The Lamentations of Jeremiah describe the gruesomeness of the times:

> Those killed by the sword are better off than those
> who die of famine; racked with hunger, they waste away
> for lack of food from the field. With their own hands

compassionate women have cooked their own children,
who became their food when my people were destroyed.
(Lamentations 4:9–10)

The ramparts of Jerusalem were breached and then toppled; the city was pillaged, and Solomon's temple desecrated and burned, its treasures carried to Nebuchadnezzar's storehouses in Babylon.

Zedekiah, the king of Jerusalem, and his sons attempted to escape the wrath of the invading army but were caught trying to flee Jerusalem. They were chained and dragged away to Babylon. Being the despot that he was, Nebuchadnezzar had the sons of the Hebrew king put to death while their father was forced to watch. As the last son met his death, Zedekiah's eyes were gouged out and he was led away to a dungeon.

The writer of 2 Chronicles gives us insight into why murder and exile were visited on the inhabitants of Judah:

Furthermore, all the leaders of the priests and the people became more and more unfaithful, following all the detestable practices of the nations and defiling the temple of the LORD, which he had consecrated in Jerusalem. The LORD, the God of their ancestors, sent word to them through his messengers again and again, because he had pity on his people and on his dwelling place. But they mocked God's messengers, despised his words and scoffed at his prophets until the wrath of the LORD was aroused against his people and there was no remedy. (2 Chronicles 36:14–16)

Yet God still did not altogether abandon His people. The prophecy of judgment delivered by Jeremiah also gave a promise of restoration. Just as God had brought the Israelites out of Egypt, there would be a second exodus: God would bring His people out of Babylon after they had endured seventy years of captivity. Jeremiah prophesied that, in time, even legal documents would be sealed with the phrase:

As surely as the LORD lives, who brought the descendants of Israel up out of the land of the north and out of all the countries where he had banished them. (Jeremiah 23:8)

As God had promised, the exiles returned home, rebuilt the temple, and reconstructed the walls of their beloved city.

CHAPTER
3

Those who have been ransomed by the LORD will return.
They will enter Jerusalem singing, crowned with everlasting joy.

ISAIAH 35:10 NLT

The sharp rebuke of exile had a cleansing effect on those who suffered through it. In losing Jerusalem, the Hebrew children began to value it as never before. Perhaps they sang the lament:

By the rivers of Babylon we sat and wept when we remembered Zion. There on the poplars we hung our harps, for there our captors asked us for songs, our tormentors demanded songs of joy; they said, "Sing us one of the songs of Zion!" How can we sing the songs of the LORD while in a foreign land? If I forget you, Jerusalem, may my right hand forget its skill. May my tongue cling to the roof of my mouth if I do not remember you, if I do

not consider Jerusalem my highest joy. (Psalm 137:1–6)

When Nebuchadnezzar sacked Jerusalem, he looted and burned the temple and knocked down the walls. That's how the city remained for seventy years. While the captive Israelites lived the existence of slaves, the land enjoyed a rest. Israel had repeatedly violated God's Law by not resting the land every seven years (see Leviticus 25:1–7), so God removed His hand of protection. Still He did not forsake His people. During the years of exile, He prompted scribes and prophets to record and perfect the Torah—the five books of Moses. The book of Daniel was documented, and the Law codified.

One hundred sixty years before the birth of King Cyrus, Isaiah had prophesied that God would elevate that king to deliver the Jews, return them to Jerusalem, and rebuild the temple. Not only did Isaiah prophesy that Cyrus would come to the aid of God's people, but that he would speak words of comfort to them. He spoke of God's promise and the utter requisite of its fulfillment. Still today God instructs His ministers to speak comfort to His children, and that command has not been negated. His message was, and is: "I discipline, but I do not stop loving. There comes a pivotal point when wrath ceases and comfort is poured out." It is a promise that God will ultimately take up residence with His children. The preeminence of His presence is an indisputable promise.

Cyrus was unique not only because he allowed the Jews to return to Israel but also because the prophet Isaiah foretold his birth and his name almost one hundred sixty years before he was born. God also revealed Cyrus's mission to the prophet. Isaiah recorded that he would accomplish specific tasks under God's direction during his lifetime. The king was destined to carry out God's plan as it related to His chosen people. It was through Cyrus that the Babylonian Empire and seventy years of Jewish captivity came to an end. The prophet Isaiah wrote:

> Who says of Cyrus, 'He is my shepherd and will accomplish all that I please; he will say of Jerusalem, "Let it be rebuilt," and of the temple, "Let its foundations be laid."' (Isaiah 44:28)

Enter Zerubbabel, an aide to King Darius I and a prince of the lineage of Zedekiah, the last king of Judah. He was also the grandson of Joshua, the last priest of Solomon's temple. He had no idea how challenging his task would be, or that it would take over twenty years to accomplish. Zerubbabel immediately began the work assigned him. The altar was rededicated even as artisans were engaged to rebuild the temple.

After two years of construction on the foundation alone, labor ceased. Stringent opposition came from the Samaritans, who were offended because they were not asked to help with the restoration.

Questions of ownership and authority gave immediate cause for conflict, as did the call for repentance and a return not only to worshiping *Yahweh* in Jerusalem but also to the tenets of the law of Moses.

Ezra, a descendant from the lineage of Seraiah, arrived in the sadly neglected Holy City only to learn that Jewish men had taken Gentile women as their wives—despite God's law forbidding mixed marriages. He fell on his face and repented for the sins of Israel and then challenged those men who had taken heathen wives to dissolve the forbidden marriages and purify themselves before God.

One day, as cupbearer to Artaxerxes I, Nehemiah met a group of men who had recently returned from the Holy City. What he heard, as recorded in Nehemiah 1:3, was heart rending.

> They said to me, "Those who survived the exile and are back in the province are in great trouble and disgrace. The wall of Jerusalem is broken down, and its gates have been burned with fire."

What was his reaction to this news? Did he just shake his head and walk away? No. Nehemiah wrote in verses 4–7:

> When I heard these things, I sat down and wept. For some days I mourned and fasted and prayed before the God of heaven. Then I said: "LORD, the God of heaven, the great and awesome God, who keeps his covenant of love

with those who love him and keep his commandments, let your ear be attentive and your eyes open to hear the prayer your servant is praying before you day and night for your servants, the people of Israel. I confess the sins we Israelites, including myself and my father's family, have committed against you. We have acted very wickedly toward you. We have not obeyed the commands, decrees and laws you gave your servant Moses."

Nehemiah's first thought was not to rush into the throne room and throw himself down before a worldly king; rather, he approached *Yahweh*—the King of kings. He wept, mourned, fasted, prayed, and repented. For four months—from the Hebrew months of Chisleu to Nisan—Nehemiah sought God's direction. As has often been the case, the answer came in a way totally unexpected. One day while in the king's presence, and though he had worked diligently to keep his grief hidden, the monarch noticed the sadness of Nehemiah's countenance:

So the king asked me, "Why does your face look so sad when you are not ill? This can be nothing but sadness of heart." I was very much afraid, but I said to the king, "May the king live forever! Why should my face not look sad when the city where my ancestors are buried lies in ruins, and its gates have been destroyed by fire?" The king said to me, "What is it you want?" Then I prayed to the God of heaven, and I answered the king, "If it pleases the king and if your servant has found favor in his sight, let him send me to the city in Judah where my ancestors are buried so that I can rebuild it." (Nehemiah 2:2–5)

Once the king had given his permission to return to Jerusalem, Nehemiah asked for letters of safe conduct through the territories that lay between Babylon and Judah. He then requested the materials necessary to repair the breeches in the walls of the city and for his own residence. Verse eight of chapter two says, "And because the gracious hand of my God was on me, the king granted my requests."

When each entreaty had been granted, Nehemiah set out for Jerusalem. After the long and taxing trip, he took three days for rest and recuperation before he began a survey of the city—and even then he went under cover of darkness. He inspected the walls and counted the cost of rebuilding.

Alan Redpath, Christian author and speaker, wrote:

> Imagine his grief of heart as he stumbled among those ruins of what was once a great and mighty fortress! Whenever a real work of God is to be done. . . some faithful, burdened servant has to take a journey such as Nehemiah took, to weep in the night over the ruins, to wrestle in some dark Gethsemane in prayer. . . Are our hearts ever stirred like that? [5]

Following his midnight ride around the circumference of the city, Nehemiah called upon the people to restore the walls. It was not an easy task. The Samaritans, led by Sanballat, a contemporary of Nehemiah, and Tobiah, his associate, accused the Hebrews of rebelling against the very king who had approved the venture. Having had their fingers in the till for so long, these men were not about to relinquish their very lucrative money-making schemes without a fight. Nehemiah sternly responded to the complaints and charges in (2:20):

> The God of heaven will give us success. We his ser-
> vants will start rebuilding, but as for you, you have no
> share in Jerusalem or any claim or historic right to it.

The work was hard, the task challenging and dangerous, but Nehemiah was certain their success lay in God's divine provision:

> Therefore I stationed some of the people behind the
> lowest points of the wall at the exposed places, posting
> them by families, with their swords, spears and bows.
> After I looked things over, I stood up and said to the
> nobles, the officials and the rest of the people, "Don't
> be afraid of them. Remember the Lord, who is great
> and awesome, and fight for your families, your sons and
> your daughters, your wives and your homes." When our
> enemies heard that we were aware of their plot and that

God had frustrated it, we all returned to the wall, each to our own work. From that day on, half of my men did the work, while the other half were equipped with spears, shields, bows and armor. The officers posted themselves behind all the people of Judah who were building the wall. Those who carried materials did their work with one hand and held a weapon in the other, and each of the builders wore his sword at his side as he worked. But the man who sounded the trumpet stayed with me. Then I said to the nobles, the officials and the rest of the people, "The work is extensive and spread out, and we are widely separated from each other along the wall. Wherever you hear the sound of the trumpet, join us there. Our God will fight for us!" (Nehemiah 4:13–20)

Finally the task was completed; Nehemiah refused to take any credit for the achievement:

When all our enemies heard about this, all the surrounding nations were afraid and lost their self-confidence, because they realized that this work had been done with the help of our God. (Nehemiah 6:16)

Once the last stone was placed in the wall, Nehemiah called Ezra to read the law of Moses to those assembled in its shadow. As the men and women gathered together in obedience and in prayer, they and the temple priests covenanted to obey the law and keep themselves separate from all other nationalities.

Under Ezra and Nehemiah, the worship of *Yahweh* and the life of His people underwent change. These men loved and endeavored to serve the God of David. They cared greatly about His laws and sought to observe them strictly.

The fire was still burning—perhaps less intensely than in the days of David—after it had nearly been extinguished by waves of adversity and judgment. Jerusalem was and remains the symbol of the persistence and perseverance of the Jews to fill David's city with the praise and worship of *Yahweh*.

CHAPTER

4

*And at the dedication of the wall of Jerusalem they sought
the Levites out of all their places, to bring them to Jerusalem,
to keep the dedication with gladness, both with thanksgivings,
and with singing, with cymbals, psalteries, and with harps.*

NEHEMIAH 12:27 KJV

In 332 BC, a mere one hundred years after Ezra and Nehemiah restored the temple and true worship of *Yahweh*, Alexander the Great captured Gaza and set his face toward Jerusalem. His entry into the Holy City was told by Hebrew historian Flavius Josephus. Although its veracity is sometimes questioned, I will share it with you here:

> And when Jaddus [the high priest] understood that Alexander was not far from the city, he went out in procession, with the priests and the multitude of the citizens. The procession was venerable, and the manner

of it different from that of other nations. It reached to a place called Sapha, which name, translated into Greek, signifies a prospect, for you have thence a prospect both of Jerusalem and of the temple. And when the Phoenicians and the Samarians that followed him thought they should have liberty to plunder the city, and torment the high-priest to death, which the king's displeasure fairly promised them, the very reverse of it happened; for Alexander, when he saw the multitude at a distance, in white garments, while the priests stood clothed with fine linen, and the high-priest in purple and scarlet clothing, with his mitre on his head, having the golden plate whereon the name of God was engraved, he approached by himself, and adored that name, and first saluted the high-priest.[6]

Alexander's empire fragmented after his death, and the followers of Ptolemy in Egypt seized Judea and Jerusalem. The battle between the Ptolemies and the Seleucids raged for 125 long years. Ultimately Antiochus III defeated Ptolemy and established his rule over Jerusalem. When Antiochus IV ascended the throne, he not only continued his father's stringent guidelines for the occupation of the region, he initiated severe religious persecution. He was determined to destroy worship of the one true God and force the Jewish inhabitants to bow to Greek paganism. Shabbat was banned; circumcision was forbidden;

the temple was dedicated to the Roman god Zeus and desecrated by the sacrifice of pigs on the altar.

Antiochus badly underestimated the Jews' piety and resolute faith in the God of their forefathers. That mistake would cost him exceedingly. The horror of seeing their temple defiled was soon replaced by the stirrings of rebellion and finally by an erupting revolt. The sons of Mattathias—John, Simon, Judas, Eleazer, and Jonathan—became the leaders of the revolution. Jewish history records:

> In 167 BC Antiochus sent some of his officers to the village of Modein [the home of Mattathias] to force the Jews living there to offer sacrifices to the pagan gods. Mattathias, as a leader in the city, was commanded by the officers to be the first person to offer a sacrifice—as an example to the rest of the people. He refused with a noble speech reminiscent of the words of Joshua in Joshua 24:14-15 (see: I Maccabees 2:15-22).
>
> Because of the determination of Mattathias, and fearing bloody reprisals against the people for his refusal, a certain Jew stepped forward and volunteered to offer the sacrifices to the pagan gods in the place of this aged priest. At this point Mattathias was overcome with a passionate zeal to defend his God, and he killed this Jewish man, as well as the officers of the king. He then tore down

the altar to the pagan gods and ran through the village shouting, "Let everyone who is zealous for the Law and who stands by the covenant follow me!" (I Maccabees 2:27). He and his sons, along with a good number of followers, fled to the mountains of the Judean wilderness.[7]

Mattathias and his sons became known as the Maccabees (meaning "hammerers") and the uprising was given several names—among them The Maccabean Revolt. From these few men grew a powerful army that began guerrilla-like incursions against the enemy in the villages and towns of Judea. They demolished pagan altars and killed those who bowed in worship before them. Just as the rebellion was gaining impetus, Mattathias died, but he had earlier chosen his son, Judas, to direct the Hebrew forces. It is thought that Judas had one of the finest analytical and tactical minds ever seen among the Jews.

After regaining control over Jerusalem, the Maccabees were determined to cleanse the temple and restore worship. While searching for the holy anointing oil to be used in the rededication of the temple, Judas and his men found only enough of the precious oil to fill the menorah in the temple for one day. Enough for eight days was required. The oil was poured into the receptacle and according to the Jewish apocryphal books, I and II Maccabees, the oil miraculously burned for the full eight days. Today, the yearly celebration of the miracle of Hanukkah (dedication) commemorates the provision of oil.

In 63 BC, Roman general Pompey retook Jerusalem and ended what has come to be called the Hasmonean Period. Antigonus, the Hasmonian king, regained control of Jerusalem in 40 BC and managed for three years to forestall attempts by the Romans to recapture the city. His efforts failed in 27 BC when Herod the Great and General Mark Anthony (minus Cleopatra) gained control once again of the Holy City. Being smarter than your average conqueror, Herod cemented his legitimate claim to the throne in Judea by marrying Mariamme, a Jewess and a Hasmonean descendant. Although Herod loved his wife—possibly as much as he could love anyone—he allowed his sister Salome to fill his mind with poisonous suspicions about Mariamme. Finally he was so enraged by Salome's baseless accusations he had his wife put to death along with their two sons, her brother, grandfather, and mother.[8]

Herod was well known for his massive building projects—in particular expanding and developing the Temple Mount and erecting a new Greco–Roman style edifice. No funds were spared in the building of the beautiful and impressive temple of which only the Western Wall stands today. During his reign, he also fortified the massive and impressive structures at Masada:

> The first of three building phases completed by
> Herod began in 35 BCE. During the first phase the West-
> ern Palace was built, along with three smaller palaces,

a storeroom, and army barracks. Three columbarium towers and a swimming pool at the south end of the site were also completed during this building phase.[9]

The New Testament Gospels relate the remarkable story of the birth of the Savior, the One who would come to restore hope to the people of God. It is incomparable: the nativity—God reaching down to Man. It is a story of the splendor and glory of heaven touching the dirt and filth of a stable floor; a story of a manger—a trough filled with hay where a tiny baby, born of a virgin, was cradled. It's the story of a guiding star, of angels and shepherds and wise men, of praise and worship, of peace on earth and goodwill toward all men. It should have been a time of rejoicing for all mankind, but there were those who were fearful, who had much to lose with the advent of a new King of the Jews.

It was during Herod's more murderous stage that an angel of the Lord had appeared to a young woman named Mary:

> The angel went to her and said, "Greetings, you who are highly favored! The Lord is with you." Mary was greatly troubled at his words and wondered what kind of greeting this might be. But the angel said to her, "Do not be afraid, Mary; you have found favor with God. You will conceive and give birth to a son, and you are to call him Jesus. He will be great and will be called the Son of the

Most High. The Lord God will give him the throne of his father David, and he will reign over Jacob's descendants forever; his kingdom will never end."

"How will this be," Mary asked the angel, "since I am a virgin?"

The angel answered, "The Holy Spirit will come upon you, and the power of the Most High will overshadow you. So the holy one to be born will be called the Son of God. Even Elizabeth your relative is going to have a child in her old age, and she who was said to be unable to conceive is in her sixth month. For no word from God will ever fail."

"I am the Lord's servant," Mary answered. "May your word to me be fulfilled." Then the angel left her. (Luke 1:28–38)

Joseph, Mary's betrothed, also had an angelic visit, and as a result quietly accepted that she would bear the Messiah as had been prophesied in Isaiah 7:14. Near the end of her pregnancy, the young couple was forced to travel from their hometown of Nazareth to Bethlehem:

He went there to register with Mary, who was pledged to be married to him and was expecting a child. While they were there, the time came for the baby to be born, and she gave birth to her firstborn, a son. She wrapped him in cloths and placed him in a manger, because there was no guest room available for them. (Luke 2:5–7)

While Matthew offers a uniquely Jewish perspective on those events, Luke anchors the narrative of the birth of Christ squarely in history. It happened, he wrote, when Quirinius was governor of Syria, at a time when Caesar Augustus had called for a census in the empire. The Messiah was born in Bethlehem into an historic lineage: the house and line of David, from which it had been prophesied that the Savior, the Messiah, would come.

Just after His birth, Mary and Joseph took Jesus to Jerusalem to comply with God's commandments for the purification of the mother after childbirth and for the redemption of a first-born child (see Luke 2:22–24). While the young family was in the temple, they encountered a stranger—Simeon—just as they were presenting the baby to the Lord. The old man walked up and took the baby right from Mary's arms. Neither Mary nor Joseph was alarmed; after all, they had very recently entertained angels and shepherds in a stable. It was a fitting introduction for this child who would turn the world upside down.

The old man cradled the child gently in his arms and with tears in his eyes turned his face heavenward. Quietly he prayed:

Lord, now You are letting Your servant depart in peace, according to Your word; for my eyes have seen

Your salvation which You have prepared before the face of all peoples, a light to bring revelation to the Gentiles, and the glory of Your people Israel. (Luke 2:29–32 NKJV)

Perhaps Simeon explained to the awed mother that God had promised him he would see the Messiah before he died. As the years passed and he grew older, maybe he had begun to wonder if God would keep His promise—the Promise he now held in his arms. However, there was more to Simeon's message. Along with the good news of the arrival of the Messiah, he gave Mary an admonition:

This child is destined to cause the falling and rising of many in Israel, and to be a sign that will be spoken against, so that the thoughts of many hearts will be revealed. And a sword will pierce your own soul too. (Luke 2:34–35)

From His birth Jesus was recognized as the promised Messiah by many in Jerusalem. As Simeon paused, an old woman hurried up to the group:

She had lived with her husband seven years after her marriage, and then was a widow until she was eighty-four. She never left the temple but worshiped night and day, fasting and praying. Coming up to them at that very moment, she gave thanks to God and spoke about the child to all who were looking forward to the redemption of Jerusalem. (Luke 2:36–38)

Anna's chosen avocation was one of prayer and fasting in the temple. We know little about why she, a widow, had made that choice, had renounced whatever hopes and dreams she might have had to perhaps fulfill Psalm 122:6: "Pray for the peace of Jerusalem: they shall prosper that love thee." (KJV) It could be that her husband had been such a tyrant that she had no desire to remarry, or that he was such a stellar example that she knew there was no other for her. Whatever the reason, she had made a choice to place her hope in Jehovah. She was surely aware of Isaiah 54:5: "For your Maker is your husband, the LORD of hosts is his name; and the Holy One of Israel is your Redeemer, the God of the whole earth he is called." (ESV).

It is not surprising, then, given her residence within the temple grounds that she had an encounter with Simeon, Mary, Joseph, and the Child. With a glance at the group, her spirit quickened; she knew something important was transpiring. Verse 38 reveals her reaction, "At that very moment she came up and began giving thanks to God, and continued to speak of Him to all those who were looking for the redemption of Jerusalem." (NASB) After all those years of service, of faithful prayer and fasting, Anna had finally seen the answer to her powerful prayers—the One who would redeem Israel!

After the purification rites, Joseph was warned in a dream that Herod was seeking the Child to kill him. Alarmed, he took Mary and Jesus and departed for Egypt, where they stayed until another angel was sent to tell them it was safe to return to their homeland. The family settled in Nazareth in the Galilee region, but each year they returned to Jerusalem for the Passover celebration.

When Jesus was twelve, Mary and Joseph discovered that He was not with them as they returned to Nazareth after celebrating Passover. They searched the caravan and then turned back to the city to search for their son. After three days of frantically seeking Him, He was found—not making mischief or apologetic for having stayed behind, but in the temple with a group of Bible scholars discussing the Scriptures. The men in the group were amazed at Jesus' understanding and knowledge of God's Word.

The years following the temple incident give us little insight into Jesus' life then. Apparently He worked with Joseph in the carpenter shop, studied with the local rabbis in the synagogue, and grew strong and robust as a young man. He began His ministry when He was baptized at the Jordan River by His cousin John. Jesus performed His first miracle at a wedding He attended with His mother, where He turned water into wine. Then the Messiah chose twelve men to accompany Him on His travels.

Jesus moved about in the Galilee region preaching, teaching, healing, and performing other miracles—establishing His credentials as the Messiah to a people hungry for rescue. He made no attempt to ingratiate Himself to the religious Jewish leaders of the day, preferring instead to reach out to the common people and those "obvious" sinners—tax collectors and prostitutes among them. Thus, He was fulfilling Isaiah 9:2:

> The people walking in darkness have seen a great light; on those living in the land of deep darkness a light has dawned.

CHAPTER
5

People from many nations will come and say, "Come, let us go up to the mountain
of the Lord, to the house of Jacob's God. There he will teach us his ways,
and we will walk in his paths." For the Lord's teaching will go out from Zion;
his word will go out from Jerusalem.

ISAIAH 2:3 NLT

The story of Jesus is unique. It is not like the myths of the ancient Near East, when gods were condemned to perpetual cycles of death and rebirth, and whose origins could not be pinpointed in time or place. The living God—the God of Abraham, Isaac, and Jacob—intervened in time and space and made Himself known to a particular people, at a precise time, in a specific place.

Jerusalem during the time of Jesus was very dissimilar from what we see today, and would not have been a very pleasant place to live. Its narrow streets were hot and dusty, filled with the noises of commerce—the bleats of goats and sheep being driven to the marketplace, the cooing of doves and lowing of cattle outside the temple, the pounding steps of Roman soldiers as they marched through the city, the sounds of men and women going about their regular daily routines. Days could be hot and the nights cold in the desert-like climate. When infrequent storms blew into the city, the result could be torrential rains and muddy streets.

And yet it was as cosmopolitan as Herod the Great could fashion it:

> The years from A.D. 1 to A.D. 33 happened to be a high point for the Holy City. "It was," says Eric Meyers, professor of Judaic studies at Duke University, "a great, great metropolitan area" and home to the lavishly restored Jewish temple, a world-renowned wonder. It was prosperous and cosmopolitan. And it was also, unknowingly, the cradle for something else, a way of believing, of seeing, that would change the West and the rest of history.[10]

Herod, the tyrant king, was simply a puppet whose strings were pulled by the rulers in Rome. The Jews resented the Roman occupation, and groups of insurgents sprang up to resist them. This was so in part because the Romans worshiped numerous gods, and had elevated the emperor to a role of divinity. This, of course, repulsed the Jews who worshiped the one true God. It was in this climate that Jesus lived and undertook His mission.

In AD, Roman emperor Tiberius appointed Pontius Pilate governor of Judah. Little is known of his origins or of his death, but he played an important role in God's plan for mankind, as we will see later. A member of the Pontii family, it is believed that Pilate was of the "equestrian" order, or one who would in later times have been called a knight. Accounts from three of the four gospels portrayed Pilate as one who sought to escape sentencing Jesus to death. Matthew depicted the prefect as washing his hands of any responsibility for the judgment of Jesus. Mark revealed Pilate's reluctance to sentence Him to death. In Luke's Gospel, not only did the ruler find no fault in Christ, he dispatched Him to Herod Antipas, who agreed with the ruling. Finally Pilate averred, "I find no fault [in Jesus]." Inexplicably, he then consigned Jesus to be flogged by the soldiers.

The Gospels record that Jesus' early ministry was carried out mostly outside Jerusalem—primarily in Galilee. He made no attempt to gain entrance into or acceptance by the ranks of the religious establishment. His disciples were mostly workingmen, not scribes or scholars. To His inner circle of twelve, and a somewhat larger group who closely followed His ministry, He was the Messiah.

During the three short years of His ministry, Jesus knew Jerusalem was to be His destiny. He spent countless hours and walked miles along the hot, dusty roads of Judea where He preached, taught, healed, and worked miracles. Jesus ventured into Samaria and Perea before He "resolutely set out for Jerusalem" (Luke 9:51). He was determined to accomplish the mission His Father had called Him to do, even though He alone might have been aware of the consequences.

The last week of Jesus' ministry holds great weight and value for His followers. As we look at those last four days of His earthly life, we see Old Testament prophecies fulfilled.

Jesus gathered His disciples, and the group set out for Jerusalem. For some, it may have been their first trip to the Holy City. But before they entered the outskirts, Jesus had a task for them. They were to find and bring an animal to Him:

> Go to the village ahead of you, and at once you will find a donkey tied there, with her colt by her. Untie them and bring them to me. If anyone says anything to you, say that the Lord needs them, and he will send them right away. (Matthew 21:2–3)

It was the fulfillment of a prophecy in Zechariah 9:9:

> Rejoice greatly, O Daughter of Zion! Shout, Daughter of Jerusalem! See, your king comes to you, righteous and victorious, lowly and riding on a donkey, on a colt, the foal of a donkey.

There was great significance in Jesus having chosen the foal of an ass to ride into Jerusalem. The Jewish people expected the Messiah to lead a vast army of warriors into the Holy City to restore their rightful claim to the land. A conquering king would have been expected to ride into the city of conquest sitting astride a white horse. Jesus chose to enter Jerusalem not as a triumphant king on horseback, but meekly on a donkey—the Son of Man whose sight was set heavenward. It is a perfect picture of the truth that His kingdom was not of this world. He was not a "knight in shining armor" who had come to deliver the Jews by force; He was far more important than that: He was the Messiah, the Savior, Deliverer, Lamb of God, Prince of Peace, King of Kings and Lord of Lords.

It was not His task to enter Jerusalem and take the city by force. Nor was it His role to become a great political orator and liberate His people with eloquence and persuasiveness—or as the apostle Paul related in 1 Corinthians 2:4 (KJV), "with enticing words of man's wisdom." The people who followed Jesus became excited because of what they thought Jesus was going to do, not about who He really was, and the ultimate purpose of His life. They wanted instant gratification; He was about redemption and eternal life. It is little wonder that disappointment led those same people who had just days before shouted, "Hosanna!" to turn against Him and demand His crucifixion.

The next job delegated to the disciples was preparation for the Passover. Jesus dispatched Peter and John into the city to locate a room where the ritual meal was to be observed: Luke 22:9–13 records the conversation:

"Where do you want us to prepare for it?" they asked.
He replied, "As you enter the city, a man carrying a jar

of water will meet you. Follow him to the house that he enters, and say to the owner of the house, 'The Teacher asks: Where is the guest room, where I may eat the Passover with my disciples?' He will show you a large room upstairs, all furnished. Make preparations there." They left and found things just as Jesus had told them. So they prepared the Passover.

When the men gathered for the Passover meal, Jesus gave His disciples a powerful lesson on the role of a servant as He neared the end of His earthly ministry: The scene is the upper room; the meal was nearing an end. Jesus—the Son of God, the Darling of Heaven, the Messiah—rose from the table and laid aside His robe. He took a towel and girded it about His waist, picked up a basin and a pitcher of water, and began to make His way around the room. As He did so, He knelt on the floor in front of each disciple and gently washed and dried their feet.

It was a dirty task relegated to the lowest of servants. Those feet had trod the dusty streets of Jerusalem. They had followed in the paths of goats and sheep, of cattle and horses. The sandals on their feet absorbed the odors of the much-traveled roads and provided little in the way of protection from the filth. What a picture of humility! What a portrait of a servant. He showed His love to the men who had followed Him for three years—even to Judas, the one who was to betray Him. Had Judas but asked, our Lord would have forgiven his deception and treachery. It is a tender picture of a Savior who never gives up on the lost—the lost coin, the lost son, or the lost sheep (Luke 15). The Creator ministered to the creation! Gently He reminded them:

> "You call me 'Teacher' and 'Lord,' and rightly so, for that is what I am. Now that I, your Lord and Teacher, have washed your feet, you also should wash one another's feet. I have set you an example that you should do as I have done for you. Very truly I tell you, no servant is greater than his master, nor is a messenger greater than the one who sent him." (John 13:13–16)

By His act of humility, Jesus made it patently obvious that the role of His followers was to give aid and support.

There were several additions to the traditional Passover feast during the one observed by Jesus and His disciples. At Step Nine of the Seder, the *maror,* or bitter herbs, are eaten. It was then that Jesus disclosed He would be betrayed by one of the twelve—Judas (see Matthew 26:20–25). Shortly thereafter, the broken *matzah* is revealed, broken into pieces, and passed around the table. Jesus said, "Take and eat; this is My body" (Matthew 26:26). When the time arrived for sharing the third cup of wine, Jesus identified it as follows:

Then he took a cup, and when he had given thanks, he gave it to them, saying, "Drink from it, all of you. This is my blood of the covenant, which is poured out for many for the forgiveness of sins." (Matthew 26:27–28)

Of the fourth cup—the cup of completion—rather than drink from that cup, Jesus stipulated, "I will not drink from this fruit of the vine from now on until that day when I drink it new with you in my Father's kingdom" (v. 29). It is worth noting that the lamb usually consumed during the Passover feast was absent from the table; the Lamb of God would indeed soon become the ultimate sacrifice.

As the observance ended, Mark 14:26 indicates, "When they had sung a hymn, they went out to the Mount of Olives." As dedicated Jews, the men would have sung portions of Psalm 114–118. Hidden among those verses is a picture of what was about to happen to the Messiah:

The cords of death entangled me, the anguish of the grave came over me; I was overcome by distress and sorrow. Then I called on the name of the LORD: "LORD, save me!" For you, LORD, have delivered me from death, my eyes from tears, my feet from stumbling, that I may walk before the LORD in the land of the living. What shall I return to the LORD for all his goodness to me? I will lift up the cup of salvation and call on the name of the LORD. Precious in the sight of the LORD is the death of his faithful servants. Truly I am your servant, LORD; I serve you just as my mother did; you have freed me from my chains. I will sacrifice a thank offering to you and call on the name of the LORD. I will fulfill my vows to the LORD in the presence of all his people, in the courts of the house of the LORD—in your midst, Jerusalem. Praise the LORD. (Psalm 116:3–4, 8–9, 12-13, 15–19)

Jesus and the disciples walked from the upper room to the garden of Gethsemane—just across the Kidron Valley from the temple. The valley held special significance for the Lamb of God: it was a symbol of sin. There in the valley, Asa had burned the idols to which the children of Israel had bowed down (1 Kings 15:12–13); Hezekiah, too, ordered the idols erected by the Jews removed from the city to the Kidron Valley (2 Kings 23:4); and Hilkiah, a high priest under the reign of Josiah, had the idols torn down and pulverized in the valley (2 Kings 23:6). It was a clear reminder of those who had turned away from God to worship man-made images.

It was also in the Kidron Valley on the afternoon before Passover that the sacrificial lambs (some say as many as 250,000) would have been prepared for the altar. It would have run red, awash with the stench of the blood and water used in slaying and then cleansing the animals. It was through this—a vivid reminder of what the morrow held—that Jesus and His disciples walked; only He understood its full significance.

As He neared the garden of Gethsemane, perhaps the full realization of what was about to happen overwhelmed Jesus. He left nine of the men, and taking only Peter, James, and John He moved forward. Instructing the three disciples to watch and pray, Jesus stumbled deeper into the garden and fell on His face in agony. His very soul cried out: "Father, if you are willing, take this cup from me." (Luke 22:42)

It is at this point, I believe, the knowledge that He was to be the sacrifice hit with all the force of a huge boulder rolling downhill and slamming into the valley below. He, Jesus of Nazareth, was the "Lamb slain from the foundation of the world." (Revelation 13:8 KJV) Perhaps it was then that His "sweat was like drops of blood falling down to the ground." (Luke 22:44) Was it here that He began to feel the burden of the sins of all mankind—what some might call the "seven deadly sins"—descending on His sinless shoulders—lust, greed, wrath, gluttony, pride, envy, sloth, laziness? He who was about to be betrayed into the hands of His accusers was served a foretaste of what was to happen the following day.

What was His response? It was not the fight-or-flight response so often observed. No, it was total acquiescence. He prayed the prayer that never fails: "Yet not my will, but yours be done" (Luke 22:42).

Jesus submitted voluntarily to the will of His Father. He knew the consequences of that surrender. He said of His life:

> No one takes it from me, but I lay it down of my own accord. I have authority to lay it down and authority to take it up again. This command I received from my Father. (John 10:18)

Rising from the rocky ground, Jesus returned to His sleeping disciples and roused them. As they stretched and rubbed sleep from their eyes, the sounds of the crowd approaching captured their attention. Led by Judas, one of their own, it is likely the disciples initially felt no alarm, but that was soon to change. The betrayer stepped from the midst of the group of priests, temple guards, and Roman soldiers to grasp Jesus by the shoulders and plant a kiss on His cheek. (Judas had indicated to the high priest that he would identify Jesus with the kiss of greeting.) At that moment, the soldiers rushed forward, bound the Lamb and marched Him off to the palace of Annas, the former high priest and father-in-law of Caiaphas, the presiding temple official.

While awaiting a decision from the Sanhedrin, the guards laid a fire in the courtyard to take away the chill of the night. It was there that Peter was challenged and denied knowing his Lord not once but three times, just as had been prophesied. After having been found guilty of blasphemy, Jesus spent the night being mocked and goaded—a cruel crown of thorns crushed onto His brow. At dawn, the taunting ceased; Jesus was dressed in His own clothing and taken to Pilate. The prelate swiftly determined that He should be transferred to the jurisdiction of Herod Antipas, who, in turn, sent Him back to Pilate for sentencing.

After being condemned to death, Jesus was scourged:

> The Roman scourge, also called the "flagrum" or "flagellum" was a short whip made of two or three leather (ox-hide) thongs or ropes connected to a handle. . . The leather thongs were knotted with a number of small pieces of metal, usually zinc and iron, attached at various intervals. Scourging would quickly remove the skin. According to history the punishment of a slave was particularly dreadful. The leather was knotted with bones, or heavy indented pieces of bronze.[11]

> And then, He was led away to Golgotha—the place of the skull, and there "the darling of Heaven"[12] was crucified.

CHAPTER

6

He has remembered his love and his faithfulness to Israel;
all the ends of the earth have seen the salvation of our God.

PSALM 98:3

s Isaiah had prophesied centuries earlier, Jesus would be "despised and rejected"[13] by religious leaders. Yet knowing that would be His fate, the Savior went up to Jerusalem to be humiliated, to die at the hands of the Romans, and to rise again victorious on the third day. God had a bigger plan than any of that day had contemplated when it came to what the Messiah would accomplish. At the dawn of time, God knew His creation would rebel; the first eleven chapters of Genesis tell the story of mankind's unrelenting defiance. Following the episode of the Tower of Babel, God turned to one particular man: Abraham. From that one man sprang the children of Israel—the people who were chosen to bear witness to the truth of God in the midst of all the races of mankind, all who had turned their backs on the Creator.

Israel's story is one of decline marked by backsliding, apostasy, and idolatry. They became a people, as Jeremiah described them, "uncircumcised in heart." But the Lord also gave a promise to Jeremiah: He would make a new covenant with His people. Where the old covenant had been written on tablets of stone, the new covenant would be written on human hearts (see 2 Corinthians 3:3).

Centuries of darkness and oppression would hover over the people before this new covenant was established. Then, like a new shoot rising from a rotted stump, came Jesus, the righteous Branch. His blood, the ultimate sacrifice, purchased the forgiveness of sin and opened the door for the entry of all mankind into the kingdom of God.

Shortly before He ascended to heaven, Jesus told His disciples not to leave Jerusalem, but to wait there for the gift the Father had promised: the Holy Spirit. The Christian church was born—in Jerusalem—on the day of Pentecost, and the good news of the gospel of Jesus Christ has literally spread "to the ends of the earth" in our time. The Holy City served both as the birthplace of Christianity and as the site of the preaching and miracles of the first apostles.

As the early church faced bitter persecution, the city's political problems were increasing. After Herod the Great's death, the kingdom was divided among his sons. There was so much squabbling over the king's legacy, and such incompetence in his successors, that Rome was forced to intercede in short order. Herod Archelaeus, the son who succeeded Herod as ruler over Judea and Samaria, proved so ineffectual that the Romans demoted him, and the region became a direct colony of Rome. Herod Antipas, whom Jesus referred to as "that fox" (see Luke 13:32), became tetrarch—a subordinate ruler—over Galilee and Perea, and Philip the tetrarch ruled over the northern provinces, which bordered Galilee and Syria.

Resistance to the Roman administration smoldered quietly most of the time among the Jews' chief proponents: the Zealots (revolutionaries who fought against the Romans), the Hassidim (the strictly Orthodox Jewish sect), and the Essenes (a brotherhood of holy men and women). However, trouble erupted when Caligula, the emperor, attempted to have a statue of his likeness installed in the temple in Jerusalem. He planned to have sacrifices made to his image, but Herod Agrippa, to whom Caligula had given the kingdom of Philip the Tetrarch, persuaded his patron to drop the idea of temple sacrifices.

Agrippa befriended Claudius, another powerful friend in Rome. When the emperor Caligula, who many say was insane chiefly because of his claims of deity was assassinated, Claudius succeeded him as emperor. Agrippa, who was part Jewish, reaped a great reward when Claudius appointed him over the entire kingdom of Herod the Great. Under his supervision Jerusalem for a time enjoyed peace and quiet.

After the demise of Agrippa, a particularly unfortunate succession of governors followed. Graft and corruption rekindled the fires of Jewish revolt, and finally the Pharisees joined forces with the Zealots. War broke out in the summer of AD 66. Caught off guard, Roman forces in Judea quickly lost control of the Masada and Antonia fortresses and were slaughtered by the rebels. At Masada, rebels discovered a vast quantity of arms and dried food supplies. Herod the Great had stockpiled the materials more than one hundred years earlier in preparation for a possible war with Cleopatra. The storehouse proved fortuitous, and Jerusalem was soon back in Jewish hands.

In Jerusalem the leaders of the rebellion coined money, collected taxes, and organized defenses for the entire country. From Rome, Nero dispatched Roman Consul Vespasian with several legions to crush the uprising, the most stubborn and desperate revolt Rome had ever faced. Bloody fighting for the next three years resulted in the isolation of the rebels in Jerusalem and Masada.

Vespasian was crowned emperor in AD 70 and returned to Rome, leaving his son Titus in charge of the Judean campaign. Titus laid siege to Jerusalem with eight thousand veteran troops; fewer than a third as many Jews defended the city. In the face of incredible shortages and starvation, they clung tenaciously to their city. By late July, Titus had captured the Antonia fortress. Hollow-eyed with hunger, the defenders regrouped. From the roof of the portico around the edge of the temple platform they rained down stones, arrows, and fiery brands against the legionnaires. The Romans then burned the roofs from under the Jewish defenders. The attackers gained access to the platform itself, and the defenders retreated behind the wall of the temple proper into the Court of the Women and the Court of Israel. More flaming projectiles set the sanctuary ablaze, and a bloody slaughter ensued.

Jewish historian Josephus, who had defected to the Romans earlier in the rebellion, was an eyewitness to the event. He claimed that the streams of blood pouring from the corpses of the defenders were more copious than the fire that engulfed everything flammable in the vicinity. Before the Roman legions had finished, the city lay in ruins with the exception of Herod's palace, where the Tenth Legion was stationed as a permanent force of occupation. It would be three more years before the imperial armies recaptured Masada, the last stand of the Jewish revolt. Nearly one thousand men, women, and children had been hiding in that isolated mountaintop fortress. When the Roman armies finally scaled the awesome heights and reached the fortress, they were met with an eerie silence. All the Jews at Masada had committed suicide, preferring to die by their own hand than be slaughtered by the armies of Rome.

Judea, prostrate from the war, was slow to recover. Early in the second century a new emperor, Hadrian, came to the throne. A great administrator, he organized Roman law under a uniform code, sought ways to improve government efficiency, instituted an empire-wide communications system not unlike early America's Pony Express, and fortified the frontiers. Seeking to unify and strengthen the empire, Hadrian invoked laws to eliminate regional peculiarities. One of these, which prohibited "mutilations," was aimed at the Jewish practice of circumcision.

During his reign, Hadrian's Wall was built to mark the northern limit of Roman Britain. A substantial portion of the wall still stands. Hadrian also drew up a plan to rebuild Jerusalem as a center of pagan worship in honor of Jupiter, Juno, Venus, and of course himself. The city's name would be changed to Aelia Capitolina in honor of the Aelian clan, Hadrian's family.

The new plan saw little progress before it drew a response from Simon bar Kokhba, a charismatic Jewish leader of that day. He united the Jews and enticed recruits from throughout the Diaspora, including Samaritans and Gentiles. His troops totaled nearly four hundred thousand when rebellion exploded in AD 132. It took three years and five legions of battle-hardened Roman troops to retake Jerusalem. Bar Kokhba remained elusive but was eventually captured and executed in AD 136.

After its victory, the Roman Army took a terrible revenge. Some of the rebel leaders were skinned alive prior to their executions. Massacres during the fighting had been common; survivors were either sold into slavery or simply allowed to starve. Burial was not permitted, so heaps of corpses lay decomposing in the streets and fields. The Temple Mount was literally plowed under and an entirely new city was constructed north of the old one. It contained two buildings, together with pagan temples. The temple platform was used as a public square on the south side of the city. It was bedecked with statues of Hadrian and other Roman notables of the day. It was an offense punishable by death for Jews to enter Jerusalem; neither were they allowed to observe the Sabbath, read or teach the Law, circumcise, or otherwise follow God's Laws.

Hadrian changed the name of Judea to Syria Palaestina and made its capital Caesarea. Jerusalem, no longer a capital city, was renamed Aelia. Syria Palaestina is the origin of the name *Palestine* and in modern times applies to the area that would eventually become the national homeland of the returning Diaspora Jews. It was said that Hadrian renamed Judea after the ancient enemy of the Jews, the Philistines. Romans in general, and Hadrian in particular, hated Jews.

Of all the nations the Romans conquered, the Jewish people were the only group who would never quite submit to the Roman yoke. For that reason, Hadrian was determined to wipe the memory of Judea and its people from the pages of history. For the next five hundred years, Jews would only be allowed into the city of Jerusalem on the anniversary of the burning of the temple.

With the Jewish population thoroughly subdued, Roman rulers turned their attention to another foe that threatened Rome's cultural survival: Christianity. Christians, who refused to sacrifice to the emperor and worshiped none of the pantheon of Roman gods, were said to be atheists. Persecution against the early church continued off and on for over two centuries.

Although Jews were forbidden in Jerusalem, Gentile Christians were not. Consequently, members of the church who had all but disappeared from the city after AD 70 began to reappear. Sometime in the second century, the first church building was erected on Mount Zion. Early in the fourth century, the emperor Constantine underwent a conversion to Christianity. He moved the capital of the empire from Rome to Byzantium, which he renamed Constantinople, partly as a consequence of his conversion.

Jerusalem suddenly began to regain prestige. Constantine sent funds to be used to excavate and preserve Christian relics and sites. Later, his mother, Helena, an elderly pious woman, went to Jerusalem to supervise and pay for the erection of a number of churches, among them the Church of the Holy Sepulchre. In addition, she also saw to the demolition of the temple of Aphrodite. It was on the site of this pagan temple that, tradition holds, Jesus had been buried after the crucifixion; thus the origin of the Church of the Holy Sepulcher, which was finished in AD 335.

Jerusalem quickly became the site of frequent pilgrimages. Churches, monasteries, and hospices for pilgrims became more and more plentiful. Gradually the evidence of Rome's paganizing of the city disappeared. Under Emperor Theodosius, Christianity became the official religion of the Roman Empire in the late fourth century.

This meant a more prosperous Jerusalem, which became one of the four most important cities in Christianity, along with Alexandria, Rome, and Antioch.

In the fifth and sixth centuries, Roman colonies suffered an economic recession that weakened the empire considerably. Taking advantage of this, the Persians began moving westward, seizing lands that had formerly belonged to the Romans. In AD 614 Jerusalem was again besieged. The patriarch of Jerusalem refused to surrender and the city fell. A terribly gruesome slaughter followed. The Persians then put as many of the churches and monasteries to the torch as they could.

However, the Persian occupation was short lived. In AD 628 Theodosius invaded Persia to reclaim the empire's lost holdings. He retrieved a cross that was thought to have been the one on which Jesus was crucified and returned it to Jerusalem. In the following years Christians sought to rebuild what the Persians had destroyed, but they never had time to restore the city's previous splendor. An emerging religion in Arabia would put an end to any hopes of rebuilding.

CHAPTER

7

*The Lord, the Lord of Heaven's Armies, will take away from Jerusalem and Judah
everything they depend on: every bit of bread and every drop of water.*

ISAIAH 3:1 NLT

As previously mentioned, Jerusalem has been laid waste numerous times by a host of enemies. Counted among its foes is not a person, but a religion—Islam. History records that its founder, Muhammad, never actually set foot in Jerusalem. He lived the last years of his life in Mecca and Medina during the time of the Persian occupation of Jerusalem. Just four years after his death, however, his followers stormed the gates of the Holy City.

Contrary to popular thought, Jerusalem is not mentioned by name in the Koran. The tenuous connection of the Holy City to Islam is based on a single line in the Islamic holy book, which describes the prophet's famous "flight to heaven" or *Isra'*:

Glory to him who brought his servant at night from
the Holy Mosque to the Remote Mosque, the precincts
of which we have bless.[14]

Perhaps for political reasons, it was not until the eighth century
that the unspecified mosque was said to have been in Jerusalem.
The *Isra'*, or nighttime visit to heaven, was an ecstatic experience
or dream. The legend of the *Isra'* says that Muhammad was carried
to Jerusalem on *al-Burak* (lightning), a winged horse with the face
of a woman and tail of a peacock. Arriving at the temple platform,
Muhammad dismounted and the angel Gabriel hitched *al-Burak* to a
ring in the gate of the Western Wall. Muhammad then proceeded up
to the outcropping of rock on the platform. There, assembled around
the rock, was a group of old prophets: among them were Abraham,
Moses, and Jesus. They all joined Muhammad in prayer.

Then the prophet climbed a ladder of light from atop the sacred
rock, through the seven heavens, and into the very presence of
Allah, who gave him a teaching about prayer. After that, Muhammad
descended by the same ladder back to the rock. *Al-Burak* carried him
back to Mecca and his bed before the night was over.[15]

Muhammad expected both Jews and Christians to receive him as
a prophet, and designated Jerusalem as the direction to face while in
prayer. Angered when he was rejected by the orthodox of both faiths,
Muhammad altered his instructions and directed his followers to face

Mecca during daily prayers. The heart of Muhammad's religious lore did have biblical roots: His concept of Islam (which means "submission") was derived from Abraham's submission of his son as a sacrifice to God. However, Muhammad believed it was through Ishmael that the true faith was descended, and that it was Ishmael—not Isaac—that Allah instructed Abraham to sacrifice on Mount Moriah.

During the last ten years of his life Muhammad enjoyed phenomenal success. He built an empire that covered all of Arabia, and found men competent to carry on his work after him. Those men were called caliphs, and by AD 700 the empire had extended to include Palestine, Syria, Mesopotamia, Egypt, all of North Africa, Spain, and Asia Minor.

In AD 636, four years after Muhammad's death, Islam arrived on Jerusalem's doorstep when the army of Caliph Omar began a two-year siege of the city. When Patriarch Sophronius decided it was time to surrender, he remembered the bloodshed that had accompanied the Persian conquest twenty-four years earlier, and sent out a request that the caliph come to Jerusalem to receive the surrender in person.

Omar and Sophronius met at the Muslim encampment on the Mount of Olives. Omar was disposed to be generous and permitted the Christians complete freedom to practice their religion and retain their holy sites. The principal change would be that taxes would be paid to Muslims instead of the Byzantines. Omar's tolerance was also extended to the Jews who would, for the first time in five hundred years, be allowed to live in Jerusalem.

As conqueror, Omar wanted to see the Temple Mount and the sacred rock from which Muhammad had ascended to heaven that celebrated night. When they arrived at the site, he and his men discovered that the area had been turned into a garbage dump, likely a gesture of disdain.

Appalled, Omar started work immediately to clean the area. The thousand men with him were enlisted in the project so that the job was completed in reasonably short order. As they knelt at the southern end of the platform to face Mecca and pray, surely Sophronius looked on in abject horror. The Temple Mount had been defiled by Muslim infidels. It was dedicated as a Muslim place of worship and renamed *Haram esh-Sharif,* or "Noble Sanctuary."

Omar and his followers opted not to establish their district capital in Jerusalem but governed from various other locations. However, Abd al-Malik, fifth of the Umayyad caliphs, did have a particular stake in Jerusalem, as a rival caliph controlled both Mecca and Medina.

In an attempt to attract pilgrims to Jerusalem and to erect a structure that would rival all other churches in the city, Omar approved the construction of the Dome of the Rock. Begun in AD 687, the edifice required four years for completion. Al-Malik succeeded in erecting a building that would dominate Jerusalem's skyline and outshine all the city's churches. However, his attempts failed to draw Muslims away from their principal devotion to Mecca and Medina.

While the Dome of the Rock is a mosque, it serves primarily as a shrine and covering for the sacred rock beneath—the site where Abraham was said to have offered Isaac. It is an octagon on a square base reached by six stairways. By any standard, the building is magnificently beautiful, but time and earth tremors have taken a toll, making frequent repairs necessary. Even so, it is still very much reminiscent of the one that was unveiled in AD 691.

The sacred rock enshrined beneath the cupola is roughly two hundred feet in circumference. During the centuries following the dome's construction, the rock was surrounded by rich brocaded curtains. Daily it was anointed with a lovely mixture of incense. More than 150 chains suspended overhead held scores of candelabra for illumination. Over three hundred people were employed to maintain the building and its grounds.

When the Muslim invaders captured Jerusalem, however, they turned Mount Moriah back into a place of worship. It was not *Yahweh*, the God of Abraham, Isaac, and Jacob, who was worshiped at the holy place; it was Allah, the Muslim god—not the same God of the Bible worshiped by both Jews, the "people of the Book," and Christians.

Prior to Muhammad, the Arabs worshiped many gods; the Ka'aba shrine in the city of Mecca was home to some 360 idols. The Arabs' chief god was the moon god, who was known by the title *al-Ilah*, "the deity." Even before Muhammad's time the moon god's title had been shortened from *al-Ilah* to Allah. Muhammad "promoted" Allah as the only god of Islam. Allah's symbol, adopted by Islam, was the crescent moon. This was one of the reasons Islam, although monotheistic, was rejected by both Jews and Christians as an unscriptural religion: the people of the Book recognized that Allah was certainly *not* the god of the Book.

Outside of one brief period, approximately one hundred years under Crusader rule, when the mosque was turned into a church, the Dome of the Rock has stood its ground for thirteen centuries.

Muslim hostility toward both Judaism and Christianity can be found in the Arabic inscriptions on the walls of the Dome of the Rock. There are over 700 feet of inscriptions, many of them quotes from the Koran:

> In the name of God, the Merciful the Compassionate. There is no god but God. He is One. He has no associate.
>
> Say: He is God, the One! God, the eternally Besought of all!
>
> Muhammad is the Messenger of God. Lo! God and His angels shower blessings on the Prophet.
>
> Praise be to God, Who hath not taken unto Himself a son, and Who hath no partner in the Sovereignty, nor hath He any protecting friend through dependence.
>
> Unto Him [Allah] belongeth sovereignty and unto

Him belongeth praise. He quickeneth. And He giveth death; and He has Power over all things. Muhammad is the Messenger of God, the blessing of God be on him.[16]

Tension between Muslims and Jews over the Temple Mount has created centuries-old conflict. Jewish ownership of the site, however, predates Muslim control by at least fifteen centuries. If title deed to this forty-five-acre tinderbox could be proved by any party, it would definitely be the Jewish people. God promised them the land, Jerusalem included. God's Word records that King David paid fifty shekels of silver for the site on which the temple would eventually be built (2 Samuel 24:24).

Gradually the administration of Jerusalem became more repressive toward Christians and Jews. Muhammad had declared there could be no other religion in Arabia than Islam. His edicts extended throughout the rapidly expanding empire.

Today, Muslims continue to see the world divided into two segments. One is *Dar al-Islam*, or "the world of Islam"; the other is *Dar al-Harb,* "the world of the sword" or "the world of war," those non-Islamic nations that have not yet been conquered by Muslim armies. Contrarily, Jews and Christians are regarded as "the people of the Book."

Non-Muslims residing in Islamic countries are regarded as *dhimmis,* "protected ones," or "tolerated ones," second-class citizens—in every sense inferior. The Koran commands imposing *jizya*, or a poll tax, on non-Muslims.

Eventually the various ruling dynasties of the Islamic empire began to rely heavily on Turkish mercenaries called Seljuks. By the middle of the eleventh century the Seljuks had gained political and military ascendancy in the empire. Rulers were called *sultan*, which means "master." Caliphates were effectively reduced to centers of purely religious affairs.

A strong and vigorous group, the Seljuks brought new life to the fading empire. They captured Jerusalem in AD 1070 and tales of their maliciousness and persecution of both Christians and Jews reached Europe quickly. As a result, Pope Gregory VII urged Christendom to launch a series of crusades against Turkish expansion into Europe and Islamic oppression of Christians in Palestine. It was his successor, Pope Urban II, who gathered a great assembly of churchmen and nobles in Clermont, France, in AD 1095.

In a stirring sermon, he urged the knights of Europe to stop their feuds, turn their efforts to the rescue of fellow Christians, and to retake the Holy Land from the Turks. The response was thunderous as the hall was filled with shouts of *"Deus vuh!"* ("God wills it!"). Soon thousands had enlisted in the holy cause. Jerusalem was about to be liberated from the Muslim infidels.

The Frankish knights of Godfrey de Bouillon, Duke of Lower Lorraine, at last gazed on Jerusalem on June 7, 1099. They had already endured arduous battles with the Saracens (Muslims) at Nicaea and Antioch. Traveling over two thousand miles, the majority of that on foot, it had taken three years to arrive at this, the knights' true goal.

Jerusalem was the grand prize for the Crusaders. They had come to rescue fellow Christians, to halt the Muslim expansion into Europe, and to liberate the sacred shrines of faith from the heathen. The first glimpse of the walled Holy City was overwhelming for many who lifted their eyes and hands heavenward and gave thanks. Others removed their shoes and bowed down to kiss the holy ground on which they were standing.

Inside the walls of Jerusalem a thousand men beseeched Allah for help to battle the great host of the enemy arrayed on the surrounding hillsides. The city's defenders had reason to be uneasy: The crusaders outnumbered them nearly twelve to one.

During the first few weeks, however, the Muslims stoutly resisted the Christians, and for the Europeans it was beginning to appear as though it would be another long siege. Before the Crusaders' arrival the Muslims had either poisoned or filled in the wells outside the city. In the ranks of the Crusaders, soldiers were parched from the fierce summer heat, and food had become scarce. There were more desertions. One entire company held a baptismal service in the Jordan River and then left for the coast to find a ship sailing for Europe.

But the Crusaders were not only short of food and water; they were short of weapons. The initial assault on the city had failed because they did not have enough ladders to scale the walls in sufficient numbers to overtake the enemy, so were forced to retreat.

Timing was critical, as additional troops from Egypt had been dispatched to reinforce the Muslims inside the walled city. The Crusaders still vastly outnumbered the city's defenders but would need to erect catapults and siege towers to successfully take the city before enemy reinforcements arrived. However, they still lacked supplies to build the needed armaments.

Just when it appeared that hope was lost, six ships sailed into Jaffa carrying food and supplies for the Christians. Now all they lacked was wood. The hills around Jerusalem were bare, so the soldiers traveled as far as Samaria to bring sufficient timber, loaded on camels and the backs of captives, to the army.

The bishop of Puy, Lord Adhemar, who had accompanied the army, had a vision that he related to Peter Desiderius, a military leader: He said he had received this message:

> "Speak to the princes and all the people, and say to them: 'You who have come from distant lands to worship God and the Lord of hosts, purge yourselves of your uncleanliness, and let each one turn from his evil ways. Then with bare feet march around Jerusalem invoking God, and you must also fast. If you do this and then make a great attack on the city on the ninth day, it will

be captured. If you do not, all the evils that you have suffered will be multiplied by the Lord.'"[17]

The soldiers responded to Lord Adhemar's vision and on Friday, July 8, 1099, marched barefooted in a solemn procession around the city. It was quite a show for the Muslims who gathered on the walls overlooking the Crusaders to watch and mock the parade. By the following Sunday the Crusaders had completed siege towers and placed them against the walls of the Holy City. Two days later, the attack was renewed and the bombardment lasted through the night. One week after the display of piety, the Crusader armies shouted as one, "God wills it!" They stormed over the walls as the Muslims fled to the refuge of Al-Aqsa Mosque, where the enemy was quickly overtaken. What followed has tainted Muslim/Christian relations ever since.

CHAPTER

8

For Jerusalem has stumbled and Judah has fallen, because their speech and their deeds are against the Lord, defying his glorious presence.

ISAIAH 3:8 ESV

The Crusaders had successfully stormed the walls of the city of Jerusalem. Mad with victory, they launched a rampage of looting and carnage as bloody as any episode in the history of the Holy City. Raymond of Aguilers, a chaplain accompanying the Europeans, wrote of the bloodbath:

> Our men cut off the heads of their enemies, others shot them with arrows so that they fell from the towers, others tortured them longer by casting them into the flames. Piles of heads, hands and feet were to be seen on the streets. It was necessary to pick one's way over the bodies of men and horses.[18]

The butchery was not limited to soldiers: All infidels were in jeopardy of their lives, regardless of age or sex. Infants were torn from the arms of their mothers and mercilessly slaughtered. Jews inside the city walls, accused of aiding and abetting the Muslim rulers, were rounded up and taken to a synagogue where they were burned alive. The total number of people killed in this "liberation" of Jerusalem is believed to have been in the tens of thousands, including men, women, and children—most of whom were civilians. Conversely, some historians think the Crusaders recorded events that greatly exaggerated their exploits for the sake of propaganda.

The barbarism of the Europeans was inexcusable, and yet they blindly followed the customs of the age in which they lived. Medieval laws of warfare dictated that if a city was surrendered, it would not be ransacked and destroyed. If not, it was fair game for pillaging and looting. Because the Muslims in Jerusalem had resisted, the Crusaders felt justified in their actions. After having traveled for three years, spanning the two thousand miles from Europe to Jerusalem, followed by weeks and weeks of preparation, the combat finally began. Once freed to attack inhabitants of the Holy City, the troops were impossible to restrain. The knights of the Middle Ages had been fed a steady diet of revenge and were determined to rain down retribution on those barbarians who had defiled Jerusalem. The horrific bloodshed was a dreadful byproduct of that hatred.

Not quite one thousand years after Hadrian had changed the name of Jerusalem to Aelia, its name was officially reinstated. Crusader Godfrey de Bouillon was named king of Jerusalem. He eschewed the title, believing that only Jesus Christ could hold that title. He took for himself the title, "Defender of the Holy Sepulcher."[19] He and his associates imposed a feudal system on the city and surrounding territory. Land was parceled out to various barons to whom the people became serfs. Mosques were converted into churches and chapels.

A steady stream of as many as ten thousand Christian pilgrims yearly began journeying to Jerusalem. Though the Crusader defenders built or rebuilt almost forty churches in the city, the Church of the Holy Sepulchre received the highest priority. It was rededicated, after elaborate restoration and refurbishing, in 1149.

The kingdom of Jerusalem continued to expand until it stretched from Lebanon all the way to Egypt. Muslims attempted to regain lost territory during the Second Crusade, but that ended in complete failure. Then a new Muslim leader, *Salah ad-din*, or Saladin, stepped onto the pages of history. A Kurdish Muslim from Tikrit in what is now northern Iraq, he quickly unified Syria and Egypt. Within a few years his kingdom stretched up into Mesopotamia and encompassed territory in what is today Jordan, Israel, Lebanon, Libya, Saudi Arabia, Sudan, Tunisia, Turkey, and Yemen.[20]

After having added Egypt and Syria to his list, Saladin set his sights on Jerusalem. He marshaled one hundred thousand troops and soundly defeated the forces of the king of Jerusalem, the Guy de Lusignan, in a heated battle north of the Sea of Galilee. Saladin not only captured the Guy, he also liberated a large wooden cross and sent it to the caliph of Baghdad. The Crusaders were convinced it was the Roman implement of torture to which Jesus had been nailed.

Saladin finally reached the city of Jerusalem in 1187. A delegation from the Holy City sought a peaceful transition, and Saladin replied that he would prefer not to besiege the city as he, too, regarded it as holy ground. Realizing that the Christian garrison was small, Saladin allowed a few months' breathing spell to strengthen its defenses and replenish its supplies. If at the end of that time they still had hopes of rescue, the Christians would be in a position to fight honorably Otherwise, he suggested they surrender immediately while he was willing to spare lives and property.

The Europeans could not tolerate the idea of relinquishing the city without a fight, nor would they accept the respite offered. The siege resumed the next day, and within a few weeks the city had fallen. Saladin's terms were unusually humane for that time: Because the city had surrendered, he exacted a ransom of ten gold pieces per man, five per woman, and one per child. Those who could not pay the ransom—some fifteen thousand Christians—were sold into slavery.

Under his administration Jerusalem, which he renamed *al-Quds* (the Holy One) was once again opened to the Jews. In addition, Saladin made the city available to Christian pilgrims, so long as they were unarmed. The end of the Crusader period marked the last time Jews would be prohibited free access to the Western Wall of the Holy City until 1948, when Jordan annexed the West Bank and East Jerusalem.

Saladin restored the temple platform—the *Haram esh-Sharif*—to Islamic status. The Crusaders had used both the Dome of the Rock and the Al-Aqsa Mosque as their headquarters. The two structures had been converted into churches, each with a gold cross raised atop the dome where the Islamic crescent had once stood. Under Saladin the cross was lowered, and the crescent restored.

The fall of Jerusalem sent shock waves throughout Europe. Pope Gregory VIII issued a call for a third Crusade, and Richard Cœur de Lion (Richard the Lionhearted) answered. In 1191 Richard retook Acre on the Mediterranean coast of Palestine and, in several other battles with Saladin, proved a worthy opponent for the Saracen leader.

Much to his chagrin, Richard was unable to wrest Jerusalem from the Muslims, and a respect and friendship grew between Richard and Saladin. As a result, they were able to affect a truce. Under its terms, the Muslims retained control of Jerusalem, while the Christians regulated the seacoast between Acre and Jaffa. Citizens and merchants of both regions were permitted to traverse the two zones unmolested.

After Saladin's death his empire disintegrated. Other Crusades followed, but by 1291 that era had ended and Christian presence in the Holy Land dwindled. Jerusalem would remain under the firm hand of Muslim war lords for a long time to come.

In Europe at the end of the fifteenth century, Spanish monarchs Ferdinand and Isabella had succeeded in driving the Moors (Muslim North Africans) out of their country. In the zeal to procure a purely Catholic state, they expelled the country's large, highly educated and cultured Jewish community in 1492.

It was, perhaps, not incidental when in that same year Christopher Columbus was dispatched across the Atlantic in search of a new and shorter route to the Far East. According to a *Daily Mail* article published in 2012, there may have been another reason Columbus sailed the ocean blue:

> . . .scholars have claimed there is compelling evidence that suggests Christopher Columbus was secretly Jewish and that he hid his true faith to survive the Spanish Inquisition. In a further revelation, historians believe the real motive behind his historic quest was to find a new homeland for Jews who were persecuted and run out of Spain.[21]

The expulsion of Jews from Spain was a disastrous blow. Many of those who were banished had to content themselves with much humbler quarters in the less-habitable climes of the Middle East, and some relocated to Jerusalem. For Spain, it constituted a self-inflicted wound from which the nation has never fully recovered.

In 1516 a new group of conquerors headed for the Holy City. As Martin Luther expounded Pauline doctrine to his students at Germany's Wittenberg University, Turkish tribesmen, the Ottomans, set their sights on Jerusalem. A vigorous and unusually warlike group, the Ottoman Turks rapidly subdued district after district and region after region throughout the Middle East. Eventually the empire would be one of the most all-encompassing in history.

By the following year, Jerusalem was under the control of yet another new landlord, Ottoman conqueror Selim I. During his reign, a heavy poll tax (*jizya*) was imposed on all non-Muslims. Selim's son, Suleiman the Magnificent, governed during the strongest and most robust period of the Ottoman Empire. He restored Islamic shrines throughout the empire and provided the Dome of the Rock with the exterior mosaic of glazed Persian tile that still bedecks the edifice.

The *Haram esh-Sharif* as it exists today is largely due to Suleiman. He rebuilt the walls of the city, and according to legend, ordered the Golden Gate on the east side of the *Haram* sealed to prevent the biblical promise of the entry of Messiah into Jerusalem through that gate.

Under Ottoman control the Jewish population of Jerusalem grew slowly but persistently. The city's infrastructure, however, suffered from neglect and corruption, and total population then shriveled to approximately ten thousand—a thousand Jews, three thousand Christians, and six thousand Muslims. As a result, Jerusalem was shunted to the backwaters of the Ottoman Empire—still "trodden down of the gentiles," or *ethnos*, meaning people of all origins.

The final year of the eighteenth century brought about events that would place Jerusalem in the headlines once again: Napoleon Bonaparte set foot on the shores of the Mediterranean Sea at Alexandria, Egypt. It was in Egypt that Suleiman's empire was most vulnerable to the establishment of a European colony. The little French general was not intent on military conquest alone; a new colony would be a tribute to the ability of the modern-day Franks to re-create the splendor that had once reigned along the shores of the Nile under the Pharaohs.

To realize his dream, Napoleon had brought with him some of the most prestigious French scientists, engineers, naturalists, orientalists, and antiquarians available. He planted the seed that would germinate and bear fruit long after he had faded from the scene. His team set to work on large-scale archaeological projects that remain today.

Napoleon's dream would become a nightmare when on the night of August 1, 1798, Admiral Horatio Nelson's fleet appeared off the coast of Alexandria. By daybreak the British had engaged and destroyed the general's massive flotilla. Faced with Nelson on the one hand and the Ottoman Army that was amassing to invade Egypt on the other, the British were confident that Napoleon would capitulate and return to France. Wrong! The emperor-to-be was not so easily intimidated. Instead, he set his face toward Jerusalem.

CHAPTER
9

The secret things belong to the LORD our God,
but the things that are revealed
belong to us and to our children forever,
that we may do all the words of this law.

DEUTERONOMY 29:29 ESV

In January 1799, Napoleon and an army of thirteen thousand men marched into Palestine to meet and crush the Ottoman Army. He moved steadily across the Sinai where he captured the cities of al-Arish and Gaza with ease, but at Jaffa the Turks countered with stiff resistance. After finally defeating them, Napoleon loosed his troops in a spree of bloodshed and looting that forewarned the inhabitants of Palestine of the true face of this new invader. When Napoleon's army suffered an epidemic of bubonic plague, many viewed it as divine retribution.

Napoleon's advance was finally halted at Acre, the old Crusader stronghold. As the French general's troops approached the city, the

Ottoman sultan announced his intention to massacre Christians in Palestine whom he suspected of having aided Napoleon. In response to Suleiman's threat, Commodore Smith of Britain's offshore fleet informed the sultan that the guns of his man-o'-war would provide protection for the Christians, just as it had protected the Turks from Napoleon.

Smith then dispatched a detachment of sailors to make a dramatic march to the walls of Jerusalem where many native Christians lived. There, they were met by Catholic and Orthodox churchmen, and greeted with profuse thanks and anxious appeals for protection. That event marked the beginning of Britain's involvement with the Holy City—one that would continue for nearly 150 years.

While Napoleon may have failed to capture Jerusalem, his forays into the Middle East served notice to the Ottoman Empire: It was no longer the impregnable bastion it had once been. It also clarified the strategic importance of Palestine in the quest for empire building, a mission that would dominate nineteenth-century politics in Europe. Leaders of the major nations of Western Europe began maneuvering for position, speculating that when the Ottoman Empire eventually fell, Palestine would be ripe for conquest.

Prompted by Napoleon's attempts to invade the region, a secret struggle commenced among Europeans for control of that vital Middle East region—a struggle carried out primarily by curiosity seekers, explorers, missionaries, archaeologists, and diplomats.

As news of open doors to the land of the Bible spread, England and the United States were electrified. Both nations were freshly imbued with Christian zeal following the Wesleyan revivals of the eighteenth century and the consequent spread of Methodism. As news of the dramatic Battle of Acre and the accompanying reports about the Holy Land reached the ears of evangelists and biblical scholars, many immediately wanted to know more about this "land of milk and honey" of which they had read in their Bibles.

The first wave of explorers and curiosity seekers found the region much less romantic and idyllic than they might have imagined. The terrain was desolate, the shrines a sham, and the inhabitants uncouth. It would require a hardier resolve than could be mustered by mere inquisitiveness to surmount those obstacles. The zeal of evangelical Christians, however, proved more than adequate for the task.

The people of the Levant, the countries on the eastern Mediterranean, were not ripe for revival in the usual sense of the word, but a handful of hardy Christians bravely paved the way for others to enter that forbidding land. There, the groundwork for the field of scientific biblical archaeology was laid.

In the 1840s a United States naval expedition explored the passage from the Sea of Galilee down the Jordon River to the Dead Sea. By mid-century, British, French, and Germans became more plentiful in the region, and consular offices were established in Jerusalem. Maneuvering for superiority in Palestine began to grow more intense.

The Palestine Exploration Fund, or PEF, which would play a commanding role in ensuing endeavors in the Middle East, was established in England in 1865. Its founders envisioned the PEF "for the purpose of investigating the archaeology, geography, manners, customs and culture, geology, and natural history of the Holy Land."[22] The organization was founded to aid a Palestine seemingly surrounded by a desolate and barren landscape, but soon an entire history was uncovered, as outlines of archaeological sites were found in the hills, valleys, and plains of the Holy Land.

It would be Charles Warren, an aggressive member of the PEF, who introduced the concept of forming an organization fashioned after the East India Company, through which Great Britain would have oversight of the project for two decades.

Queen Victoria consented to be the official patron of the society and sent a contribution of 150 British pounds sterling in support of the project. One of the other speakers addressed the need of the PEF to counteract efforts by the French to stake a claim in Palestine.

In 1881, the PEF dispatched teams led by lieutenants Claude Reignier Conder and Horatio Herbert Kitchener of the Royal Engineers to map Western Palestine in its entirety. (The survey marked the beginning of a project that T. E. Lawrence, the legendary Lawrence of Arabia, helped to complete in 1914.)

The two men were assigned to the area west of the Jordan River, from Beersheba in the south to Tyre in the north. Conder, who first arrived in Palestine in 1872, had spent six years there before being wounded at Safed. He left the Middle East only to return with Kitchener. Conder was convinced that the area being mapped should be placed in the capable hands of the Jews. He felt they would be better stewards of the land than those who then inhabited the area, because the Jews were "energetic, industrious, and tactful."[23]

Conder was engaged not only to help survey the land but also to determine basic needs in the territory. His list included draining swamps and providing irrigation to the arid land, restoring the network of aqueducts and wells, and meeting the sanitation requirements of the population. He also noted the need for a system of roads connecting Dan and Beersheba, as well as reforestation and agricultural projects. Conder is credited with establishing the guidelines through which the "flowering of the desert" has since been achieved in the land of Israel. In an address to the London branch of Hovevei Zion (Lovers of Zion) in 1892, Conder proposed the establishment of a rail system from Damascus to Haifa. He believed the region was so fertile that a means to transport produce to markets would be advantageous. It was his hope that Israel would one day become an agricultural leader.

Charles Warren was the first agent of the PEF to engage in serious archaeological excavations. He also was an officer of the Royal Engineers and highly experienced in the work of digging mines and tunnels for military purposes. Because of the nervousness of the

Turkish officials as well as the townspeople in Jerusalem about excavations of holy sites, Warren's techniques proved invaluable. To explore the walls of the Haram and other sites, he simply sank shafts into the ground and then tunneled to the location he wished to examine. All that could be seen of his work above ground was an innocuous opening in the earth which allayed fears that he would create mayhem in the city. At the same time Warren was working in Jerusalem, the terrain was being excavated in the southwest for a project that would affect Jerusalem more deeply than Warren's explorations: For ten long years, the French had been busy digging the Suez Canal. Aristotle wrote of the early efforts to provide a navigable, artificial waterway from the Mediterranean to the Red Sea:

> One of their kings tried to make a canal to it (for it would have been of no little advantage to them for the whole region to have become navigable; Sesostris is said to have been the first of the ancient kings to try), but he found that the sea was higher than the land. So he first, and Darius afterwards, stopped making the canal, lest the sea should mix with the river water and spoil it.[24]

The successful construction of the canal, which first opened on November 17, 1869, with upgrades completed in 2015, provide a shorter and more rapid journey for vessels traveling between the North Atlantic and the Indian Ocean.

At first the British, who had the most to gain from the canal, had nothing to do with its construction or management. When the Franco-Prussian War (1870–1871) destroyed the empire of Napoleon III, Britain was virtually unobstructed in its efforts to gain control of the canal. Egypt, which might have been a player in the control of the canal, was instead quickly becoming a British colony.

The secret struggle for Palestine, however, would continue much longer. Europeans were aware that the Ottoman Empire was crumbling. When it did collapse, there would be a scramble among Britain, France, Germany, and Russia to divide the remains. The situation was fraught with risks, and the consensus was that Istanbul's domain should be left intact as long as possible until other matters were settled.

Meanwhile, Jerusalem blossomed. The influx of Europeans and Americans dramatically changed the face of the city. Signs such as Deutsche Palaestina Bank and Barclays appeared on its streets. The Turks did what they could to hold the line, but the tide of westernization proved overwhelming. In the 1880s, in addition to diplomatic and archaeological activity, the French found time to construct a railroad from the coast to Jerusalem.

By the middle of the century the number of Jews had risen to constitute nearly half the population. Many new immigrants fell into the pattern of the scholars and sages who lived in the city and were supported by the charity of Jews in Europe and the United States. It would take time for the idea of reclaiming the desolate countryside to truly seize the Jewish imagination.

Sir Moses Montefiore, a wealthy English banker, contributed a good deal of money and energy to expanding the concept of what it meant for Jews to live again in their own land. He donated large sums of money to promote industry, education, and health amongst the Jewish community in Palestine, including the founding of *Mishkenot Sha'ananim* (peaceful habitation), the first settlement of the *New Yishuv* [those immigrants who built outside the walls of Old Jerusalem.]

In 1858, Montefiore's dream of building a windmill, also "outside the walls," became a reality. Its purpose was to free the Jews from dependency on Arab flour mills. Thoroughly incensed, Arab millers tried to sabotage the project—not with explosives but with a curse, as S. Y. Agnon penned in his book *Only Yesterday*:

> And the Arabs saw and were jealous. They hired an old man to curse the windmill. He turned his eyes to the windmill and said, I guarantee you that when the rains come and the winds come, they will make it into an everlasting ruin, and the rains came and the winds came and didn't do anything to it.[25]

After an extensive renovation in 2012, Montefiore's windmill was rededicated by Prime Minister Benjamin Netanyahu to again be used for grinding grain. During his remarks, the prime minister said of Montefiore:

> Moses Montefiore made a great and significant contribution to Jews' leaving the walls. He contributed to their economic base during a very difficult time, even as the Baron Rothschild supported the early communities. Beyond the economic support, he also assisted Jews with know-how on managing enterprises and developing the economy of the future Israel. This double contribution was expressed here in this neighborhood and this windmill.[26]

Montefiore's name is linked with another Israeli settlement—*Har Hatikva*. The colony, also known as Mount Hope, was established in 1855 by a group of American and German Christian Zionists. Located just north of Jaffa, the first outpost in this area was destined for violence that would leave an indelible mark on the colonists.

The original community fathers chose the location that houses the Shevah Mofet School just south of the central bus station in southern Tel Aviv. The plan was to establish farms that would ultimately instill the desire in local Jews to choose farming as an occupation. The effort became a topic for journalists in both the United States and Europe, and numerous articles found their way into various newspapers.

Mishkenot Sha'ananim ("Dwellings of Tranquility") is used today by the Israeli government to house honored guests of the country.

The constant influx of Westerners increased with the opening of the Suez Canal. Almost one million Europeans visited Jerusalem in the nineteenth century. It was no longer a tourist attraction solely for the wealthy or the religious. After the opening of the canal, a Baptist lay preacher, Thomas Cook, launched a travel agency that made it affordable for middle-class Europeans to tour Jerusalem. Travelogues about the Holy Land, and especially Jerusalem, were written by famous authors such as Benjamin Disraeli, Gustave Flaubert, and Herman Melville, and quickly became bestsellers.

Perhaps one of the best-known American writers to tour the Middle East and publish a manuscript of his travels was Samuel Langhorne Clemens. Under the penname of Mark Twain, he was a writer who gained global fame for his body of work—especially *The Innocents Abroad.*

This contribution of Twain's was a biting satire on the prolific accounts of devoted pilgrims. It regaled readers with the details of his trip to the Middle East. Though labeled a Holy Land excursion, he visited a number of towns and cities along the Mediterranean Sea before reaching his final destination of Jerusalem.

Given his assessment upon arriving in the Holy Land, it's a wonder his travels generated any desire at all to travel to Palestine. He observed:

Of all the lands there are for dismal scenery, I think Palestine must be the prince. The hills are barren, they are dull of color, they are unpicturesque in shape. The valleys are unsightly deserts fringed with feeble vegetation that has an expression about it of being sorrowful and despondent. The Dead Sea and the Sea of Galilee sleep in the midst of a vast stretch of hill and plain wherein the eye rests upon no pleasant tint, no striking object, no soft picture dreaming in a purple haze or mottled with the shadows of the clouds. Every outline is harsh, every feature is distinct, there is no perspective—distance works no enchantment here. It is a hopeless, dreary, heart-broken land. . . . Palestine sits in sackcloth and ashes. Over it broods the spell of a curse that has withered its fields and fettered its energies. . . . Palestine is desolate and unlovely.[27]

CHAPTER
10

Shake off your dust; rise up, sit enthroned, Jerusalem.
Free yourself from the chains on your neck, Daughter Zion, now a captive.

ISAIAH 52:2

The precarious status quo in Jerusalem became even more unstable as Britain, France, and Russia connived to wrest more territory from the Ottoman Empire. Only Germany held out a helping hand to Turkish sultan Mehmed IV. During the 1880s Kaiser Wilhelm sent a number of German military and economic missions to Istanbul; in 1889 he traveled there in person.

On October 29 of that year, escorted by Prussian and Turkish cavalries, the kaiser entered Jerusalem via the Jaffa Gate astride a white stallion, his spiked helmet glistening in the sun. During the next two days he and Kaiserin Augusta Victoria (daughter of Britain's Queen Victoria) visited the city's shrines and sites. The two monarchs dedicated an orphanage in Bethlehem, an impressive Protestant church near the Holy Sepulchre, and also presented the city's German Catholics with a plot of ground on Mount Zion for the erection of a new church.

In one of his speeches, Wilhelm declared, "From Jerusalem a light has arisen upon the world—the blessed light in whose splendor our German people have become great and glorious."[28] After their visit, the Augusta Victoria Hospice was erected on Mount Scopus. The kaiser had staked his claim as firmly as he could. A year later, the German-Turkish alliance began to take formal shape. The die was cast: The Englishmen knew that if they were going to have Palestine, they would have to fight both the Germans and the Turks to get it. That would become even more evident as the clouds of World War I began to form over Europe.

As 1913 dawned, many felt war was inevitable. T. E. Lawrence traveled to the Negev (Wilderness of Zin/Desert of Zin) to initially engage in archaeological research. He and his traveling companion, Leonard Woolley, had been employed by the Palestine Exploration Fund. The two men stood atop the lofty site of the ancient Nabataean city of Nizzana (Nitzana), which lay roughly thirty-five miles southwest of Beersheba. Their assigned task was to prepare notes about the site, and pave the way for a full-scale excavation at some later date.

While Lawrence was a lover of archaeology, he was even more fascinated by military strategy. He and Woolley had also been commissioned to work on the project to map western Palestine. By 1913 everything west of the Jordan River Valley had been mapped with the precision and attention to detail for which the Royal Engineers were justifiably famous. The Negev was of particular interest, as it would have to be crossed by any Ottoman army en route to Egypt. By June 1914, Woolley and Lawrence had filed a report on their archaeological findings, but more important were the maps the two produced of the area, especially designating water sources.[29]

Although war had been anticipated, it was on June 28, 1914, that it became a reality. Shortly after noon crowds had gathered in Sarajevo, the capital of the Austro-Hungarian province of Bosnia, to see the heir to the Hapsburg throne, Archduke Franz Ferdinand and his wife, Sophie (another daughter of British Queen Victoria and Prince Albert). As their 1911 Gräf & Stift Double Phaeton open touring car was driven to the town hall for a meeting with the local mayor, an assassination attempt shook the archduke and his wife. More than sixteen people were killed or injured when a bomb thrown by Muhamed Mehmedbašić bounced off the vehicle and exploded beneath the third car in the motorcade. The perpetrator, realizing his failed mission, swallowed a cyanide pill and jumped into the Miljacka River. Unfortunately for him, the river was only a shallow stream due to drought conditions, and he vomited up the pill before any harm could be done. The crowd, however, took matters into its own hands, severely beating Mehmedbašić before the police stepped in to arrest him.

The shaken couple met with the mayor, and afterwards expressed what would become an ill-fated desire to visit the hospital where the injured bystanders had been taken. The archduke and Sophie were being driven past their cheering subjects when another avowed assassin, Gavrilo Princip, ran from the crowd, leaped onto the car's running board and fired two shots at the archduke from point-blank range. Franz Ferdinand's pregnant wife took a third bullet to the stomach. The vehicle was driven at breakneck speed through the streets of Sarajevo to the governor's residence. The couple and their unborn child were dead by the time their car reached its destination.

When the assassination was investigated by Austrian authorities, it was discovered that Princip, a Bosnian, had lived in Serbia for several years. The inspectors deduced that he had acted as an agent of the Serbian government. That same day, Austria declared war on Serbia. By the end of October 1914, the Central Powers—Austria-Hungary, Germany, and the Ottoman Empire—were at war with the Allies—Belgium, France, Great Britain, Russia, and Serbia.

In the Middle East, Lawrence and Woolley were quickly called back into service in the Negev, their knowledge vital to the British Army stationed in Egypt. Meanwhile, the Turkish VIII Corps had set up headquarters in Jerusalem, where the German-Turkish High Command under the leadership of General Friedrich Freiherr Kress von Kressenstein made plans to attack the Suez Canal. By mid-January 1915, some one hundred thousand troops were stationed in and around

Beersheba. Von Kressenstein sent his troops across the Sinai in a human-wave assault against the well-entrenched and heavily armed British and Indian troops. British machine guns and artillery crushed the Turks and sent survivors limping back to Palestine.

Assessing the situation and redoubling his efforts, von Kressenstein realized his troops needed to be combat hardened and better trained to take on the Brits. He called on help from Berlin, where the importance of the Suez mission was recognized and understood. Germany sent machine gunners, heavy artillery, and even aircraft to the Sinai front. During the summer of 1916, British defenders repelled two more desperate attempts to pierce their lines around the canal.

On the Western Front in Flanders, English blood flowed at a ghastly and alarming rate in places with names like Ypres and Somme. Had the government not suppressed the casualty rate—approximately two million men during the four battles at those sites—the public outcry would have likely forced Britain out of the conflict.

One man, British Field Marshal Horatio Kitchener, devised a plan to break the stalemate in the trenches of France. He believed a full-fledged expeditionary force in Egypt for the purpose of achieving a stunning victory against the Turks would help the war effort and lift morale. In order to understand what drove Kitchener, it is necessary to take a look back to a meeting in Cairo in 1914. An Arab, Abdullah ibn Hussein and Kitchener met in February of that year. Abdullah was sharif (governor) of Mecca and descended from

Muhammad. His father, Sharif Hussein, had recently been appointed grand sharif of Mecca by the Young Turks who had taken over the Ottoman government in Istanbul. Abdullah would attend the meeting as a representative of Hejaz, the mountainous coastal district of the Arabian Peninsula that extended from near Mecca toward Sinai in the north.

Abdullah's plan encompassed more than just having a voice in parliament for Hejaz: He had stopped in Cairo to discuss with Lord Kitchener an all-out Arab revolt against the Turks. Kitchener was interested but noncommittal.

Kitchener died in 1916, but newly elected prime minister David Lloyd George saw the merit of Abdullalhl's plan and took the necessary steps to implement it. If it failed to achieve the goal of breaking the stalemate in France, it would at the very least secure the Suez Canal. That alone was a worthy goal.

Under the command of Sir Archibald Murray, the Egyptian Expeditionary Force of the Royal Army struck out across the Sinai in December 1916. Following the coastline as had Napoleon in 1799, they took Al-Arish and Rafah with little opposition. From there the EEF moved up into southern Palestine.

In Gaza, Murray found the Turks heavily entrenched. He hurled his troops at the line, but victory eluded them. Heavy casualties drove them back, and Murray was faced with the predicament that had beset von Kressenstein in 1915. The English leader responded just as his German counterpart had before him: He replenished his troops and attacked the fortress at Gaza again in April 1917. The results were the same: Gaza sand soaked up the blood of the Englishmen and Indians. The Turks had prepared by bringing in troops from the German Asien-Korps.

Lloyd George was livid. He was certain his plan had been foiled by an incompetent leader. Another event that same month gave him a new perspective: The United States declared war on the Central Powers. It appeared that the stalemate would be broken after all.

Murray was relieved of command of the EEF and replaced by General Edmund Allenby, a dogged and tenacious fighter nicknamed "The Bull." Before embarking for the Middle East, Allenby was summoned to No. 10 Downing Street, where Prime Minister George made it abundantly clear that the British had no intention of suffering a third defeat in Palestine. Allenby was to marshal his strength, his wisdom, and his troops to present the British people with a Christmas present—Jerusalem.

Allenby arrived in Egypt in June 1917 and went directly to the front near Gaza. He quickly recognized that another frontal assault would be a suicide mission. He set about to devise a better plan. While he worked on it, unexpected news arrived: T. E. Lawrence and his band of Bedouins whose loyalty he had gained had managed to cross what had been thought to be an impassable desert to reach Aqaba by land. Aqaba's heavy guns faced the Persian Gulf waters, the only anticipated avenue of attack. Lawrence and his troops quickly drove the Turks from the port city. They had taken the town by complete surprise.

The effect of the capture of Aqaba was more than valuable for Allenby. It served to protect his rear and right flank should he accomplish his plan—to break the Ottoman line at its eastern point, Beersheba. On October 31 elements of the British fleet began to bombard Gaza unrelentingly. At the same time, a British scout "allowed" himself to be spotted by Turkish sentries. In his flight, he dropped a courier pouch. Inside, sentries found what appeared to be secret British plans for an imminent and massive assault on Gaza, not unlike those employed by General Murray.

The Turks took the bait. To ready for the attack, they pulled a sizeable body of troops from Beersheba to Gaza to help man the trenches there. Only a small garrison was left at Beersheba. Meanwhile, a large complement of British troops moved to within easy striking distance of the town. They were guided by maps compiled four years earlier and by up-to-date intelligence reports from a network of Jewish spies living in Palestine. When the troops received the signal to attack, they swarmed over Beersheba with lightning speed and accuracy. The Turkish garrison was stunned and quickly retreated to Gaza.

That was Allenby's moment to take Gaza. Fortified by naval support, aircraft for reconnaissance and support—a first for the EEF—and with tanks (the first deployment in the Holy Land), Allenby drew up his battle plan. Within nine days, Gaza had fallen.

In January 1916, before Lloyd George had become prime minister, British representative Sir Mark Sykes and French representative Francois Georges-Picot concluded an agreement that allocated postwar spheres of influence in the Middle East to their two nations. Britain would supervise Mesopotamia, most of Transjordan, and southern Palestine. France would claim southern Turkey, Syria, northern Palestine, and the Mosul area of upper Mesopotamia.

The area around Jerusalem in central Palestine would require special treatment. The Russian czar exercised a protective role over various Orthodox monasteries and churches. The French had a similar interest in regard to Catholic institutions. The British represented the somewhat smaller Protestant interests in the area, along with the Germans. However, Britain's prime interest had been the Suez Canal. Consequently, they all had their hands in the pot when it came to central Palestine.

Lloyd George was appalled to learn of the Sykes–Picot Agreement: ". . . a secret agreement between the governments of the United Kingdom and France . . . defining spheres of influence and control in the Middle East . . ."[30]

He turned to Chaim Weizmann, a lucid and convincing propagandist for the Zionist movement. Two newspaper editors had introduced Weizmann to Lloyd George, Arthur James Balfour, Winston Churchill, and Lord Robert Cecil. Weizmann was a man of unusual charm and charisma. With his commanding physical appearance and his charming English laced with a Russian accent, he adapted his arguments to each listener with unusual skill. With Britons and Americans he could use biblical language to awaken deep emotions. With Lloyd George, a Welshman, he emphasized Palestine's topography, which was much like that of Wales. With Balfour, who came from an evangelical background, he explored Zionism, and with Lord Cecil he spoke in terms of a new world organization. With other British leaders, Weizmann stressed the extension of British imperial power inherent in the plan.

The evangelical heritage of many of Weizmann's listeners worked in his favor. These men had read the Old Testament and were familiar with it to a degree unparalleled by their Catholic allies in France and Italy. To them, the children of Israel and the land of Canaan were to be venerated.

So it was that Weizmann's talk of a "British protectorate over a Jewish homeland" began to interest government officials more and more. Several officials in particular began to advocate a partnership with the Zionists, among them Mark Sykes, who had concluded the Sykes–Picot Agreement with France. That was before he met the charismatic Mr. Weizmann. Through him and other influential spokesmen, Sykes had become convinced that a Jewish national presence in Palestine was in the best interests of the British Empire. He was, however, hampered by the agreement he had signed with the French, which he could not disclose to the Zionists.

Sykes had hinted that the government was not a free agent in the Middle East, that it needed the endorsement of Paris and Rome before it could officially sponsor the Zionist cause. Sykes asked Weizmann if he and his cohorts would secure the endorsements needed in Europe. Weizmann and his fellow Zionists left for Europe only to find Sykes at every turn, carefully stage-managing the entire enterprise.

Sykes' plan succeeded. The French gave the Zionists a letter assuring that they were sympathetic to the cause. A bigger surprise was the cordial welcome from Pope Benedict XV. It is easily explained: The British were preferable to the Russians and their Orthodox Church when it came to who was going to replace the Turks in Palestine.

Other factors moved Lloyd George and his government steadily toward the fateful step they would take on November 2, 1917. Even with the United States' entry into the war, France's strength was all but spent. No American troops had yet reached the trenches, Italy had suffered a major setback, and German submarine warfare was taking an enormous toll on Allied shipping in the Atlantic. The prime minister's two greatest needs were to get the Americans fully engaged and committed and to keep Russia from dropping out altogether.

Weizmann kept up his campaign for an endorsement from the British government. He was finally rewarded on June 17, 1917, when Balfour urged the Zionists to draw up an appropriate declaration. He promised he would support the document and submit it to the cabinet. Weizmann's two closest associates, Harry Sacher and Nahum Sokolow, set to work. Their final version of the paper was presented to Balfour the following day. The statement read:

> His Majesty's government views with favour the establishment in Palestine of a national home for the Jewish people, and will use their best endeavors to facilitate the achievement of this object, it being clearly understood that nothing shall be done which may prejudice the civil and religious rights of existing non-Jewish communities in Palestine, or the rights and political status enjoyed by Jews in any other country.[31]

When the letter was presented to the cabinet, most ministers heartily approved it, with the exception of one: Joined by Lord George Curzon, secretary of state for India, Edwin Montagu persuaded other members to take no action on the proposal. It had taken a long time for Montagu, a Jew, to win full acceptance in the high levels of government in which he now moved. He took exception to the phrase, "a national home of the Jewish people." He felt that if he were to endorse that, it would call into question his own loyalty as an Englishman. He told his fellow cabinet officers that Zionism was "a mischievous political creed"[32] and that endorsement of the statement would alarm the Muslims of India and embarrass the Jews of England.

A second hearing on October 4 convinced the pro-Zionists in

the cabinet that a milder text was needed. Weizmann and his friends didn't like it, but decided it was the best they could get. Now only one hurdle remained: Lloyd George had sent the first draft to President Woodrow Wilson. The prime minister knew it would require Wilson's support for a British protectorate in Palestine after the war. Wilson thought the Sacher–Sokolow text had made too big a commitment. When he saw the second, milder draft, he asked his closest advisor, Colonel Edward House, to advise the British that he "concurred in the formula suggested." House informed British intelligence, who cabled London that day:

> Colonel House put formula before president, who approves of it but asks that no mention of his approval shall be made when His Majesty's Government makes formula public, as he had arranged that American Jews then ask him for his approval, which he shall give publicly here.[33]

The cable arrived at Whitehall on October 16 and gave pro-Zionists the muscle needed to override objections from Montagu and Lord Curzon. On October 31, the War Cabinet gave the document, which would become known as the Balfour Declaration, a solid majority vote.

On November 2, 1917, Balfour sent a letter to Lord Lionel Walter Rothschild, president of the British Zionist Federation:

Dear Lord Rothschild,

I have much pleasure in conveying to you, on behalf of His Majesty's Government, the following declaration of sympathy with Jewish Zionist aspirations, which has been submitted to, and approved by, the Cabinet.

"His Majesty's Government view with favour the establishment in Palestine of a national home for the Jewish people, and will use their best endeavours to facilitate the achievement of this object, it being clearly understood that nothing shall be done which may prejudice the civil and religious rights of existing non-Jewish communities in Palestine, or the rights and political status enjoyed by Jews in any other country."

I should be grateful if you would bring this declaration to the knowledge of the Zionist Federation.

Yours sincerely,
Arthur James Balfour[34]

By the time Lord Rothschild received the letter, Allenby's troops were pursuing Turks and Germans northward along the Palestinian coastline. On November 11 they overran Tell el-Hesi. A week later, a different contingent of Allenby's force cleared Germans from the trenches at Tel Gezer. The same day, Allenby's main force captured Jaffa. From there, he turned eastward and began to concentrate on his primary objective—Jerusalem.

The Turkish-German High Command in Jerusalem was in a state of panic. Prisoners of war and wounded soldiers from both sides crowded a city already threatened with starvation. When Djemal Pasha, the ruler of that region of the Ottoman Empire, realized British forces were marching on the city from the north, south, and west, he ordered an evacuation. Officers grabbed whatever they could find—autos, wagons, carts, camels, horses—and loaded them with furniture, records, gold, and silver and frantically retreated to Damascus. Valuables that could not be transported were hidden or destroyed.

By December 9, the Turks and Germans were gone. Residents of Jerusalem were left to fend for themselves in the face of an impending British attack. They could not know that Allenby, a religious man, was unwilling to damage the Holy City. He consulted with both the War Office and the king about how to take Jerusalem. His sovereign counseled him to make it a matter of prayer. Presumably he did just that. He decided to drop leaflets on the city from an airplane. They addressed the absent Turkish authorities and invited them to surrender. The Arab who penned Allenby's instructions wrote the general's name incorrectly. The leaflet was therefore signed "Allah Bey" which means "son of Allah."

The Turks, having seen few if any aircraft, were frightened to see them overhead with leaflets raining from the heavens. According to one account:

> On November 27th, 1917, General Allenby gave orders before the victorious advance and gave instructions that "on no account is any risk to be run in bringing the city of Jerusalem or its immediate surroundings within the area of operations." General Allenby was familiar with the Scriptures, and he would therefore see fit to protect a dedicated city. He had taken the Bible with him from England for the campaign. Eventually, when the time came to attack and occupy the city, Allenby sent six bombers over it armed with leaflets. The leaflets were to call on the city to "surrender" and the bombs carried were in case of emergency.[35]

Jerusalem's Muslim civilian mayor, Haj Amin Nashashibi decided to accept Allenby's offer. He borrowed a white sheet from an American missionary and walked outside the city through the Jaffa Gate toward the southwest. He assumed it was the direction from which the main body of the troops would come. He and his associates were accompanied by a small group of boys before and behind them in an effort to protect themselves.

Not far down the road the small entourage encountered two British scouts, sergeants Hurcomb and Sedgewick of the London

Regiment. With hand signals, the mayor made his intentions of surrender clear to the two men. Within hours British troops marched into the city. The Jews, the largest segment of the population, had heard of the Balfour Declaration. The arrival of these troops signified to them the seriousness of the declaration to give them a national homeland.

Arabs were cheering too. They were all familiar with the exploits of Lawrence of Arabia and the way in which he represented British support for the Arab desire for national independence. Of course, Christians cheered with the knowledge that Jerusalem's holy sites would no longer be under Muslim domination.

Two days later, on December 11, Allenby arrived at the Jaffa Gate to mark the beginning of a new regime. A fierce Turkish counterattack on November 25 had slowed his progress into the Judean Hills from Jaffa. His troops had fought hard to reach that point. Allenby dismounted, reached for the visor of his cap, and removed it. Humbly he entered the Holy City as the bells of various churches and the clock tower rang a joyous welcome.

Once inside, he mounted the steps of the Turkish citadel and read a proclamation, which assured the city's inhabitants that the rights of the religious communities would be preserved and their various shrines scrupulously protected. He also gave formal greetings to the chief rabbis, the mufti, the Latin and Orthodox patriarchs, and other religious leaders.

An official report revealed:

From 2 to 7 that morning the Turks streamed through and out of the city, which echoed for the last time their shuffling tramp. On this same day, 2,082 years before, another race of conquerors, equally detested, were looking their last on the city which they could not hold; and inasmuch as the liberation of Jerusalem in 1917 will probably ameliorate the lot of the Jews more than that of any other community in Palestine, it was fitting that the flight of the Turks should have coincided with the national festival of the Hanukah.[36]

Winter rains held up further advances by Allenby's troops, so the Turks remained in control of Palestine above a line running north of Jaffa and Jerusalem. Consequently, Jewish residents of Galilee suffered bitterly because the Turks believed them to be firmly aligned with the Allied cause. Ottoman troops confiscated Jewish farms, and Turkish Army deserters terrorized Jewish settlements, looting and murdering the populace. In addition, hunger, illness, and exposure took a toll. By September 1918, Jewish settlers in Palestine had been reduced by thirty thousand men, women, and children.

Also by September, Allenby reached Megiddo and scored yet another striking victory. His conquest of the Holy Land was complete. Before the end of the year he would capture Damascus and Aleppo, and succeed where Richard the Lionhearted had failed.

CHAPTER

11

They shout, "Prepare for battle!"

JEREMIAH 6:4 NLT

O n November 2, 1917, something even more momentous was happening in London. Lloyd George had for some months wrestled with his plans for Palestine. He regarded it as the strategic buffer to Egypt, and meant for Great Britain to control Egypt and the Suez Canal when the war ended. To make that workable, he had to have Palestine as well or the entire plan would be jeopardized. To accomplish that goal, he had to offer a loftier justification to get postwar allies to endorse his plan.

Other factors, including reports in October 1917 that the German command might be considering a statement in support of a Jewish homeland in Palestine, moved Lloyd George and his government steadily toward the fateful step that would be taken on November 2,

1917. Even with the United States' entry into the war, France's strength was all but spent. Its leadership had little time and less inclination to dwell on Palestine.

Chaim Weizmann proved to be the answer. Weizmann, a man of unusual charm and charisma, had uttered his first cry on November 27, 1874, in the Russian village of Motyl, and was one of fifteen children born to lumber merchant Oizer and wife, Rachel. As a child he attended a Hebrew school but by the age of eleven had moved on to the high school in Pinsk, Russia. He attended the Polytechnic Institute of Darmstaat, Germany, where he studied Chemistry. He received a doctorate with honors in 1899 from the University of Fribourg in Switzerland. From his post as an assistant lecturer at the University of Geneva, Weizmann was elevated to senior lecturer at the University of Manchester and emigrated to Great Britain in 1904. While in Geneva he met his future wife, Vera Chatzman. The Weizmanns produced two sons, Michael and Benjamin. (Michael lost his life while flying with the Royal Air Force in 1944.)

It was said of the elder Weizmann in his 1952 obituary in the *New York Times*:

> In the three-quarters of a century through which he lived, he experienced every emotion: reward, for priceless scientific achievement; despair, when the great prize seemed lost; and triumph, when the prize—his lifelong

dream of a Jewish home in Palestine—was achieved. [In June 1949, Weizmann relinquished his British passport and became a citizen of the rebirthed State of Israel.][37]

Weizmann kept up his campaign for a statement from the British government. He was finally rewarded on June 17, 1917, when Balfour urged the Zionists to draw up an appropriate declaration. He promised he would submit the document to the cabinet with his endorsement. Ten years earlier, Balfour had wrestled with the political situation of the Jews in Britain. During a campaign speech while seeking election to parliament, he talked of his certainty that the Jews had long been a wronged people:

> My anxiety is simply to find some means by which the present dreadful state of so large a proportion of the Jewish race . . . may be brought to an end. . . . [He added] if a home was to be found for the Jewish people . . . it was in vain to seek it anywhere but in Palestine.[38]

In April 1917, as the Ottoman Empire faced collapse and the question of the disposition of its lands in the Middle East rose to the fore, Balfour traveled to the United States for talks with President Woodrow Wilson. He was also eager to meet new Supreme Court Justice Louis Brandeis, who was considered to be the head of organized Jewry in the States. Balfour and Brandeis met for an early breakfast. After pleasantries were exchanged, the two men began to talk of the political turmoil in the Middle East. Possibly lingering in the back of Brandeis' mind was a cablegram that had preceded Balfour's arrival: English Zionist James Rothschild had sought to enlist the Justice to secure an endorsement from the president for the establishment of a Jewish homeland in Palestine under a British protectorate.

It was Rothschild, after all, who had cautioned Chaim Weizmann about asking for too little when he approached diplomats and world leaders regarding a Jewish state. His advice fell on deaf ears. After the war ended, Weizmann was asked by David Ben-Gurion why he hadn't demanded a Jewish state in Palestine more forcefully than he had. Weizmann replied, "We didn't demand a Jewish state because they wouldn't have given us one. We asked only for the conditions that would allow us to create a Jewish state in the future. It's just a matter of tactics."[39]

Truthfully, his reticence provided little inspiration for the British to move forward and provided even less incentive for others who might have had an interest, i.e., Louis Brandeis. Knowing little about the situation, the erudite Brandeis surely must have felt as if he were at a distinct disadvantage.

In May 1917, Brandeis and President Wilson had a lengthy conversation regarding the United States' position on the Palestine situation. It was their first practical discussion about the principles of Jewish national aspirations. Wilson's administration was unwaveringly against any US responsibility for Palestine or any other portion of the crumbling Ottoman Empire.

As a devout Christian Zionist, Arthur Balfour's encounter with Brandeis had been a brilliant move on his part. He had made contact with a Supreme Court justice who was a close adviser to the president, known for his administrative expertise and lofty ethics, and had a deep personal interest in his people, the Jews.

In London, Chaim Weizmann's two closest associates, Harry Sacher and Nahum Sokolow, had set to work on a document to be presented to Balfour. Their final version of the paper was given to him the following day.

When what came to be known as the Balfour Declaration was presented to President Wilson, his approval came as a complete surprise to Secretary of State Robert Lansing, who had been usurped in the area of foreign affairs by Texan Edward M. House—frequently referred to as "Colonel" House (a Southern title often bestowed) even though he had no military experience. Determined to remove any doubt as to his feelings about the Palestine initiative, Lansing dashed off a letter to President Wilson enumerating his objections to an endorsement of the Balfour Declaration. Among them were: No formal announcement of war with the Turks, no support for a Jewish state from Jews in the United States, and perhaps his most anti-Semitic blast of all, "Many Christian sects and individuals would undoubtedly resent turning the Holy Land over to the absolute control of the race credited with the death of Christ."[40]

Colonel House informed a British intelligence officer of Lansing's objections to the declaration; London was notified that same day. The cable arrived at Whitehall on October 16 and gave the pro-Zionists the muscle needed to override the objections of Montagu and Lord Curzon. On October 31, the War Cabinet gave the document, which would become known as the Balfour Declaration, a solid majority vote.

It is interesting to note that most of the nine-member War Cabinet were raised in Evangelical homes. Lloyd George was Baptist; the Presbyterians included Arthur Balfour, plus Anglican, Dutch Calvinist, and Scottish Methodist. Only one member, Edwin Samuel Montagu, was Jewish.

One must not think for a moment that the British government was completely altruistic in the pursuit of a Jewish homeland in Palestine. The British were, after all, still in the throes of empire building. The boast that the sun never set on the British Empire remained true until after World War I, when Britain began to divest herself of colonies. The dissolution gained speed following World War II, when financial straits escalated the granting of independence to the far-flung and often violent outposts. (An early indicator of the empire's fragility was Britain's departure from India in 1947.)

Britain's control of Palestine would prove difficult for both Jews and Arabs, and it would last only until just after World War II.

There is no doubt, however, that the efforts of Chaim Weizmann and the Balfour Declaration—and the passion of those British who were staunch supporters of Zionism—were bringing the Jewish population ever closer to seeing the rebirth of the nation of Israel in the Holy Land.

Finally, on October 31, the War Cabinet gave the Balfour Declaration, as it would become known, a solid majority vote. Arthur Balfour's niece later wrote that, near the end of his days, her uncle had looked back on his career and reflected that what he had been able to do for the Jews had been the thing most worth doing. On November 2, 1917, Balfour addressed a personal letter to Lord Rothschild, president of the British Zionist Federation, which said:

> I have much pleasure in conveying to you on behalf of His Majesty's Government, the following declaration of sympathy with Jewish Zionist aspirations which has been submitted to, and approved by, the cabinet: "His Majesty's Government view with favour the establishment in Palestine of a national home for the Jewish people, and will use their best endeavors to facilitate the achievement of this object, it being clearly understood that nothing shall be done which may prejudice the civil and religious rights of existing non-Jewish communities in Palestine, or the rights and political status enjoyed by

Jews in any other country." I should be grateful if you would bring this declaration to the knowledge of the Zionist Federation.[41]

This was a momentous occasion for the Jewish people and the first solid support they would have for establishing their claim upon Jerusalem. In Palestine, Allenby's troops were now pursuing Turks and Germans northward along the Mediterranean coast. By late November they had taken Jaffa. From there, they turned east and began to concentrate on their primary objective—Jerusalem.

Once General Allenby marched into Jerusalem, the most important issue had not changed: Jerusalem was still "trodden down of the gentiles" (see Luke 21:24). Some Englishmen were enamored of the notion that the Anglo-Saxon tribes that had moved into Britain long ago were actually the lost tribes of Israel.

The Jews did not stand silently by during those dark years of World War I combat. An espionage network, *Netzakh Yisrael Lo Yishaker* (NILI—Israel will survive forever), was founded by Sarah, Aaron, and Rebecca Aaronsohn, along with Avshalom Feinberg. Because of suspicion and mistrust, the NILI was denied entrance in the *Hashomer* (Watchman), an organization that provided security for Jewish villages in Palestine. After witnessing Armenians being slaughtered by the Turks, NILI leaders approached the British, who were fighting against the Ottoman Empire. They were able to provide strategic information, which aided British Major General Edmund Allenby in taking Palestine.

Major General George MacDonough, chief of British military intelligence, said during an address to the Royal Military Academy in 1919:

> You will no doubt remember the great campaign of Lord Allenby in Palestine and perhaps you are surprised at the daring of his actions. Someone who is looking from the sidelines, lacking knowledge about the situation, is likely to think that Allenby took unwarranted risks. That is not true. For Allenby knew with certainty from his intelligence (in Palestine) of all the preparations and all the movements of his enemy. All the cards of his enemy were revealed to him, and so he could play his hand with complete confidence. Under these conditions, victory was certain before he began.[42]

Another group of some 500 volunteers, the Jewish Legion, was formed into the mule transport detachment. The company grew to 650 men by March 1915. In Egypt, Russian journalist and Zionist Ze'ev (Vladimir) Jabotinsky worked tirelessly for establishment of a Jewish Legion on the Palestine front. In August 1917, his efforts came to fruition. The British officially declared the formation of a Jewish regiment—the 38th Battalion of the Royal Fusiliers.

It was made up of British volunteers, members of the Zion Mule Corps, Russian Jews, and more than 50 percent were American volunteers.

John Henry Patterson, born in Ireland in 1867, proved the perfect commander for the Zion Mule Corps (ZMC). His familiarity with the Bible—its stories, laws, geography, prophecies, and morals—stood him in good stead when his army superiors chose him to take over the Corps.[43] The group formed would be the first Jewish fighting force to take to the field of battle since AD 135 with noted Jewish commander Bar Kochba—and it was led by a Christian. From their displacement in foreign lands, he led them home to the Holy Land.

When the volunteers were sworn in, Patterson offered an invitation: "Pray with me that I should not only, as Moses, behold Canaan from afar, but be divinely permitted to lead you into the Promised Land." Of the training camp, he wrote, "Never since the days of Judah Maccabee had such sights and sounds been seen and heard in a military camp—with the drilling of uniformed soldiers in the Hebrew language."[44]

The ZMC had originated in Egypt among displaced Jews fleeing the Turkish stranglehold in Palestine. The plan for a corps to help liberate Palestine from the Turks had been proposed by Jabotinsky. The British, however, were opposed to the idea of deploying Jewish recruits to fight on the Palestinian border. Subsequently, Patterson and a group of three hundred volunteers were sent instead to Gallipoli (today's Turkish town of Gelibolu) to aid the British on that front. They landed at V Beach, east of Cape Helles.

In his book *With the Judeans in the Palestine Campaign*, published in the 1930s, Lieutenant Colonel Patterson had written of his experiences with the ZMC. The *Jewish Chronicle* published an article on September 15, 1915, in which Patterson revealed:

> These brave lads who had never seen shellfire before most competently unloaded the boats and handled the mules whilst shells were bursting in close proximity to them . . . nor were they in any way discouraged when they had to plod their way to Seddul Bahr, [a village in Turkey] walking over dead bodies while the bullets flew around them . . . for two days and two nights we marched . . . thanks to the ZMC the 29th Division did not meet with a sad fate, for the ZMC were the only Army Service Corps in that part of Gallipoli at that time.[45]

Patterson, who later commanded the Jewish Legion, was such an ardent supporter of Zionism, he believed that Lloyd George and Sir Arthur Balfour had been elevated to positions of power just as Esther had been in ancient Persia—"for such a time as this." His excitement was palpable as he watched unprecedented events taking place before his very eyes, precursors to the Jewish people returning to the land that had been promised to Abraham and his offspring for all eternity. He wrote:

> All down the centuries from the time of the Dispersion it has been the dream of the Jew that one day he would be restored to his ancestral home. In his exile the age-long cry of his stricken soul has ever been "next year in Jerusalem."[46]

Patterson said of the Balfour Declaration:

> A friendly Palestine today is of immensely more importance to the peace and prosperity of the British Empire. Our statesmen were, therefore, but following in the footsteps of the greatest men of the past when they issued the world famous Balfour Declaration pledging England to use her best endeavors to establish a National Home in Palestine for the Jewish people.[47]

Many wanted to believe the mandate over Palestine awarded to Britain in 1920 represented the fulfillment of Jesus' words in Luke 21:24 (NKJV):

> And they will fall by the edge of the sword, and be led away captive into all nations. And Jerusalem will be trampled by Gentiles until the times of the Gentiles are fulfilled.

CHAPTER
12

The Gentiles shall come to your light,
And kings to the brightness of your rising.

ISAIAH 60:3 NKJV

n 1915, the conversation Field Marshal Kitchener and Abdullah ibn Hussein had a year earlier was taken up by two different men: Abdullah's father, Hussein, and Sir Henry McMahon, Britain's high commissioner in Egypt. In a letter dated October 24, McMahon revealed his country was ready to recognize and support Arab independence throughout Syria, Arabia, and Mesopotamia, with the exception of districts in Damascus, Homs, Hama, and Aleppo. In return for this pledge, Hashemite Arabs would help the British fight the Turks. Although no formal agreement was signed, Hussein's son, Faisal, led an Arab revolt in June 1916. With the full support of the British Army, Faisal became a quasi-constitutional king.

Faisal and Chaim Weizmann met in Aqaba. Faisal entertained the Zionist cordially and was receptive as Weizmann stressed that there was plenty of room for everyone, and that a lot of Arabs would undoubtedly be enhanced by the work of Jewish settlers. That winter Sir Mark Sykes invited both Weizmann and Faisal to a meeting in London. At a luncheon hosted by Lord Rothschild, Faisal addressed the guests with remarks prepared for him by T. E. Lawrence, in which he said, "No true Arab can be suspicious or afraid of Jewish nationalism."[48]

Emir Faisal later wrote to Felix Frankfurter, Harvard Law School dean and later a supreme court justice:

> We feel that the Arabs and Jews are cousins in race, having suffered similar oppressions at the hands of powers stronger than themselves, and by a happy coincidence have been able to take the first step towards the attainment of their national ideals together.
>
> We Arabs, especially the educated among us, look with the deepest sympathy on the Zionist movement. Our deputation here in Paris is fully acquainted with the proposals submitted yesterday by the Zionist Organization to the Peace Conference and we regard them as moderate and proper. We will do our best, insofar as we are concerned, to help them through: we will wish the Jews a most hearty welcome home.[49]

Not long after, Weizmann and Faisal signed a formal agreement that guaranteed, among other things, unlimited Jewish immigration and settlement in Palestine so long as Arab tenant farmers and their plots were safeguarded and received economic aid from their Jewish neighbors. Faisal, however, noted on his Arabic copy of the agreement that he would concur only if the Arabs were granted independence in accordance with his memorandum to the British foreign office.

Within a month, Faisal made it clear that what he really wanted from the Jews in exchange for his goodwill was their support in his struggle against the French. In July 1919, he presided over an Arab congress in Damascus that called for recognition of the kingdom of Syria, which would include Palestine with Faisal as sovereign, repudiation of the Sykes-Picot Agreement and the Balfour Declaration, and foreign assistance, preferably from the United States, not France.

In April 1920, while Faisal was busily making demands, representatives of the Allied Powers—Britain, France, Italy, Russia, and the United States—and other world leaders gathered in Paris to begin to fulfill Balfour's vision and grant a mandate over Palestine to Britain. The wheels of what had begun as a dream for multitudes were set in motion.

Arab nationalists living in Palestine were enraged by the Balfour Declaration's call for a state for the Jewish people. When their protests fell on deaf ears—the League of Nations had endorsed both the declaration and the Jewish homeland—the Arabs resorted to violence. They were determined to expel both the Jews and the British, and establish an Arab state encompassing the whole of Palestine.

It was also in April that Arabs convened in Jerusalem to celebrate *Nabi Musa*,[50] an annual Muslim pilgrimage to the tomb of Moses, located about eleven kilometers south of Jericho. It was short work to whip the crowd into an anti-Zionist frenzy, threatening the permanent establishment of the kingdom of Faisal. Arab police stood by silently while crowds began to attack Jews. One hundred sixty were injured in three hours of rioting. When British troops arrived, the rioters were jailed overnight, but when released the following morning, the riots resumed. It took three days to quell the uprising. By then, a number of Jews and Arabs were dead, and hundreds had been injured.

The aftermath of the rioting was as appalling as the riots themselves. British authorities dismissed the Arab mayor of Jerusalem and gave stiff sentences to the two leading Arab agitators. Most rioters got off with light sentences. Vladimir Jabotinsky and several other Jews who had organized the Jewish self-defense were given fifteen-year jail terms. This obvious favoritism produced such an uproar in England that the government decided to set up a court in Jerusalem to investigate the matter. The British officers defended their actions during the hearings by declaring the Jews guilty of having started the riots.

The Jews accused the British officers of encouraging Muslim unrest. The chief intelligence officer in Cairo, Colonel Richard

Meinertzhagen, took the stand and was able to show that military administrators in Palestine clearly favored the Arabs to the detriment of the Jews, which was in violation of the Balfour Declaration.

The French had no intention of acquiescing to Faisal. By July 25, 1920, they were in full command of Damascus, and Faisal was forced to flee. His coveted Arab state evaporated. The British found a place in its mandate for Faisal in Mesopotamia, which in 1921 was renamed Iraq. Faisal was proclaimed king. Most of the men who had surrounded him in Damascus, however, found refuge from the French in Jerusalem. That has played a critical role in the unfolding of events to this day, but especially in the period from 1920 to 1940.

Arab leaders, who fled to Jerusalem and began to set up their nationalistic headquarters, saw the issues as these: Neither the British nor the French were going to be leveraged out with ease; the Jews occupied a minority settlement on land that seemed to be shrinking by the day, nor did they have a great army. They were much more vulnerable to Arab muscle than were the French or British. Therefore, the Jews were their first target.

In late April an announcement came from London that the military government in Palestine would be dismantled with a civil administration placed in control. Lloyd George tapped Herbert Samuel as the civil high commissioner. Samuel, a leader of George's Liberal party and former cabinet member, was a Jew, a loyal Zionist, and the first Jew to govern to Israel in two thousand years.

Faisal was angered by the appointment and alarmed Allenby, who then warned of Arab violence. Samuel was dispatched to Jerusalem on June 30, 1920, under heavy guard. The early days of his administration demonstrated his determination to strengthen the Palestinian economy, to encourage Jewish immigration, and to be utterly impartial. It was his impartiality that ultimately caused problems.

In order not to offend the Arabs, he eventually restricted Jewish immigration and imposed other measures that impeded Zionist progress. He had hoped to appease the Arabs, but instead it encouraged them to want more and compromise less. Winston Churchill was serving as colonial secretary during this time. It presented him with some of his most taxing issues. One such quandary was the rise of Faisal's older brother, Abdullah, who undertook a crusade to restore his brother to the throne in Damascus.

In the summer of 1920 Faisal and his retinue journeyed from Hejaz to Amman in Transjordan. No one had taken much interest in that area since the flight of the Turks. That left Bedouin tribes free to raid settlements in Palestine and take booty. Churchill revived a suggestion put to him by T. E. Lawrence: Invite Abdullah to be king of Transjordan as a British protégé. If he accepted, it would keep him from troubling the French and embarrassing the English. It would also provide much-needed administration in the area.

Churchill and Abdullah met in Jerusalem on May 26, 1921, for a day-and-a-half conference. The proposal was made; the terms were simple: Abdullah would desist from any further action against the French; he would set up an orderly government in Amman; he would recognize Transjordan as an integral part of Britain's Palestine Mandate and govern the area in the name of the Mandate. On their side, the British would pay Abdullah a monthly subsidy, provide him with trained advisors, and guarantee him and his country eventual independence.

After an all-night session with his advisors, Abdullah met with Churchill and informed him he would accept the offer and abide by its terms. Churchill was delighted and returned to London rife with self-satisfaction. Writing about the event at a later time, Abdullah spoke of the miracle Allah had provided him by getting the British to separate Transjordan from the Palestine Mandate. The terms of the Mandate, as finally approved by the League of Nations, included the exact wordage found in the Balfour Declaration.

Neither the Jews nor anyone else had expressed a particular interest in that largely barren land. Churchill seems to have drawn on the correspondence between Sir Henry McMahon and Abdullah's father, Hussein, in 1915. The Arabs had been promised autonomy over significant tracts of real estate. A year later, Herbert Samuel traveled to London to secure a definitive interpretation of the Balfour Declaration in order to dispel Arab fears once and for all. Churchill accepted Samuel's argument and told him to draft such an interpretation. He would sign it once the details were hammered out.

Later known as the Churchill White Paper, it declared that the Jewish national home was restricted to the area west of the Jordan, that the Balfour Declaration had not meant to envision a predominately Jewish state, and that Jewish immigration should be limited to the economic capacity of the country. The Zionist Organization signed the paper with great reluctance and only because it did not wish to lose British support altogether. The Arabs rejected it flatly, establishing a pattern that would be repeated incessantly in years to come, one that is still followed today.

Once the Churchill White Paper was released, the House of Commons ratified the Mandate just five days later. The Council of the League of Nations followed suit on September 29. With the Mandate in place, the British needed a basic document of law under which Palestine would be governed. Interestingly, while the Syrian and Iraqi directives called for the mandatory regime (by France and Britain respectively) to foster self-government in those countries, nothing of the sort was envisioned in Palestine. The League's goal there was to ensure a Jewish homeland. Self-government in the 1920s in Palestine would have meant another Arab state, because the Arabs formed the majority.

Consequently, in Palestine Britain was vested with full legislative and administrative powers. After King George V signed the White Paper, Herbert Samuel delivered the declaration from Jerusalem. Under law Palestine would operate as a Crown colony in all but name, with the headquarters for its own sector and the capital of the entire country to be Jerusalem. When Hebrew University on Mount Scopus opened, Allenby came from Cairo to attend, and Arthur Balfour traveled from London. He was moved to tears by the abundant visual evidence of progress.

While the Zionists were making progress in Palestine, another man entered Jerusalem's story: Haj Amin al-Husseini. Haj Amin was one of the instigators of the *Nabi Musa* riots in Jerusalem in 1920. Although convicted and sentenced in absentia, he managed to slip across the border into Jordan and disappear. His exile didn't last long. In 1921 Grand Mufti Kamal al-Husseini died. Herbert Samuel began to look for a replacement for the office. He called on Ernest T. Richmond, responsible for formulating Arab policy, to assist him with his task. Incredibly, Richmond persuaded Samuel that Haj Amin was the man for the job. He convinced the high commissioner that the young Arab firebrand would gain a sense of responsibility in the post of grand mufti. In the short term, Richmond's plan worked; in the long term, it failed dismally.

Haj Amin worked quietly and steadily for seven years to build his power base. His most significant achievement was to rise to the presidency of the supreme Muslim Council. With that post went unrestricted control of all Muslim religious funds in Palestine. Haj Amin controlled schools, courts, mosques, and cemeteries so that no teacher or official could be appointed who had not demonstrated unswerving loyalty to him. The mufti made sure his most devoted following was based among the illiterate residents of the villages and farms in the region.

On Yom Kippur in 1928, Haj Amin was ready to make his move. He found a pretext for violence at the Western Wall. As the Jewish holy day approached, the sexton who kept the area of pavement in front of the wall so as to separate the men from the women, set up a portable screen running perpendicular to the wall. It was a minor change, but in Jerusalem any change in the status quo can quickly achieve major significance. The mufti carefully orchestrated a series of protests and counter-protests over the following year. He fed the fire by suggesting that the Jews were trying to take over sacred Arab property. The British tried vainly to keep everyone happy. On August 23, 1929, the weekly Muslim Friday Sabbath service came around. At noon Haj Amin mounted his pulpit in the Dome of the Rock to preach a commonplace sermon to the faithful gathered there. The "faithful" had been carefully chosen by the mufti, armed and ready to carry out their mission.

As Jews began to congregate at the Western Wall late that afternoon in preparation for the Shabbat, Haj Amin went to his little garden just above the Western Wall. From there he could watch them writhe and scream in the early twilight as they were pounded with the fists and clubs of Allah's servants. That night the rioting spread to the Jewish Quarter and across nearly all of Palestine. The Arab police were of no use. A contingent of the Royal Air Force stationed in Amman could not restore order. By the time troops arrived from Cairo five days later, 133 Jews had died and 399 had been injured. Arab casualties were significantly lighter: eighty-seven dead, ninety-one injured. Haj Amin had become the undisputed ruler of the Palestinian Arabs.

Samuel was followed by Field Marshal Sir Herbert Plumer. He carried on Samuel's record of achievement in a soldierly and forthright manner. Jerusalem's Jewish population doubled between the years 1924–1928. The era was referred to as the Fourth Aliyah (wave of immigration) spawned by a nasty wave of anti-Semitism in Poland. About seventy thousand Polish Jews left their country and traveled to Palestine. As sad as their story was at the time, one can only marvel at how blessed they were to have escaped Poland before the Nazi invasion in 1939.

Back in London, Jewish immigration grew persistently, especially as Hitler tightened his grip in Germany. By 1936 the tide had begun to turn. Britain was preoccupied with Hitler. Nazi propaganda in the Middle East was playing heavily on the anti-Semitic fears of the Arabs. Germany was manipulating the Arabs toward Hitler's cause, much as Britain had done during World War I. England's response was to become increasingly friendly toward the Arabs in an attempt to win their favor; one of the chief means was to limit Jewish immigration.

CHAPTER
13

And you will hear of wars and rumors of wars.

MATTHEW 24:6 ESV

Haj Amin cunningly took advantage of Britain's preoccupation and Adolf Hitler's rise. He instigated a labor strike in Palestine that lasted six months and was accompanied by an armed uprising among the Arabs who were aided and abetted by Iraqis, Syrians, and other predominately Muslim neighbors. The Jews and British suffered losses during ensuing battles, but the real bloodletting was among the Arabs. Haj Amin had seen this as an opportunity to destroy his enemies, particularly in the rival Nashashibi clan, but he didn't stop there. The mufti had a rabid fear of anyone who was literate, especially in English, and targeted landowners, teachers, clerks, and the like. Men were gunned down in the marketplace and at home in their beds. The mufti's goons became so adept at these executions that they began to hire out to others. Today we call them mercenaries or terrorists.

More than two thousand Arabs died in the melee. Haj Amin's grip on the Arab community was as strong as steel. It choked the life out of the community. Those who might have led the Arabs into vital and dynamic growth were either gone or cowed into silence. This was not the case with the Jewish community, where a generation of leaders and thinkers was being carefully nurtured and groomed.

In the midst of the slaughter, Haj Amin's own outwardly decorous and refined behavior was a strange anomaly. However, he was rooted in reality: He never ventured out into the streets without wearing a bulletproof vest and being accompanied by his six Sudanese bodyguards. His automobile was armor plated, and he never arrived at an appointment on time—he would be either late or early.

In January 1933 while Haj Amin was stirring up turmoil in Jerusalem, Adolf Hitler, an Austrian by birth, was appointed chancellor of Germany and quickly assumed the role as head of the government. Hitler's rise to power would ultimately overshadow all other events in Europe and the Middle East as he quickly set about eliminating those who opposed his authority.

Historian Paul Johnson wrote:

> Germany's defeat in 1918 was bound to unleash a quest for scapegoats, alien treachery in the midst of the Volk.

Christianity was content with a solitary hate-figure
to explain evil: Satan. But modern secular faiths needed
human devils . . . The enemy, to be plausible, had to be an
entire class or race. The Jews tried everything to combat
the poison. Some brought up their children to be artisans
or farmers. They enlisted in the army. They attempted
ultra-assimilation. But each policy raised more difficulties
than it removed, for anti-Semitism was protean, hydra-
headed and impervious to logic or evidence.

The syphilis of anti-Semitism was not the only weakness of the German body politic. The German state was
a huge creature with a small and limited brain. The state
was nursemaid as well as sergeant-major. It was a tower-
ing shadow over the lives of ordinary people and their
relationship towards it was one of dependence and docil-
ity. The philosophy was Platonic; the result corporatist....
[Vladimir] Lenin's religious-type fanaticism would never
have worked in Germany. The Germans were the best-
educated nation in the world. To conquer their minds
was very difficult. Their hearts, their sensibilities, were
easier targets. Hitler's strength was that he shared with
so many other Germans the devotion to national images
new and old . . . In a rare moment of frankness, Lenin once
said that only a country like Russia could have captured

so easily a country as he took it. Germany was a different proposition. It could not be raped. It had to be seduced.[51]

The Nazi despot had been born in Braunau am Inn, Austria, on April 20, 1889, the son of Alois Schicklgruber Hitler and Klara Pölzl, both from a remote area of lower Austria. Hitler's father had been born out of wedlock to a young peasant woman, Maria Anna Schicklgruber. It was not until Alois was in his thirties that his father returned to the village, married Maria Anna, and changed their young son's last name to Hitler. Had he not come forward to claim an inheritance, Johann Hitler's grandson would have grown up as Adolf Schicklgruber. (One can't help but wonder if he would have had the same impact and garnered the same notoriety had he conducted his life with that surname rather than the more familiar Adolf Hitler. An unnamed philosopher once said, "Words have meaning and *names* have power."[52])

As a child, Adolf was angry and sullen, undependable, short-tempered, and indolent. He was antagonistic toward his father, who was a strict disciplinarian, and intensely devoted to his industrious mother. The young Hitler "took singing lessons, sang in the church choir, and even briefly entertained thoughts of becoming a priest."[53] He was devastated when Klara died during his teen years.

Sixteen-year-old Adolf made his way to Vienna with dreams of becoming an artist. He applied to the Viennese Academy of Fine Arts but was roundly rejected by that august body. He survived in the large cosmopolitan city by taking odd jobs and selling his artistic sketches in backstreet pubs. Between drawing likenesses of patrons, he would spout political rants of his ostentatious dreams for a superior Germany to anyone too drunk to walk away.

Adolf was enchanted with the manipulative methods of Vienna's mayor, Karl Leuger, and quickly adopted his affinity for anti-Semitism, with its fanatical demand for "purity of blood." From the eccentric teaching of an excommunicated monk, Lanz von Liebenfels, to those of German Nationalist Georg von Schönerer, the impressionable young Hitler subscribed to the credo that the Jewish people were responsible for anarchy, dishonesty, and the ruin of civilization, government, and finance. According to those so-called "learned men," the resolve of the Jew was to completely weaken Germany and dilute the superior Aryan race.

Hitler enlisted in the Sixteenth Bavarian Infantry Regiment during World War I, where he served as a dispatch runner. He was awarded the Iron Cross for bravery but was caught in a gas attack shortly before the end of the war. He spent months recovering from the effects, including temporary blindness. After his recovery, Adolf was delegated the job of spying on various political factions in Munich— among them the German Workers' Party.

Hitler joined the other forty members of that group in 1919 and its name was changed shortly thereafter to the National Socialist German Workers' Party. By 1921, he had claimed chairmanship of the organization and began to dazzle crowds with his formidable gift of oratory. Soon thereafter, the party adopted a new logo—the swastika —which Hitler believed symbolized the triumph of the Aryan man. It also adopted a new greeting, *"Heil!"* and eventually *"Heil, Hitler!"* (This can be translated as "Hail Hitler," or more ambiguously as "Salvation through Hitler.")

The mustachioed little man mesmerized his listeners with his gravelly, impassioned voice—never mind that his speeches contained little of actual value. Near the end of 1921, he had come to be known as *der Führer* ("leader" or "guide"). He formed gangs to maintain control at his assemblies and to apply goon-squad tactics to disrupt those of his adversaries. These were the beginnings of the infamous storm troopers, the SS, Hitler's black-shirted and dreaded bodyguards.

Although British Prime Minister Lloyd George was driven from office in 1922 by the opposition party and would never hold another government position, even in his retirement years, he stirred a bit of controversy: In 1936, he traveled to Berlin to meet with Adolf Hitler. Upon return to England he wrote an article for the *Daily Express*, in which he infamously gushed:

> I have now seen the famous German leader and also something of the great change he has effected. Whatever one may think of his methods—and they are certainly not those of a parliamentary country, there can be no doubt

that he has achieved a marvelous transformation in the spirit of the people, in their attitude towards each other, and in their social and economic outlook. . . . One man has accomplished this miracle. He is a born leader of men. A magnetic and dynamic personality with a single-minded purpose, a resolute will and a dauntless heart.[54]

Of course, by the time Hitler had breached the Munich Agreement, Lloyd George was no longer a proponent of appeasement or of the German leader's tactics.

It was also in 1922 that Hitler outlined his plan fully in a conversation with a friend, appropriately named Joseph Hell:

If I am ever really in power, the destruction of the Jews will be my first and most important job. As soon as I have power, I shall have gallows after gallows erected, for example, in Munich on the Marienplatz—as many of them as traffic allows. Then the Jews will be hanged one after another, and they will stay hanging until they stink. They will stay hanging as long as hygienically possible. As soon as they are untied, then the next group will follow and that will continue until the last Jew in Munich is exterminated. Exactly the same procedure will be followed in other cities until Germany is cleansed of the last Jew![55]

Hitler stridently declared the Jewish people to be Germany's No. 1 enemy, the race accountable for all the nation's internal problems. He strongly stressed what he saw as "the anti-Semitism of reason" that must lead "to the systematic combating and elimination of Jewish privileges. Its ultimate goal must implacably be the total removal of the Jews."[56] He was so convinced Germany was near collapse that he joined forces with nationalist leader General Erich Friedrich Wilhelm Ludendorff in an attempted coup.

The ensuing riot that became widely known as the "Beer Hall Putsch" began in a Munich beer hall and resulted in (1) the deaths of sixteen individuals, (2) the Nazi Party being outlawed, and (3) Hitler being tried and sentenced to five years in prison. His sentence was inexplicably commuted to nine months, but during his incarceration, he dictated a draft of *Mein Kampf* ("My Struggle") to Rudolf Hess, who would become his devoted sycophant. The tome—filled with a coarse, ill-conceived jumble of anti-Semitism, fabrication, and fantasy—evolved into the literal bible of the emerging Nazi Party. By 1939, this hodgepodge of pretense had sold five million volumes and had been translated into eleven languages. (Even today that missive is enthusiastically embraced by many leaders in Islamic countries.)

Philosopher Houston Stewart Chamberlain wrote to encourage Hitler in a letter dated October 7, 1923. He zealously advised the Führer that he was perceived as the "opposite of a politician . . . for the essence of all politics is membership of a party, whereas with you all parties disappear, consumed by the heat of your love for the fatherland."[57] In a later missive to Hitler, Chamberlain inaccurately asserted: "One cannot simultaneously embrace Jesus and those who crucified him. This is the splendid thing about Hitler—his courage. In this respect he reminds one of [Martin] Luther."[58] It is quite obvious from his writings that Chamberlain also viewed the Jewish industrialists as Germany's "Public Enemy No. 1."

The German hierarchy made a disastrous error in judgment in 1925: They removed the prohibition against the Nazi Party and granted permission for Hitler to address the public. Moreover, when he needed it most in order to expand the scope of the party, a worldwide economic crisis reached Germany. Ironically, the resulting magnitude of unemployment, panic, and anger afforded Hitler the very opportunity he most needed to step forward and claim the role of redeemer and savior of the nation. On January 30, 1933, Weimar Republic of Germany President Paul von Hindenburg was persuaded to nominate the Führer as Reich Chancellor. Germany had lost her last chance to avoid a Second World War and the devastation visited upon the Jewish people that came to be known as the Holocaust.

Hitler's determination to outfox his opponents and remove conservatives from any role in government took little time or effort. He abolished free-trade unions, removed communists, Social Democrats, and Jews from any participation in politics, and brutally consigned his rivals to concentration camps. By March 1933, he had solidified his hold on Germany with the use of persuasive argument, indoctrination, fear, and coercion. The façade was firmly in place, and the people of Germany were intimidated into total subjugation.

With the death of von Hindenburg in August of 1934, the Third Reich had a determined dictator who claimed the titles of both Führer and chancellor, as well as all the powers of the state accorded to a leader. He abandoned the Treaty of Versailles, conscripted a massive army, supplied it with war materiel, and in 1938 forced the British and French into signing the Munich Agreement. Soon to follow were laws against Jews, concentration camps, the destruction of the state of Czechoslovakia, the invasion of Poland, and a short-lived non-aggression pact with the USSR. The only obstacles standing between Hitler and the rest of the world were Franklin D. Roosevelt, Winston Churchill, Joseph Stalin, and the armies of Western civilization.

Just one week after President Roosevelt was sworn in for his first term as America's chief executive, German laborers had completed Dachau, the original concentration camp. Within its confines some forty thousand individuals would be murdered, most of them Jews. Hitler would follow the opening of the camp by nationalizing the Gestapo and bringing it under his full control. Just three months later, he had successfully combined all commands under the aegis of the Nazi Party.

In 1935, the Nuremberg Laws were instituted and German Jews lost their citizenship with its rights and privileges. They were now totally under the cruel fist of Hitler and his rabid Jew-hatred. Along with perhaps many of the Jews in the earlier days of Hitler's rule, Roosevelt was deceived by the picture presented to the world at the 1936 Olympics. American historian and author Deborah Lipstadt wrote:

> The sports competition was a massive exercise in propaganda and public relations, and many American reporters were uncritical about all that they saw. . . . Americans, particularly non-German speaking ones who only knew Germany from the Games—departed convinced that the revolutionary upheavals, random beatings, and the murders of political opponents had been greatly exaggerated or were a thing of the past. Those bedazzled included not only the athletes and tourists, but personages such as newspaper publisher Norman Chandler and numerous American businessmen. This period marked the beginning of Charles Lindbergh's love affair with the Reich. One reporter was convinced that as a result of the Games visitors would be . . . inclined to dismiss all anti-German thought and action abroad as insipid and unjust. [The visitor] sees no Jewish heads being chopped off, or even roundly cudgeled. . . . The people smile, are polite, and sing with gusto at the beer gardens. Visitors to Berlin

described it as a warm, hospitable place and Germany as a country well on its way to solving the economic and unemployment problems which still plagued America.[59]

Hitler's meteoric rise to prominence produced increasing Nazi radio broadcasts into the Middle East, and growing Arab unrest as Zionism was portrayed as the handmaiden of French and British imperialism. In July of 1937, the Peel Commission—"a British Royal Commission of Inquiry, headed by Lord Peel, appointed in 1936 to investigate the causes of unrest in British Mandate for Palestine following the six-month-long Arab general strike in Mandatory Palestine"[60]—issued a report detailing the British despair of ever finding a solution to the Arab-Jewish conflict. Britain had made irreconcilable commitments to both groups. Since the British were unwilling to turn over four hundred thousand Jews to Arab domination, or conversely to place nearly a million Arabs under Jewish rule, the only apparent solution was partition—to divide the territory into two separate states. Jerusalem and Bethlehem, said the Royal Commission, should be set aside in a British enclave with access to the coast.

The League of Nations rejected the partition concept. King Abdullah of Transjordan and his friends the Nashashibis likely favored the move but were afraid to say so.

Haj Amin and his followers were contemptuous in their rejection, which assured that the Arab Higher Committee would also turn it down. The Jews were willing to accept it as the least undesirable alternative. It was all a moot point; the status quo would continue. That would mean more fighting.

Also in July, the mufti stopped in to see the German consul-general in Jerusalem. He wanted to tell the Nazi official how much he admired the Third Reich, and how he would appreciate a little help in his struggle against the British and the Jews. From there the negotiations progressed until Admiral Wilhelm Canaris, head of German intelligence, delivered quantities of weapons from German manufacturers to the mufti via Iraq and Saudi Arabia. Finally, in the wake of the assassination of several British officials in Galilee by Arab gunmen, the British deposed the mufti and abolished the Supreme Muslim Council and the Arab Higher Committee. The mufti retreated to the sanctuary of the Dome of the Rock.

On October 15, 1937, Haj Amin slipped past British police disguised as a beggar. He got to Jaffa by auto and then was smuggled aboard a fishing boat to Lebanon. Haj Amin kept retreating north until, by 1941, he was the honored guest of Adolph Hitler in Berlin. He was convinced that the Nazis held the key to the two great goals of his life—to destroy the Jews and to drive the British out of the Middle East.

During the war, the mufti lived in Europe and aided the German war effort any way he could. He recruited Arabs to sabotage the British behind their lines. He helped raise two divisions of Balkan Muslims for the SS, and his agents provided useful intelligence.

Haj Amin's greatest zeal was spent in destroying Jews. When the "Final Solution" was invoked by the Nazis in 1941, the mufti was one of its most enthusiastic supporters. He worked diligently to ensure that none of the Jews destined for the gas chambers and ovens were mistakenly diverted to Palestine or other places of refuge. Haj Amin received word that four thousand Jewish children from Bulgaria were to be allowed to immigrate to Palestine in 1943. Tragically, they never left Europe, due in great part to the grand mufti.

After the war, Haj Amin narrowly escaped arraignment before the court in the Nuremberg Trials. Thanks to the French, he made his way to Cairo to resume leadership of the Arab cause in Palestine. It was he who would determine Arab response to the momentous events of 1947 and 1948.

For the Jewish community in 1938 Jerusalem, the primary problem was trying to persuade the British to increase immigration quotas. The British, however, saw increased allotments only as putting a match to the Arab fuse—and a short one at that. So we read the agonizing accounts of Jewish refugees escaping Hitler's iron fist only to perish in the waters of the Mediterranean in unseaworthy ships that could find no safe harbor; sadly, not even in the United States.

CHAPTER
14

He will honor those who submit to him, appointing them to positions
of authority and dividing the land among them as their reward.

DANIEL 11:39 NLT

As Palestine moved toward partition, one Jewish leader emerged from the pack and stepped onto the stage of political history. Her name was Golda Meir. She was an American, although she had been born in Kiev in 1898. When she was eight, her family moved to Milwaukee, Wisconsin. At the age of seventeen, Golda discovered her Zionist faith—the doctrine to which she devoted the remainder of her life.

In 1921 Golda and her husband, Morris Meyerson, immigrated to British Mandate Palestine. By 1924, Golda was immersed in the political scene, and by 1928, had become an official in the Histadrut Trade Union. In the early 1930s, she returned to the United States as the trade union's emissary.

After many of the Jewish leaders in Palestine were imprisoned in 1946, Meir was appointed to lead the Jewish Agency's political department as the chief liaison with the British. She actively raised funds to support Israel's War of Independence. Admired for her powerful speeches, Meir was chosen by members of her community as their representative at the first kibbutz convention in 1922. During the meeting, David Ben-Gurion became aware of Golda's silver-tongued oratory, and appointed her a member of his government.

In the early days of May 1948, Ben-Gurion instructed Golda to masquerade as an Arab and dispatched her to a meeting with Jordan's king. On May 11, three days before the end of the Mandate, and disguised as an Arab peasant woman, Golda slipped across the Jordan at Naharayim to meet again with King Abdullah. Ironically, Meir and the king met on a little stretch of the east bank of the Jordan River, the site of a hydroelectric station built and run by the Jews. It was from this facility that the royal palace received electricity. David Ben-Gurion had sent Golda to meet with Abdullah in the home of the plant's director. They greeted one another much like old friends with a common enemy—the mufti Haj Amin. Abdullah confided that in the event of partition, he would prefer simply to annex the Arab sector to his kingdom.

Abdullah was pale and seemed to be under great strain. Golda asked him if he had broken his promise to her—the one made during their visit the previous November. He told her that when he had made that promise he believed he was in control of his own destiny. He had since learned otherwise. He informed Mrs. Meir that he felt a war could be averted if the Jews were not in such a rush to proclaim statehood.

Golda replied that the Jews had waited two thousand years, and she didn't think they were being impatient at all. The time of statehood had arrived; it would not be postponed. The king sadly informed her that war was inevitable; Golda assured him that the Jews would fight . . . and that they would win. Meir thought that sounded much better than a separate state led by Haj Amin.

Meir pledged that the Jews would leave the Arab sector to its own devices, and the Jews would devote themselves entirely to the establishment of their own sovereignty within the borders assigned them by the UN. Abdullah was not anti-Semitic; he recognized the Zionists as fellow Semites who had returned to their homeland after a long exile. Their presence in Palestine had already profited him and his people immensely. He knew better than to think he could put a stop to the establishment of a Jewish state. The mufti, on the other hand, was a foolish man who viewed Jews in terms of the pale rabbinical students so easily cowed by his ruffians' clubs. Abdullah knew the Zionists for what they were: a vigorous and capable people who would put up a stiff fight. When the king and Israel's future prime minister parted company, Golda expressed a desire that they meet again. It was not to be. Abdullah was assassinated by an Arab in Jerusalem three years later on July 20, 1951.

As events of the 1930s led ominously toward a second world war, the Nazis under Hitler had already been searching for a "final solution" to what they considered the Jewish problem. After years of this continuous rhetoric, it took a mere ninety minutes for Adolf Hitler's henchmen to determine the fate of six million Jews. During that period, roughly the time it would take to drive from Jerusalem to Tel Aviv during peak traffic, the Holocaust became a heinous reality.

The date: January 20, 1942.

The place: The beautiful Wannsee Villa located in a serene lakeside suburb of Berlin

The objective: To find a "Final Solution to the Jewish Question."

Presiding over the conference was SS Lieutenant General Reinhard Heydrich, chief of the Security Police and Security Service. In attendance were fourteen high-ranking German military and government leaders, among them Adolf Eichmann. As the meeting began, Heydrich was determined that none should doubt his superiority or his authority, which was not limited by geographical borders. He briefed those in the room on measures that had already been taken against the Jews in an attempt to eradicate them from both the German culture and homeland.

Imagine: Over lunch, fifteen men changed the world forever. January 20, 2017, marked the 75th anniversary of that fateful conference.

We dare not let these dubious anniversaries pass without marking how little time it can sometimes take to alter the course of history.

Initially, steps had been implemented to allow German Jews to immigrate to whatever countries would accept them, but the move proved to be too slow for the Führer and the Reich. Now the men gathered to implement Hitler's new solution. Heydrich provided a list of the number of Jews in each country; a total of eleven million Jews were to be involved. In his zeal he determined, "In large, single-sex labor columns, Jews fit to work will work their way eastward constructing roads. Doubtless, the large majority will be eliminated by natural causes. Any final remnant that survives will doubtless consist of the most resistant elements. They will have to be dealt with appropriately because otherwise, by natural selection, they would form the germ cell of a new Jewish revival."[61] Translation: All must die.

According to the minutes of the meeting, Jews were to be purged, beginning in Germany, then in Bohemia, and Moravia. After that, they were to be expunged in Europe from east to west. Many questions arose as to how to identify those who were to be considered Jews. That issue was not resolved during the Wannsee meeting.

Of course, this was not the beginning of the extermination of the Jewish people. Many of those in attendance had already participated in murders since the summer of 1941. Even before the gathering at Wannsee, more than a half million Jews had been murdered behind enemy lines. The question was how to attain the goal of mass extermination in areas outside the battle zone. A more efficient means needed to be found to eliminate larger numbers. No, the meeting was not called to determine *how* to begin the process but rather to spell out how the "final solution" would be achieved. By January, several death camps equipped with gas chambers were under construction.

Obviously, the ordinary citizenry of Germany did not enter the war determined to annihilate six million of their neighbors. It began with a subversive program of anti-Semitism aimed at blaming the Jewish people for all the ills that had beset Germany following its losses in World War I. Perhaps even Hitler did not begin the purge with total extermination in mind. That seed probably began to germinate only after Jews were denied entry into other countries. It seemed to the Führer that he had been given a green light to do whatever he wished with the Jewish population.

Hitler was aided in his nefarious plan by a Western media determined to bury its head in the sand. One of the most prominent was the *New York Times*, which seemed determined to underplay the horrors taking place in a Nazi-controlled Germany. According to Northeastern University journalism professor Laurel Leff:

> The story of the Holocaust made the *Times* front page only twenty-six times out of 24,000 front-page stories. . . . In only six of those stories were the Jews identified on page one as the primary victims. . . . Nor did the story lead

the paper, appearing in the right-hand column reserved for the day's most important news—not even when the concentration camps were liberated at the end of the war. . . . the *New York Times* was less likely than other news organizations to miss what was happening to the Jews. But it was also more likely to dismiss its significance. . . . the newspaper's Jewish publisher believed the Jews were neither a racial nor ethic group, and therefore should not be identified as Jews for any other than religious reasons. . . . The result: *The New York Times* was in touch with European Jews' suffering, which accounts for its 1,000-plus stories on the Final Solution's steady progress. Yet, it deliberately deemphasized the Holocaust news, reporting it in isolated, inside stories. The few hundred words about the Nazi genocide the *Times* published every couple [of] days were hard to find amidst a million other words in the newspaper. *Times* readers could legitimately have claimed not to have known, or at least not to have understood, what was happening to the Jews.[62]

In October 1943 three men—Winston Churchill, Chaim Weizmann, and Clement Atlee—sat down in London to discuss the latest partitioning plan, which called for Jerusalem to be a separate territory under a British high commissioner. The plan would have to be kept secret until after the war, Churchill explained, but he wanted the other two men to know that Israel had a friend in him. He explained that when Hitler had been crushed, the Jews would have to be established in the land where they belonged. Churchill added, "I have an inheritance left to me by Balfour, and I am not going to change. But there are dark forces working against us."[63]

The prime minister probably didn't then realize how dark and powerful those forces were. No matter how firm his commitment to Zionism, the British Foreign Office and the authorities in Jerusalem who had charge of the Mandate hindered Churchill from stating his position. The all-too-familiar story of the bitter struggle and disappointment for the Jewish people continued—Palestine was not to be opened to the hapless survivors of the concentration camps.

In the months between November 29, 1947, when the UN General Assembly voted for partition, and May 14, 1948, when the last British troops exited and the State of Israel was reborn, Jerusalem was the scene of interminable conflict. It was Haj Amin's opportunity to seize final control and turn Palestine into an Arab state with him at its helm.

To lead this crusade he selected a kinsman, Abdul Khader Husseini. Abdul Khader was a uniquely charismatic leader who aroused the admiration and zeal of his fellow Arabs. His father had been mayor of Jerusalem—the same one deposed and exiled by the British in 1921 following the Nabi Musa riots. Khader was but a small child at the time, but he grew up fighting the British. He was wounded twice during the Arab revolts from 1936 to 1939. Under Haj Amin's sponsorship, he had received considerably more education than most of the mufti's lieutenants, including training with explosives in Germany during World War II.

In December of 1947 Khader slipped back into Palestine and began to organize the holy war his cousin had called for against the Jews. The centerpiece of his strategy was Jerusalem, and his goal was to strangle the city. Before Khader's arrival, the mufti had already launched his crusade by calling for a three-day strike in the immediate wake of the partition vote. The Arabs opposed partition because it acknowledged the right of the Jews to exist unmolested in the Middle East. Haj Amin denied that right with his very being. After the strike, relations between the Jews and Arabs grew even more strained and distant. Jewish and Arab workers who had co-existed peacefully for years were now compelled to search one another for weapons at the beginning of each day.

The UN had called for internationalization of the city, but its inhabitants, both Jewish and Arab, knew that no country—not Britain, not the United States, not France, not any nation—was willing to back the UN policy with its own troops. It was probably the greatest victory for the Arabs that winter—the conclusion that the United Nations' Palestine resolution could not be implemented without armed force.

Only Jews and Arabs were willing to shed their blood for Jerusalem. The rest of the world stood by and essentially said, "So be it."

Prime Minister David Ben-Gurion's strategy was simple and applied to the whole *Yishuv*—the Jewish community in the land of Israel, including Jerusalem: Every Jew should stand fast. Not one shred of territory that had been gained should be given up. In Jerusalem, where Jews were in the clear majority, this meant harassing the Arabs in an effort to get them to back off first. Sometimes it worked.

Abdul Khader's initial thrust was a desultory raid against a house where a detachment of Haganah men was stationed. He brought in a truckload of 120 men from Hebron, an Arab center thirty miles south of Jerusalem. The brief skirmish was broken up by British soldiers in an armored car, and there were no casualties. Meanwhile, the Jews were doing everything possible to strengthen their hold on their most vulnerable and isolated population center—the Jewish Quarter of the Old City, which was surrounded by walls. Living inside the Jewish Quarter were rabbis, sages, and students. Pale and stooped from long years of studying the Torah, they were not sturdy recruits for the Haganah. Instead, the task of the organization was to smuggle as many fighting men into the Quarter as possible, past the watchful eyes of both the British and the Arabs.

Another thing the Haganah lacked was weapons. The Arabs had access to arms by way of shipping routes from all around the Middle East; military hardware could only reach the Jews through

Mediterranean ports, where British agents maintained a close watch. Smuggling became a fine art. Rifles, mortars, machine guns—all sorts of materiel—arrived disassembled and disguised. The arms were then assembled and carefully hidden in secure storage areas pending the departure of the British. Meanwhile, Golda Meir made a memorable trip to the United States to raise money to pay for all this—entirely from private funds.

The man appointed by Ben-Gurion to defend Jerusalem was David Shaltiel. He had gained his military training in the French Foreign Legion fighting Arabs in Morocco. Shaltiel later settled in France and only really became involved in Zionism in the late 1930s, with the rise of Nazi anti-Semitism. He was captured by the Gestapo, tortured, and sent first to Dachau and then Buchenwald. It was there, ironically, that his leadership skills began to shine. When released from the camps, he managed to return to Palestine just before war was declared on Hitler's Germany. In Palestine, Shaltiel continued war efforts as a Haganah counterintelligence operative.

As Shaltiel rose through the ranks of the Haganah, his background in the French military became apparent. He was a spit-and-polish disciplinarian in what was then, and still is today, the most egalitarian army in the world. He was a man who would put the starch into the Jewish defense of Jerusalem. And starch it would need! Shortly after he arrived, Shaltiel got a taste of the way things would be in Jerusalem. A British sergeant major arrested four Haganah men who had been exchanging gunfire with the Arabs. He simply took the four into the Arab sector and turned them over to the mob. One was shot to death, the other three were stripped, beaten, emasculated, and then hacked to death.

Abdul Khader Husseini was after bigger game. His chief demolitions expert was Fawzi el-Kutub, a graduate of an SS terrorism course in Nazi Germany. Fawzi blew up the offices of *The Palestine Post*, a Jewish newspaper, on February 1, 1948. Later in the month, with the help of two British deserters, he managed to plant an enormous explosive device on Ben Yehuda Street in the heart of Jewish Jerusalem. Fifty-seven died and eighty-eight were injured. His greatest accomplishment, from his point of view, was on March 11, when a United States consulate car carried a bomb into the headquarters of the Jewish Agency—the most heavily guarded building in the city. Thirteen people died.

The most severe threat to Jerusalem, however, was starvation. Abdul Khader's militia held Bab el-Wad, Kastel, and other strategic points along the main highway between the coastal plain and the Judean hills on which Jerusalem sits. His tactic was working. Virtually every convoy bringing supplies was ambushed and sustained losses before reaching the city—if it reached Jerusalem at all. By the end of March, nothing was getting through. The Jewish Quarter of the city had only a few days' supplies remaining.

CHAPTER
15

I will be your enemy, surrounding Jerusalem and attacking its walls.

ISAIAH 29:3 NLT

On March 29, 1948, David Ben-Gurion summoned his Haganah commanders to a meeting to determine how to reopen the road to Jerusalem. Yigael Yadin, an archeologist in civilian life but then the chief of operations for the entire Haganah, put it plainly: The Yishuv, both in Jerusalem and in Galilee, was being strangled. Convoys and mere defensive measures were no longer getting the job done, and bolder measures were required. It was Ben-Gurion's most critical moment. The Zionist cabinet debated the situation for three hours and would have gone longer had Ben-Gurion not said, "Enough!" The time had come to take action, and the reticent cabinet approved his plan.

The first requirement was to secure weapons in sufficient quantity to launch a sizeable operation. Ben-Gurion had already cabled Ehud Avriel, his agent in Prague. On April 1, an American-built twin-engine

Dakota (or C-47) transport plane arrived at a deserted British airstrip less than twenty miles south of Tel Aviv. Two days later the main arms shipment arrived via freighter off a coastal inlet loosely patrolled by British guards. Hundreds of machine guns and thousands of rifles were ferried ashore. From there they were transported by truck directly to the untested troops who would use them. The men wiped the packing grease off their new weapons with their own underwear. By April 5, three battalions of five hundred men each began clearing the way for a convoy of 250 trucks to bring relief to Jerusalem.

During the fighting a very decisive event occurred—Abdul Khader was killed. Caught in the crossfire of a more intense Jewish assault than he had ever experienced, Khader called on Fawzi al-Kaukji, an Iraqi leader on his northern flank, to send help. Kaukji was Khader's rival. Haganah agents monitoring the conversation heard his terse lie in response, "Mafish—I have not any!" The betrayed Abdul Khader died in the fighting soon after that conversation. When his body was found the following morning, unprecedented mourning and wailing broke out in the ranks.

Such was the nature of his leadership that with Khader's passing, Haj Amin's cause was lost. Never again would the Palestinian Arabs offer so serious a threat to the Haganah. As the Arabs mourned Abdul Khader, the Jews of the New City were rejoicing. Truckload after truckload of supplies arrived. The siege had been broken, at least for the moment. Before long, Arabs would resume the ambush of convoys, and supplies would begin to dwindle again.

Added to starvation tactics was increased shelling of the city. As the British continued to withdraw, they turned over arms and other materiel to the Arabs. In this way the Palestinians came to possess more and more artillery with which to fire on the Jewish sectors. In the midst of all this, the final day of the British withdrawal arrived—May 14, 1948. While Ben-Gurion read the independence proclamation, Sir Alan Cunningham, the final British high commissioner, exited his residence in Jerusalem and was driven to Haifa, where he boarded a British cruiser.

Years later Menachem Begin described the scene eloquently in an address to the Knesset:

> One day after our independence was renewed, in accordance with our eternal and indisputable right, we were attacked on three fronts, and we stood virtually without arms—few against many, weak against strong. One day after the declaration of our independence, an attempt was made to strangle it with enmity, and to extinguish the last hope of the Jewish People in the generation of Holocaust and Resurrection.[64]

Arab armies from five nations were poised on Palestine's borders, awaiting the moment to drive the Jews into the sea. That objective has never changed. They had exerted as much pressure as could be brought to bear to keep the United States from recognizing the new State of Israel. It had come mostly through the Arab American Oil Company (Aramco) to the State Department: If the West wanted Arab oil, it had better not try to help the Jews. Oil is still the leverage of choice against support for Israel.

In the United States, President Harry S Truman was being urged by his foreign policy advisers to give in to Arab pressure. Nevertheless, after an emotional encounter with his former business partner in Kansas City, a Jew named Eddie Jacobson, Truman decided to meet with Chaim Weizmann. A cordial meeting between the president and Weizmann took place on March 18, 1948. Truman assured Weizmann that America was for partition and would stick to it. The next day, however, Truman was embarrassed by remarks the American ambassador to the UN made in the Security Council:

> On March 19, 1948, Warren Austin, U.S. ambassador to the United Nations, without the president's knowledge or White House clearance, announced on national radio as well as to the UN Security Council that the US government opposed the partition of Palestine. On March 20, Secretary of State George Marshal made a similar announcement. Truman was furious. According to [White

House Council Clark] Clifford, Truman said, "I assured Chaim Weizmann that we were for partition and would stick to it. He must think I am a plain liar." He quickly contacted Jacobson and Weizmann to reassure them that Austin had misrepresented the U.S. position.[65]

Truman later wrote in his diary:

> What is not generally understood is that the Zionists are not the only ones to be considered in the Palestine question. There are other interests that come into play, each with its own agenda. The military is concerned with the problems of defending a newly created small country from attacks by much larger and better trained Arab nations. Others have selfish interests concerning the flow of Arab oil to the U. S. Since they all cannot have their way, it is a perfect example of why I had to remember that "The Buck Stops Here."[66]

Truman was deluged with communications from Zionist and Jewish communities that objected vehemently to the change in United States policy postponing partition and Israel's independence. As it turned out, on May 14, a very short while after Ben-Gurion read the declaration of Israel's independence, Truman extended American recognition to the new government.

Now the man in the middle was King Abdullah, who was sitting with a newspaperman in Amman. He supposedly told the reporter:

> The Arab countries are going to war, and naturally, we must be at their sides, but we are making a mistake for which we will pay dearly later. One day we will live to regret that we did not give the Jews a state to satisfy their demands. We have been following the wrong course, and we still are."[67] King Abdullah smiled faintly at the newspaperman and added, "If you quote me on that, I will deny it publically and call you a liar."[68]

The Arab Legion, Abdullah's army, led by British Lieutenant General John Bagot Glubb, was the only professional army in the Arab Middle East at that time. He identified what he believed to be the chief weakness of Arab military establishments: He felt their armies tended to be overstaffed with the elite and political theorists, rather than with officers whose first interest was in soldiering. Glubb Pasha, as he was known in Arab circles, had managed to expunge this tendency from the ranks of his Arab Legion. Theirs would be the only army to prove durable against the Haganah.

In the early years of the war to retain their independence, Jewish authorities in Tel Aviv had to put Jerusalem on hold while they gave their attention and manpower to ward off an Egyptian onslaught coming up through the Negev. This gave Abdullah's forces an advantage in Jerusalem. Because of the Dome of the Rock, it had become the third holiest shrine in Islam. Also, Abdullah's father had lost Mecca and Medina to the Saudis in 1925, so Jerusalem would serve as compensation for his family as well—a vindication of the Hashemite dynasty.

Glubb was reluctant to commit his Bedouin soldiers to street fighting in Jerusalem. If he had known how poorly defended the city was at that point, he might have felt differently. The first units of the Legion—a small detachment—arrived in the Old City on May 19. At the same time 2,080 of Glubb's soldiers invaded the heights north of the city and began to advance on the New City—the center of Jewish population with roughly 100,000 inhabitants. The Legion's approach struck terror. This was a real army, not an undisciplined bunch of irregulars.

David Shaltiel had roughly the same number of men under his command, but they were virtually weaponless. A group of teenagers armed with Molotov cocktails, a bazooka, and an armored car encountered Glubb's first column of the Legion. The Jordanians had made a wrong turn near the Mandelbaum Gate and were taken completely by surprise by the ambush. Before the Arabs could withdraw, the teenagers had managed to knock out three of their armored cars. The victory gave new heart to the Israelis; they would need it.

While the New City was momentarily safe from capture by the Arabs, the Jewish Quarter remained in grave danger. On May 18, a second company of Haganah men had managed to fight its way into the Quarter to join the lone company defending the Jews there. Here, however, Glubb's Legion held the real advantage. Its artillery prevented further reinforcement by the Jews, and the Arab death grip tightened. The Quarter was forced to surrender on May 28. It was an enormous symbolic capitulation not only for the inhabitants of Israel but to the Jewish community worldwide.

Ten days of savage fighting followed, during which the Jews managed to turn back the Arab assault. On May 28, Glubb called off his attack, His men had been seriously mauled in the fighting. Besides, the strategy for his assault was wrong; the battle for Jerusalem would be decided on the heights of Latrun, which overlooked the supply road from Tel Aviv. David Shaltiel believed he had done what he could in the Jewish Quarter and that his primary responsibility was the New City.

The Egyptian threat from the south had been lessened by the end of May, and the Israeli high command could focus its attention on getting relief to Jerusalem. By early June the Jewish sector had been the recipient of more than ten thousand rounds fired from Jordanian artillery. Two thousand homes had been destroyed with twelve hundred civilian casualties reported. The city was entirely cut off from supplies, and its people were on the verge of starvation.

Haganah operations chief Yadin and Ben-Gurion summoned
General Yigal Allon, who had been leading the fighting in Galilee,
to head the assault on Latrun and break the Arab stranglehold on
Jerusalem's supply route. Haganah troops had been augmented with
large numbers of raw recruits, many fresh off the immigrant ships.
These men were rushed to the front by bus and taxi. In the blistering
heat, these untrained troops were tossed into a direct frontal assault
on the entrenched Jordanians without badly needed artillery support
or even adequate reconnaissance. The Arabs raked them with artillery and mortars. The Jews suffered heavy losses and were forced to
withdraw.

In the midst of the campaign to take Latrun, Ben-Gurion assigned
a new and special volunteer to oversee the assaults. He was David
Marcus, a Jewish American, West Point Graduate, veteran of the
Normandy invasion, and a colonel in the United States Army. Marcus
had left his prestigious post at the Pentagon to help his brothers in
Israel. He joined with Shlomo Shamir, the commander of the first
assault against Latrun, and together they tried harder to make the
next one equally successful.

In spite of reinforcing their operations considerably, the Fourth
Regiment of the Arab Legion stood firm in the face of the next Israeli
attack. More Jewish bodies littered the slopes in front of their positions. It seemed that the hope of relieving Jerusalem was being bled
dry at Latrun. An upcoming deadline made their task even more

urgent: A UN cease-fire was due to go into effect on June 11. When that happened, if the road to Jerusalem was not open, it would be too late.

Marcus began to search for a different route. There was a path by which troops had been getting to Jerusalem on foot. Marcus recruited two young officers, Vivian Herzog and Amos Chorev, to take a jeep ride with him, and together they discovered it was indeed possible to traverse this path from Tel Aviv to Jerusalem on wheels. Now all they needed to do was make it passable for trucks. Dirty and unshaven from their trek across mountainous terrain, the three men headed directly for Ben-Gurion's office as soon as they arrived back in Tel Aviv. The prime minister listened carefully to the report, probably thinking, *Maybe, just maybe, if a jeep could get through . . .*

A searing heat wave bore down on Palestine as hundreds of workers set out from Tel Aviv to begin the daunting task of building a road in the wilderness. Given the shortage of heavy machinery, it was a mind-boggling job. Meanwhile, in Jerusalem the situation was growing more desperate by the hour; only a few days' supply of food and water remained. The ordnance officer estimated there was enough ammunition for a sustained battle of no more than twenty-four hours.

Dov Joseph, a Canadian Jew and the civilian governor of Jerusalem during the crisis, could take much of the credit for the orderly and disciplined way of life in the city. The people were remarkably steadfast and courageous. On Saturday, June 5, just six days before the UN cease-fire would be imposed, Joseph was still reeling from the fate of his daughter, who had died fighting in the south just a few days prior. Now he was forced to cut the citizens' rations once more. He and his fellow Jerusalemites would subsist on four thin slices of bread each day, supplemented by half a pound of dried beans, peas, and groats for the week. He waited in anticipation for news from what many were calling the "Burma Road," the proposed Tel Aviv-to-Jerusalem route. It was named after the path hacked out of jungle-covered mountains in Burma by Chinese coolies in order to provide supplies to Chiang Kai-shek's troops during World War II.

Marcus began the excavation with just one bulldozer at his disposal. The work inched forward at an agonizingly slow pace. Each hundred yards of progress toward Jerusalem often required three hundred yards of winding roadway. Alternate crews worked day and night. Then a second bulldozer became available, but by then conditions in Jerusalem were desperate. On Sunday, June 6, Joseph had cabled Ben-Gurion that the city couldn't hold out beyond the following Friday. Ben-Gurion weighed his alternatives: Marcus had three miles to go. Could he make it in four days?

Ben-Gurion decided he could not afford to risk the wait. He called out the Home Guard and sent the members on foot, each with forty-five-pound packs loaded with food for Jerusalem. Three hundred middle-aged men were bused to the end of the makeshift road and set out to hike the three miles over ridges and through ravines until they reached the point where they could off-load their packs onto a truck bound for the Holy City.

On June 9, David Marcus and his two bulldozers miraculously emerged from the wilderness through which they had been digging since the end of May. The first trucks, filled with food and water, made their way over that primitive roadway to be greeted in Jerusalem with tears and cheers of joy. Two days later, at 10:00 a.m., the UN cease-fire went into effect. It was just the breathing space the Israelis needed to rearm and replenish for completion of the War of Independence.

In Jerusalem, the war was over. The Jordanians held half the city—including the Old City with its holy sites, the Western Wall, the now-abandoned Jewish Quarter, and all the surrounding countryside north, south, and east. The Israelis held the New City and a secure western corridor leading to the coast. Jerusalem now had a knife thrust through her heart: for the first time in her history, she was a divided city.

Theodor Herzl

Western Wall

Chaim Weizmann

Allenby enters Jerusalem

Arthur James Balfour

Haganah troops

Foreign Office,
November 2nd, 1917.

Dear Lord Rothschild,

I have much pleasure in conveying to you, on
behalf of His Majesty's Government, the following
declaration of sympathy with Jewish Zionist aspirations
which has been submitted to, and approved by, the Cabinet

"His Majesty's Government view with favour the
establishment in Palestine of a national home for the
Jewish people, and will use their best endeavours to
facilitate the achievement of this object, it being
clearly understood that nothing shall be done which
may prejudice the civil and religious rights of
existing non-Jewish communities in Palestine, or the
rights and political status enjoyed by Jews in any
other country"

I should be grateful if you would bring this
declaration to the knowledge of the Zionist Federation.

Balfour Declaration

Transfer of government

Raising flag

Israel soldiers liberate the Western Wall

Rabbi Shlomo Goren blows the shofar at the Western Wall

A nation is born

Begin and Sadat

Mike Evans and Prime Minister
Menachem Begin

David Ben-Gurion

Mike Evans and Mayor Teddy Kollek

Mike Evans and Prime Minister
Benjamin Netanyahu

Israeli tanks advancing on the Golan Heights

Mike Evans and the Chief Rabbi of Jerusalem

Mike Evans and Prime Minister Yitzhak Rabin

CHAPTER
16

Who has heard such a thing? Who has seen such things?
Shall a land be born in one day? Shall a nation be brought forth in one moment?
For as soon as Zion was in labor she brought forth her children.

ISAIAH 66:8 ESV

W hen examining the history of the State of Israel, one has to marvel at the hand of God in human events. Modern historians find it remarkable that Israel was created during a tiny window of opportunity. It happened at precisely the right moment—so much so that it had to have been more than merely coincidental.

For example, had Israel declared independence when Franklin D. Roosevelt was president, it is unlikely the United States would have recognized the newborn state. Without that recognition, any global support for the Jewish state would have evaporated.

Conversely, Harry Truman, Roosevelt's successor, would have been unlikely to recognize Israel had it not been for the intercession of his old business partner, Edward Jacobson. Lieutenant Truman and Sgt. Jacobson had served together in the 129th Field Artillery, and after the war ended they opened a haberdashery in Kansas City. The joint- venture store would fall victim to the 1921 recession, but their friendship would flourish. During his later life, Truman would credit Jacobson as the person whose advice had a major impact on his decision to recognize Israel as an independent state.

It was Jacobson who suggested Truman meet with Zionist leader Chaim Weizmann. In a meeting with Truman, Jacobson pointed to a statue of President Andrew Jackson, saying:

> Your hero is Andrew Jackson. I have a hero too. He's the greatest Jew alive. I'm talking about Chaim Weizmann. He's an old man and very sick, and he has traveled thousands of miles to see you. And now you're putting him off. This isn't like you, Harry.[69]

Truman agreed to a meeting at the White House, making sure Weizmann entered by a side door, unnoticed by the press.

In a letter to Jacobson, Chaim's wife, Vera, wrote in reference to efforts to swing the pendulum in favor of the Jewish people, "One day the world will know the part you played in helping my husband achieve his goal."[70] Ambassador James Grover McDonald said of Jacobson, "Just because Eddie Jacobson is so thoroughly American—and so Jewish—he has played a quiet but effectively large constructive role."[71]

In the end, however, it would be Weizmann, with Jacobson's help, who would secure Truman's backing and loyalty. In April 1943, almost two years before he would take office and five years before Israel reached statehood, the then-senator Truman delivered a scalding volley directed at those ambivalent listeners who had not raised a hand to help the Jews:

> This is the time for action. Today—not tomorrow—we must do all that is humanly possible to provide a haven and place of safety for all those who can be grasped from the hands of the Nazi butchers. Free lands must be opened to them. To do all of this, we must draw deeply upon our tradition of aid to the oppressed, and on our great national generosity. This is not a Jewish problem, it is an American problem—and we must and we will face it squarely and honorably.[72]

Just two days after he was sworn into office as chief executive, Truman delivered another passionate speech:

> Merely talking about the Four Freedoms is not enough. This is the time for action. No one can any longer doubt the horrible intentions of the Nazi beasts. We know that they plan the systematic slaughter throughout all of Europe, not only of the Jews but of vast numbers of

other innocent peoples. . . . Their present oppressors must know that they will be held directly accountable for their bloody deeds. To do all this, we must draw deeply on our traditions of aid to the oppressed, and on our great national generosity.[73]

The State Department, headed by Secretary Edward R. Stettinius Jr., held a decidedly pro-Arab stance. On Wednesday, April 18, 1945, Secretary Stettinius wrote to the newly inaugurated president:

It is very likely that efforts will be made by some of the Zionist leaders to obtain from you at an early date some commitments in favor of the Zionist program which is pressing for unlimited Jewish immigration into Palestine and the establishment of a Jewish state. . . . The question of Palestine is, however, a highly complex one and involves questions which go far beyond the plight of the Jews in Europe. If this question shall come up, therefore, before you in the form of a request to make a public statement on the matter, I believe you would probably want to call for full and detailed information on the subject before taking any particular position in the premises. I should be very glad, therefore, to hold myself in readiness to furnish you with background information on the subject at any time you may desire.[74]

Perhaps it was Secretary of Defense James Vincent Forrestal, who best summed up views of the State Department when he said, "You don't understand. There are four hundred thousand Jews and forty million Arabs. Forty million Arabs are going to push four hundred thousand Jews into the sea. And that's all there is to it. Oil—that is the side we ought to be on."[75] (Many of the following secretaries of state have seemed not to waiver from that stance to this day: Oil trumps reliable allies.)

Years later, Truman would write of this memo from "the striped pants boys" (as he referred to the State Department), saying that they were "in effect telling me to watch my step, that I didn't really understand what was going on over there and that I ought to leave it to the experts." However, the new president was not to be intimidated. He felt that "as long as I was president, I would see to it that I made policy."[76]

While it may seem unlikely that the memo pushed Truman to support Zionism, what it did ensure was that whatever his decision on the subject, it would be made quite independent of anti-Semitic State Department pressure.

Another point well taken: Had Israel's move for independence come just a year or so later, the Cold War would have been underway and Truman, despite his Zionist leanings, might not have had the courage to buck the powerful forces allied against Israel. Consider the Soviet Union, which followed America's lead in recognizing the State of Israel. The Soviets' ploy was seen only as a way to dislodge Britain from the Middle East and extend its own influence.

By the early 1950s the Soviets were courting Arab interests in the Middle East and had withdrawn their support for Israel. So Israel's declaration of independence on May 14, 1948, came at precisely the right moment—not a moment too soon or too late. As historian Paul Johnson notes, "Israel slipped into existence through a crack in the time continuum."[77]

Had more people studied the writings of the prophet Ezekiel, they would not have been so surprised by the birth pangs of the nation of Israel or the ingathering of Jews from all over the world. The creation of modern Israel made possible the fulfillment of a prophecy made some twenty-five centuries before the fact: Ezekiel's foretelling of the scattered dry bones is one of the most vivid and moving passages in the entire Bible (see Ezekiel 37:1–10).

Ezekiel relates how he was taken to a vast open cemetery, a great valley full of bones. After long exposure to the sun and wind, the skeletons had become dry, bleached, and disconnected. As he viewed this grisly sight, the Lord asked Ezekiel if the bones could live again. He simply relied, "O Sovereign Lord, you alone know." Ezekiel was then given the responsibility of prophesying over the bones, promising then that they would receive flesh, breath, and life. As he obeyed the Lord, there was a great shaking and a loud noise as the bones came together and were covered with flesh. God breathed life into the bones; they then stood to their feet and formed a great army.

God revealed to the prophet that the bones represented the house of Israel. The dry, scattered bones depicted the dispersion of the Jews around the globe. The aura of hopelessness and despair symbolized the fear of never being united again. The Lord instructed Ezekiel to say to them, "I will bring you back to the land of Israel . . . and I will settle you in your own land" (Ezekiel 37:12, 14).

Ezekiel proclaimed the message God had given him. His prophetic words kept a glimmer of hope alive in the hearts of the Jewish people through the centuries—from the boneyards in every nation of the world where they had been dispersed. In the midst of incredible persecution and suffering, God offered a promise to which they could cling. The words of the Lord were as a bright light cutting through the gloom and darkness of the Jewish ghettos and death camps.

The establishment of the new nation of Israel in 1948 and the subsequent emigration of Jews from more than one hundred nations to populate the Jewish state has exactly fulfilled Ezekiel's prophecy.

During a private conversation before he became prime minister of Israel, Benjamin Netanyahu once said to me:

> The truth of the matter is that if it had not been for
> the prophetic promises about returning to our homeland,
> the Jewish people would not have survived. There is

something about reading the statements of the prophets in the original Hebrew language—the powerful impact of those words bore deep into your heart and is implanted in your mind. There is absolutely no question but that those ancient prophetic promises kept hope alive in the hearts of Jewish people and sustained us over the generations when we had nothing else to cling to.

From the beginning of their independence—while still at war—Israel threw open her doors to Jewish refugees. Within the first four months following her independence, some fifty thousand Jews fled to Israel, most of them Holocaust survivors. Within the first three years the total number of immigrants climbed to almost seven hundred thousand, doubling Israel's population.

In 1950 the Knesset unanimously passed the Law of Return, which states:

1. Every Jew has the right to come to this country as an oleh [an immigrant to Israel].

2. Oleh's visa

    (a) Aliyah shall be by oleh's visa.

    (b) An oleh's visa shall be granted to every Jew who has expressed his desire to settle in Israel, unless the Minister of Immigration is satisfied that the applicant

(1) is engaged in an activity directed
against the Jewish people; or

(2) is likely to endanger public health or
the security of the State.[78]

Over 2.5 million men, women, and children from the four corners of the earth did just that: settle in a land they had never seen, but for which they had always longed. The cry, "Next year in Jerusalem" became a reality for them. The nation of Israel has gone to great expense to help them get there; sometimes putting together massive airlifts of thousands of Jews at a time, sometimes taking them out of hostile countries during war situations. The logistics of those airlifts were staggering, but the Israelis quickly mastered the process.

The first major airlift, in 1950, was dubbed "Operation Magic Carpet." The entire Jewish population of the Arab country of Yemen was airlifted to Israel. That was followed by transporting over fifty thousand Jews from Baghdad. A tight deadline had been set by the Iraqi government before immigration to Israel became a capital offense.

Two more airlifts brought Jews, believed to have existed in Ethiopia since the time of Solomon, to a new home in Israel. "Operation Moses" and "Operation Joshua" from 1984 to 1985 moved 7,500 Ethiopian Jews to Israel. When they arrived, they only knew two words in Hebrew: *Yerushalayim* and *shalom*—"Jerusalem" and the word of greeting that means "peace."

When civil war again broke out in the African nation in 1991, thousands more Jews were stranded. After months of difficult negotiations, and with the assistance of the United States, permission to rescue the remaining Ethiopian Jews was given. In less than thirty-six hours the Israeli Air Force completed "Operation Solomon." A total of 14,324 men, women, and children were rescued from Addis Ababa and flown to Tel Aviv before the news was leaked to the press.[79]

The largest and most prophetically significant group of immigrants came to Israel from the former Soviet Union. Approximately 100,000 Jews were allowed to emigrate in the 1970s. Many had waited years to receive exit visas, and with the collapse of Communism, the floodgates opened:

> Soviet Jews were permitted to leave the Soviet Union in unprecedented numbers in the late 1980s, with President Gorbachev's bid to liberalize the country. The collapse of the Soviet Union in late 1991 facilitated this process. After 190,000 *olim* reached Israel in 1990 and 150,000 in 1991, the stabilization of conditions in the former Soviet Union and adjustment difficulties in Israel caused immigration to level off at approximately

70,000 per year. From 1989 to the end of 2003, more than 950,000 Jews from the former Soviet Union had made their home in Israel.[80]

Even though Israel's Ministry of Absorption was a great help in integrating the new arrivals into Israeli society, it is still today a tremendous economic burden on the Jewish state. However, the government of Israel is determined to provide a haven for Jews from any corner of the world. Despite being surrounded by hostile Arab countries, and subjected to political pressure from the West, the *raison d'etre* for the State of Israel is to provide safety from any future Holocaust. For that purpose, her doors will never be closed to any Jew seeking to make *aliyah*—or "going up to Jerusalem."

CHAPTER

17

*Like birds hovering, so the L*ORD *of hosts will protect Jerusalem;*
he will protect and deliver it, he will spare and rescue it.

ISAIAH 31:5 RSV

After the 1948 Armistice was declared between Israel and Jordan, it was thought that Jerusalem was permanently divided:

> Barbed wire and concrete barriers ran down the center of the city, passing close by Jaffa Gate on the western side of the old walled city, and a crossing point was established at Mandelbaum Gate slightly to the north of the old walled city.[81]

The Armistice provided Israeli access to two important Jordanian-controlled areas of Jerusalem: Mount Scopus, where the campus of Hebrew University and Hadassah Hospital were located, and the

Western Wall and synagogues of the Old City. Actually, the only good to come of this agreement was that the Jews were allowed to maintain a police outpost on Mount Scopus. British historian Simon Montefiore wrote of the duplicity surrounding the division of Jerusalem under the Armistice:

> The Armistice, signed in April 1949 and supervised by the UN, who were based in the British Government House, divided Jerusalem: Israel received the west with an island of territory on Mount Scopus, while [Jordan's king] Abdullah kept the Old City, eastern Jerusalem and the West Bank. The agreement promised the Jews access to the [Western] Wall, the Mount of Olives cemetery and the Kidron Valley tombs but his was never honored. Jews were not allowed to pray at the Wall for the next nineteen years, the tombstones in their cemeteries were vandalized.[82]

In November 1949, Jerusalem again appeared on the agenda of the United Nations. The Israelis argued against internationalizing the Holy City. They instead offered to sign an agreement that would guarantee access to all holy sites in their portion of the city. This was not to be. On December 10, the UN General Assembly passed a resolution calling for internationalization under UN trusteeship.

The government of Israel reacted promptly. In December 1949 it announced the immediate transfer of offices from Tel Aviv to Jerusalem and proclaimed Jerusalem the eternal capital of Israel. Faced with Israel's actions and Jordan's vehement opposition to the resolution, the UN Trusteeship Council recognized it was unenforceable except by armed intervention. The resolution was set aside.

In 1995 the 104th US Congress passed the Jerusalem Embassy Act. It was designed to acknowledge Jerusalem as the capital of Israel and provide for a US Embassy to be established in Jerusalem no later than May 1999. Both Houses of Congress voted overwhelmingly to recognize Jerusalem. Each year since its passage, Presidents Clinton, Bush, and Obama have waived the implementation of the Act. The denial has been based on petty grievances over which branch of government has the authority to set foreign policy, and on "national security interests." President Donald Trump has promised to honor the Embassy Act. Incredibly, Israel remains at this writing the only nation on the face of the earth not permitted to proclaim its own capital.

Under the UN mandate and by January 1950, all government services housed in East Jerusalem during the British Mandate had been transferred to Amman. King Abdullah annexed the city and the West Bank, the hill country of Samaria and Judea that lie north and south of Jerusalem. He then changed the name of his country from Transjordan to the Hashemite Kingdom of Jordan. East Jerusalem was heralded the "second capital" of Jordan, although it meant little in actual practice. The city was cut off from access to the Mediterranean and somewhat isolated up in the hills.

For several years following the armistice, East Jerusalem was without electricity, and water was in short supply. The economy was based on tourism and institutions devoted to religious research. Its only significant manufacturing facility was a lone cigarette plant. Under Jordanian oversight, building projects were nearly nonexistent, confined to a few hotels, churches, and hospitals.

On the other side of the wall separating Israeli and Jordanian oversight, the times were very different. The Israelis were much more aggressive in their allotted portion of Jerusalem, even though it was situated at the end of a long corridor and surrounded by hostile Arabs. Larger water pipelines replaced circa 1948 conduits and an immense reservoir for water was constructed south of the city. The already-functioning electrical network was connected to the national grid, and train service in and out of the city resumed in May 1949.

Major highway construction and other building projects got underway quickly. Both Hadassah Medical Center and Hebrew University required new campuses to replace the facilities on Mount Scopus, which lay vacant. The complex multiplied to include a medical school, a training school for nurses, a dental school, and a wide range of specialty clinics.

The university added a stadium, synagogue, planetarium, and a major national library. A convention center for concerts, dramatic performances, exhibitions, and conferences was erected on the western outskirts of the city. In 1951 the Twenty-third Zionist Congress assembled in the center. It was the first to be held in Israel.

To the southwest of Jerusalem, Mount Herzl was turned into a national memorial park in honor of Theodore Herzl's work. Since then, many noted Zionists and Israeli leaders have been honored with burial there.

Israeli government buildings were raised in the late 1950s. The Knesset building, financed by the Rothschild family, was completed in 1966. These structures, including the Shrine of the Book and the Jerusalem Museum, lent credence to the assertion that Jerusalem was indeed the capital of Israel.

After Israeli president Chaim Weizmann died in 1952, the presidential residence was moved permanently to Jerusalem. It is there that foreign diplomats are compelled to present their credentials as well as to confer with the prime minister or foreign minister. By 1961 West Jerusalem's population had reached 166,300.

Life on the west side of the dividing wall was occasionally disrupted by sniping incidents instigated by Jordanian soldiers. A major point of contention was the Israeli police garrison on Mount Scopus. Each fortnight, a convoy passed through the Mandelbaum Gate under UN supervision to bring the relief shift and resupply the garrison with food and water. In one incident Jordanian troops fired on Israeli patrols, killing a UN observer and four Israeli policemen.

Dag Hammarskjöld, the then-secretary-general of the UN, and his envoy, Ralph Bunche, shuttled from Amman to Jerusalem in efforts to resolve the problem. They were unsuccessful.

In 1965 Teddy Kollek was elected mayor of West Jerusalem. Two years later, following the reunification of Jerusalem, he became the first mayor of the reunited city. During his tenure in office, the atmosphere between Jordanian East Jerusalem and the western part of the city was, while not cordial, relatively calm. There were isolated incidents, but the real boiling cauldrons were in Egypt and Syria, where the Soviets were pulling out all stops to court the two countries. Israel had been on the receiving end of wooing by the Soviets following World War II, but little came of it.

The governments of both Egyptian president Gamal Nasser and Syrian president Amin al-Hafez were recipients of an enormous amount of military and economic aid from Russia. In 1967 Soviet rhetoric reached a crescendo when the Israelis were accused of fostering an ominous arms buildup along the Syrian border and the Golan Heights. It was a patent falsehood.

In mid-April 1967 Soviet ambassador to Israel Leonid Chuvakhin complained to Prime Minister Levi Eshkol about the purported buildup. Apparently Ambassador Chuvakhin had no need to learn the truth; the abounding rumors were enough for him. Eshkol offered to drive him to the Syrian border to show him that the accusations were untrue. It was a useful diplomatic tool. If the rumors of Israeli aggression failed to materialize, the Soviets could brag that it was their support of the Syrian Ba'athist regime that saved the day.

The Soviets, however, stoked the fire just a tad too long and the pot would soon boil over and scald them. Nasser amassed an army on the Sinai Peninsula, opposite Israel's border. He closed the Strait at Sharm el-Sheikh at the mouth of the Gulf of Aqaba. It was the classic provocation. Israel had already notified the UN Security Council that if measures warranted, it would act in its own self-defense. UN secretary general U Thant failed to act forcefully to execute conditions of the truce that had existed since 1956. The UN peacekeeping forces standing between Nasser's army and the Israelis timidly packed up their tents and left town. On May 19, 1967, nothing stood between the Egyptians and the border of Israel.

In an amazing display of self-assurance, Levi Eshkol and Defense Minister Moshe Dayan remained cool, not acting until every alternative to avoid a confrontation had proved fruitless. On May 30 King Hussein of Jordan flew to Cairo to mend fences with Nasser and sign a mutual defense pact. Israeli intelligence, headed by Isser Harel, had spent a considerable amount of time studying the Arab character. They knew, for instance, that collective efforts among Arabs were seldom cohesive for any length of time. The best the Israelis could hope for was that the pact would be Hussein's lone demonstration of Arab solidarity—and that he would leave the fighting to Egypt and Syria.

Israel launched a lightning attack against the Arab states at ten minutes after seven on the morning of June 5. Well before noon nearly the entire Egyptian aircraft fleet was a flaming wreckage. Their air force was destroyed on the ground by Israeli fighter jets as God blinded the eyes of the Egyptians. In similar attacks, Israel destroyed Syrian jets and Jordanian planes.

Simultaneously, Israeli ground forces struck the Egyptian army amassed in the Sinai with an iron fist that virtually demolished Egypt's capacity to respond. As an important part of Israeli strategy for victory, Dayan had ordered a complete blackout of news. None of the stunning victories of June 5 were acknowledged for a twenty-four-hour period. That allowed Egyptian announcements loudly proclaiming that Israel's armed forces had been destroyed to go unchallenged. The Israelis allowed the false reports because they wanted to forestall a Soviet move toward a cease-fire if it thought its client states were winning.

Dayan's ploy had one unexpected drawback: King Hussein also heard Radio Cairo's bizarre and whimsical interpretation of the facts and believed the reports. Israel had already contacted the king and offered not to infringe on his territory if he would stay on the sidelines. Perhaps out of a desire for self-glory, Hussein ignored Israel's proposal and instructed his troops to begin shelling West Jerusalem. Hoping to have seen the limit of Hussein's military action Dayan ordered the front commander in Jerusalem, Uzi Narkiss, to hold his fire. But just to be on the safe side, Israeli jets destroyed Amman's air force of twenty Hunter jets the same day.

At one o'clock that afternoon, the Jordanians made their move to overrun Government House on the south side of the city. It was the headquarters of General Odd Bull, the Norwegian chief of the United Nations Truce Supervision Organization. Surrounded by seven hundred acres, it would give Hussein easy access for his Patton tanks to invade Israeli Jerusalem.

An hour later, Dayan gave the signal for Israeli troops to secure Government House. The Jerusalem Brigade drove the Jordanians from their objective and even farther south beyond "The Bell," a series of deep ditches dug as protection from enemy gunfire. By midnight the brigade had accomplished its mission with the loss of only eight men.

About the time Dayan had ordered the Jerusalem Brigade to attack, Uzi Narkiss issued the command to Uri Ben-Ari, leader of the Harel Mechanized Brigade—tanks and motorized infantry—to take the ridges north of the corridor. He was then to intercept Jordanian tank columns advancing on Jerusalem from the south through Ramallah. Ben-Ari's men and tanks moved into the Jerusalem corridor, and he then began to send units into the ridges controlled by the Jordanians.

Ben-Ari chose four separate routes to ensure that at least one column would break through and reach the objective—Tel el-Ful. It was the place where the road south from Ramallah and west from Jericho met to form one road into Jerusalem. It was a strategic point. The main obstacles to their advance were Jordanian troops and a minefield that stretched the entire length of the border in that area. The ground had been mined for so long no one knew where the explosives were located. Sadly, Uri Ben-Ari and his troops would find many of them before the battle ended.

At five o'clock the command was given to commence firing. Israeli tanks—supported by jet fighter-bomber attacks—blasted the Jordanian bunkers blocking their way. The infantry moved forward while engineers set out to find the mines, equipped only with bayonets, cleaning rods, and other improvised equipment. Many of the men lost legs that grisly night

As dawn crept over the battlefield, Ben-Ari's units had managed to reach the outskirts of Tel el-Ful. They had only four Sherman tanks, some halftracks, and a few vehicles from the reconnaissance unit. They soon spotted three of Jordan's Patton tanks moving toward them from Jericho and opened fire. They scored direct hits, but to their astonishment the 75mm shells bounced off the Pattons' heavy armor plate. Supplied with 90mm guns, the tanks returned fire and scored a direct hit on one of the Israeli tanks. With its commander wounded and its main gun destroyed, the Sherman withdrew. The firing pin on the second Sherman cannon broke, leaving just two Israeli tanks to level ineffective fire on the advancing Jordanian Pattons. If the three Jordanian tanks kept coming, there was little the Israelis could do to stop them. Lying just behind the advancing Patton tanks were twenty more awaiting orders of engagement.

Suddenly, and for no apparent reason, the Jordanian tanks began to turn and withdraw behind Tel el-Ful. The cessation of fire gave the Israelis an opportunity to crew the tank with the damaged gun and rejoin the operative Sherman tanks. Soon thereafter, Patton tanks came from behind Tel el-Ful to rejoin the fray. The Israelis resumed firing only to again see their shells bounce off the Jordanian tanks.

Sitting in the turret of the tank with the disabled cannon was Sergeant Rafael Eitan. He had been studying the Patton tanks through his binoculars when he spotted metal containers mounted on the backs of the Jordanian tanks. Could they be auxiliary fuel tanks?

There was only one way to find out: He cocked the heavy machine gun on his tank's turret and opened fire on the containers. A direct hit on one of the containers caused the Patton to burst into flames. The terrified crew of the tank beside it bailed out and ran for their lives. One Jordanian tank kept coming toward the Israeli line. Just as its commander broke through, Israeli air support arrived and directed a well-aimed round at the Patton tank. The remainder of the Jordanians turned and headed back to Jericho. Ben-Ari's troops had secured the road to Jerusalem and firmly blocked it.

In Tel Aviv, Colonel Mordechai Gur and his 55th Paratroop Brigade had been scheduled for deployment in the Sinai. Things were going so well there, however, that the high command offered their services to Narkiss. Colonel Gur and his staff arrived in Jerusalem a few hours ahead of their paratroopers. The greatest difficulty facing Gur's plan to penetrate the Green Line—as the border with Jordan was called—was whether to attack at night or wait for dawn. Since Dayan had ruled out air support because of the holy sites, it made little sense to wait for daylight; launching a night attack might even give the Israelis an advantage.

The battle for Jerusalem was bloody and costly. The Jordanians had withdrawn to entrenched positions on Ammunition Hill. There, the Israelis encountered massive resistance. In the early morning hours, two prongs of the paratrooper attack crossed just north of the Mandelbaum Gate. One unit headed toward the Old City, the other toward several Arab strongholds. Both groups encountered fierce street-to-street combat. By noon, however, Jordanian resistance had been quelled.

Perhaps the most critical struggle for Jerusalem was not fought on the battlefield but in the cabinet of Prime Minister Eshkol. Defense Minister Moshe Dayan and Menachem Begin were in favor of surrounding the Old City and choking it into surrender. Others were in favor of liberating all of Jerusalem. Dayan's plan remained in effect until he and Narkiss drove to Mount Scopus to survey the area. As Dayan gazed out over the Old City—Jerusalem the Golden—he realized the city had to be taken or all would be lost.

At the cabinet meeting that night, Eshkol issued orders through Chief of Staff Yitzhak Rabin to take the city. Colonel Gur arranged for detachments to enter the Old City through its gates. The main thrust would be through the Lion's Gate opposite the Mount of Olives. Resistance was minimal. The remainder of the day was relegated to rejoicing and the costly work of eliminating the last pockets of Jordanian opposition.

At the same time the Western Wall was being liberated, columns of Israeli tanks and infantry continued pressing the Jordanians throughout Samaria and Judea—called the West Bank by Arabs. My beloved friend General Gur, a 37- year-old colonel at that time, led his brigade to defend Jerusalem. Years later in his office in Jerusalem he told me, "On Wednesday morning, June 7th, I and my paratroopers stormed into the Old City and advanced on the Temple Mount. I wept as I shouted over my communications system, 'The Temple Mount is in our hands!'"[83]

Gur continued to tell me of his experience:

> I had long looked forward to liberating Jerusalem as something sublime. For me it was the culmination of my most personal goals as a youngster, as a Jew, and as a soldier. To me, the Temple Mount was more important than the Western Wall because the temple was the center of religion, the center of tradition. It was also the center

of the kingdom, of the state, of all our hopes. The day we took it, I wrote in my diary, "What will my family say when they hear we again liberated Jerusalem just as the Maccabees once did?" Jerusalem has only been a functioning capital when the Jews have ruled it.[84]

By sundown on June 7, the Israelis had reached the Jordan River. King Hussein had paid dearly for his gamble on the Egyptian propaganda. His army suffered over fifteen thousand casualties—dead, wounded, and missing. His air force had been decimated and half his tanks destroyed. He had lost his dynasty's last claim to the Islamic holy places. He had, however, lost more than that. The West Bank had been his richest agricultural land. Tourist income from Jerusalem and Bethlehem had accounted for 40 percent of Jordan's revenue. His only consolation was that the Jews had suffered more casualties against his army (1,756) than they had in the much larger Sinai campaign (1,075). One-fourth of Israel's losses had come in Jerusalem.

Few Israelis found room for mourning. Chief Rabbi Shlomo Goren related to me:

I managed to reach the Western Wall even before the firing had died down. Like one of Joshua's priests, I was running with the ram's horn, the shofar, in my hand. When I placed it to my lips and blew, I felt like thousands of shofars from the time of King David were blowing all at once.[85]

Jews from every nation were dancing and weeping as they touched the Western Wall. They sang, *"Yerushalayim Shel Zahav"* . . . Jerusalem of Gold. Prime Minister Yitzhak Rabin told me years later:

> This was the most holy day of my life. I heard rabbis crying that the Messiah was coming soon, and that ancient prophecy was fulfilled that day. You would have thought King David had returned with his harp and the Ark of the Covenant.[86]

Hardened veterans ran to touch the ancient wall, tears flowing down their faces in gratitude. "Next year, Jerusalem" was no longer a heartrending cry; it was reality. To pray at the Western Wall was no longer a yearning; it was a certainty. The Temple Mount, on which stands the Dome of the Rock, would remain closed to the Jewish people, but they could at least stretch out their fingers and touch a portion of it.

Most importantly, Jerusalem was again united and in Jewish hands.

CHAPTER
18

I will bring them back to live in Jerusalem. They will be My people,
and I will be their faithful and righteous God.

ZECHARIAH 8:8 HCSB

On the morning of June 9, 1967, Mayor Teddy Kollek bounded out of bed with an entirely new portfolio. His responsibilities had increased one hundredfold! He was now mayor over all Jerusalem, including some 67,000 Arabs who were opposed to the new oversight. Kollek was unclear as to their legal status as Jerusalemites and his responsibility toward them, but he would soon prove capable of the task set before him.

Having seen the condition of East Jerusalem, it would have been understandable to the observer had the Jews sought revenge against the Arabs in their midst. The infrastructure was in abysmal condition. There was much to be done to bring it up to standards.

Upon inspection, the Jews discovered not a single usable synagogue in the old Jewish Quarter of the city. Jewish shrines and cemeteries had been shamefully desecrated. Given the vitriol spewed by their Arab neighbors, retaliation might have been foremost in their minds. The choice by the Israelis, however, was not retribution but mercy.

Mayor Kollek realized that the Jordanians were the true perpetrators of defilement in the Jewish Quarter. He determined that under Israeli administration, all the city's inhabitants, no matter their nationality or religion, were entitled to law and order, freedom of religion, and efficient and humane public services. He went to work that very day—even before the cease-fire was announced.

Municipal employees crossed into East Jerusalem to repair broken water pipes and electrical circuits. They tore down and hauled away the barriers of roadblocks and barbed wire that had divided the city. The electrical grid and telephone systems were integrated. Water from West Jerusalem reservoirs ended the chronic shortages that had plagued Arab Jerusalem since 1948. The physical quality of life for Arabs improved immeasurably overnight, something that seemed to have escaped all but the Israelis who were working long hours to provide essential services.

The chief goal of Mayor Kollek and the Israeli government was to incorporate Arab Jerusalem as thoroughly as possible into the fabric of Israeli life. They wanted it understood unmistakably that Jerusalem was now united, and that they had come to stay. This was apparent in Kollek's enthusiasm to share his staff's talents with the Arabs, and also in the way he incorporated hundreds of Arab municipal employees and inspectors into the united city's enlarged administration. It was also apparent in the tough measures taken to remove squatters from the Jewish Quarter and to clean out the warren of bedraggled flats that abutted the Western Wall in order to make room for Jews to worship there.

The mayor wrote me a letter expressing his concerns for Jerusalem:

> Now it is more important than ever that we rally support for Jerusalem . . . international opinion is being swayed in favor of two capitals in one city. We know that is not the solution and that two capitals in Jerusalem will only lead to another division of the Holy City.

Every evicted Arab was offered compensation and alternative housing, but the move was inevitable. The Israelis were determined to remove every temporary, ramshackle lean-to in the area. The course for the future of the city was toward permanent change.

The Knesset passed into law a bill amending the Law and Administration Ordinance of 1948 to proclaim that the government could, by order, extend the law, jurisdiction, and administration of the state to any part of the land of Israel so designated. An order accompanying this bill placed East Jerusalem and its environs under Israeli supervision. Another directive authorized the minister of the interior, at his discretion, to enlarge by proclamation a particular municipality by the inclusion of a designated area.

Following the passage of that second bill, the interior minister expanded the Municipality of Jerusalem to include the city's holy places in an effort to protect them from desecration and assure equal access to all—Arabs, Christians, and Jews. The UN saw this move as the Israelis having annexed East Jerusalem. The General Assembly voted 99 to 0 that the changed status of Jerusalem was invalid and that Israel should rescind its actions. Israel responded by informing the UN that measures adopted by the Knesset related only to the integration of East Jerusalem into the administrative and municipal spheres, and served only to provide for the protection of the holy places in the city.

What UN General Assembly members failed to comprehend was that the Jordanians had taken the land in 1948 not by international law, but by force. It had been incorporated into their state. Israelis had taken back their land in an act of self-defense. It was an argument any reasonable person should have been able to comprehend and respect.

There was, however, one chief legal problem. The Arabs of Jerusalem were Jordanian citizens who now lived in the State of Israel. This technicality didn't seem to bother them at all. They mingled freely with the rest of the population. Arabs visited homes they had abandoned nineteen years before. In a show of solidarity on Friday,

June 30, Mayor Kollek attended prayer services at *Haram esh-Sharif* (the Noble Sanctuary located on the Temple Mount).

Jerusalem's Arabs certainly didn't turn up their noses at the many improvements the Jews had brought to their area. True, Israelis could be imperious and unaccommodating, but the Arabs were not indifferent to their essential physical security. By year's end, Kollek had provided fifteen miles of newly paved streets, twelve hundred new streetlights, thousands of trees planted in city gardens, new waste-removal equipment, and Arab homes were being connected to the municipal water system at the rate of fifty per week. The mayor was investing several times more on East Jerusalem than had the Jordanians.

Israelis poured into the Old City to spend their hard-earned cash on virtually everything the Arabs had for sale. It was a far cry from the sinister brutality Arabs had been warned to expect from the Jews. The West Bank and Jerusalem Arabs were enjoying economic prosperity such as they had never before known.

In the early years there were some incidents of strikes and violence. Eight hundred buildings were leveled in a West Bank village that was a base for terrorists. Convicted felons were jailed or deported. Sadly, in Jerusalem, violence has remained because of imported terrorists.

Since the Israelis regained control of the Old City in 1967, Hebrew University resumed activities on its Mount Scopus campus, and was expanded and improved. Hadassah Hospital was reopened.

Today the modern facility serves Arabs and Jews alike, as it did before 1948. The Jewish Quarter in the Old City has undergone total restoration and is once again a thriving part of the city. The Muslim Quarter, as indicated, has been upgraded. Throughout the Old City, television cable has all but eliminated unsightly antennas.

Streets and alleyways have been improved, and the Via Dolorosa—the traditional route taken by Jesus to His crucifixion on Calvary—has been resurfaced with ancient paving stones from the time of Herod. The Old City's crenellated walls were renovated, and a walkway permits citizens and visitors to stroll along its ramparts. The marketplace received a thorough cleaning and painting, and the ancient Roman thoroughfare that bisects the city—the Cardo—has been excavated, restored, and turned into a shopping mall with souvenir shops that cater to the tourist trade.

Outside the walls of the Old City, the Israelis expanded water districts, built elementary schools, vocational schools, community centers, adult and youth clubs, childcare centers, and libraries. An average of one million tourists visit Jerusalem each year, among them a multitude of people from Arab states that maintain no diplomatic relations with Israel.

A Saudi Arabian king is said to have complained that he did not feel free to visit Al-Aqsa Mosque because it stood on ground occupied by Israel. That seems contradictory when neither he nor his predecessors visited the mosque when it was under Jordanian control.

This leads to one important detail: Arabs are united only in anti-Semitism. They all can agree that the Jews are the "Little Satan," but here their unity ends. They talk openly about replacing Israel with a Palestinian state but distrust each other, and well they should. The Syrians really want Lebanon, Israel, and Jordan. The Jordanians want the West Bank and Jerusalem. The Palestinian Authority wants all of Israel, preferably with every Jew slaughtered, and anything else that can be wrested from Jordan, Syria, and Lebanon.

Today Americans and Europeans tend to take Arabs at face value. Few seem to understand that in the Arab culture, it is deemed perfectly acceptable, even preferable, to lie to an infidel—and that every non-Arab is considered to be an infidel. The United States, European Union, United Nations, and Russia continue to call for a negotiated settlement, believing Arabs to be reasonable people who are willing to negotiate a compromise by which Israel will be allowed to live in peace. Unfortunately, even some Israeli leaders have bought in to this fatuous dream. In reality, Israel has little choice but to retain sovereignty over all of Jerusalem.

Teddy Kollek wrote of Jerusalem:

> Let me be perfectly candid. The thing I dread most
> is that this city, so beautiful, so meaningful, so holy to
> millions of people, should ever be divided again; that
> barbed wire fences, mine fields, and concrete barriers

should again sever its streets, that armed men again patrol a frontier through its heart. I fear the re-division of Jerusalem not only as the mayor of the city, as a Jew, and as an Israeli, but as a human being who is deeply sensitive to its history and who cares profoundly about the well-being of its inhabitants . . . It must never again be divided. Once more to cut this living city in two would be as cruel as it is irrational.[87]

The treaties with terrorists that have been forced on Israel are nothing more than attempts to divide the Holy City, which God Almighty gave to Abraham and to David. Jerusalem became David's capital over three thousand years ago. A journalist for *U.S. News and World Report* wrote: "Peace is more than the mere absence of war . . . the path to Middle East peace remains as perilous as Moses' forty-year trek through the desert."[88] Peace has continued to be elusive, but there can be no doubt that the moment the Jews took Jerusalem back, the Holy City was energized and began once more to thrive.

CHAPTER
19

*"When you see Jerusalem being surrounded by armies,
you will know that its desolation is near."*

LUKE 21:20

After all Israel has done to incorporate Arab residents in Jerusalem and the West Bank, it is still not enough for the enemies that surround the tiny nation. It seems none will be satisfied until Israel ceases to exist.

One of the more determined foes of the Jewish state in Palestine was Egyptian-born Mohammed Yasser Abdel Rahman Abdel Raouf Arafat al-Qudwa al-Husseini. On the world stage, he was known as Yasser Arafat. He liked to advertise that he was born in Jerusalem, but like many of his "facts," that assertion proved to be entirely false: His birth certificate was legally registered in Cairo. During years spent in Kuwait, he helped to found the terrorist group Fatah.

Once settled in Jordan, Arafat and what would ultimately become the Palestinian Authority apparently sought to muddy the political activity by using fear tactics and sheer numbers to intimidate the late King Hussein. The Palestinians were positioned to surface as an overriding power in Transjordan politics. Their very presence, if allowed to expand, could well have ended the Hussein monarchy. Arafat and his underlings were determined to undermine the king while sowing seeds of empathy and support in the Jordanian ground that were ripe for unrest.

Backed by Syria, Arafat and his Fatah minions soon began to slip over the border from Jordan into Israel to make their terrorist presence known by targeting Israeli sites. One of the first was in January 1965 when organization operatives tried to bomb Israel's National Water Carrier. The attempt failed. By the late 1960s, and especially following the Six-Day War in 1967, Arafat and his crew began to openly stir up trouble for King Hussein by using his country as a base of operations against Israel. Reciprocal raids by Israel resulted in damage to Jordanian cities. Having deemed the organization a threat, King Hussein instructed his forces to disarm the Palestinian militia groups. The move resulted in open conflict with Arafat's Palestine Liberation Organization (PLO).

In September 1970, Egyptian president Gamal Abdel Nasser died. His successor, Anwar Sadat, was determined to regain the territory lost during the Six-Day War. Through a UN intermediary, Sadat let it be known that he would sign a peace treaty with Israel if the nation agreed to withdraw to the pre-1967 boundaries. The Knesset emphatically responded that Israel would not withdraw to the pre-June 5, 1967, lines.

Sadat's plan was to cause just enough damage to the Israelis to alter their decision. The leader of Syria, Hafiz al-Assad, had no such aspirations; he was determined to reclaim the Golan Heights militarily. The Syrians had launched a massive upsurge along their border with the Golan Heights, and they planned nothing short of a decisive victory against the Israelis. Al-Assad had another goal in mind: to establish Syria as the supreme military force among Arab countries. He was certain that with Sadat's assistance, the two allies could strike a convincing blow to tiny Israel and ensure that the West Bank and Gaza would once again be in Arab hands.

Sadat was plagued by economic ills that he thought would be allayed by a war with Israel, the nemesis of all Arabs. Author Abraham Rabinovich wrote:

> The three years since Sadat had taken office . . . were the most demoralized in Egyptian history . . . A desiccated economy added to the nation's despondency. War was a desperate option.[89]

The Egyptian people had been put to shame by the rout of their troops during the Six-Day War. If Sadat had been successful militarily, he planned to persuade the population that reforms were necessary. University students protested against Sadat, seeing war as the only way to regain respect in the region. They were upset that Sadat had waited so long to retaliate against the Israelis.

King Hussein of Jordan, on the other hand, was hesitant to join any coalition to attack Israel. His country had lost much in 1967, and he was afraid of further losses in another attempt. While Sadat backed the PLO in its claims to the West Bank and Gaza, King Hussein was fighting his own battles against the terrorist organization. After several hijackings, attempts to assassinate the king, and efforts to wrest the Irbid—the area with the second-largest city in the Hashemite Kingdom—from Hussein, Jordanian troops expelled the PLO from the country during what became known as Black September 1970.

In the bloody fighting that followed the king's decision, terrorists murdered Major R. J. Perry, military attaché at the United States Embassy in Amman. Then they took over two hotels, the Intercontinental and the Philadelphia, and held thirty-two American and European guests hostage. The leader, George Habash, announced they would kill the hostages and blow up the hotels if Jordanian troops did not retreat. An uneasy quiet ensued, but was shattered in September when King Hussein reached his breaking point politically. A group of Palestinians hijacked three airplanes and ultimately landed all three in Jordanian territory:

✧ September 6: Trans World Airlines (TWA) Flight 741, en route from Frankfurt to New York, a Boeing 707 carrying 149 passengers and crew. Hijackers rename the plane Gaza One and order it to the Jordanian air strip.

✧ September 6: Swissair Flight 100 from Zurich to New York, a DC-8 with 155 passengers and crew. It is over France when hijackers seize it, rename it Haifa One, and order it to Dawson Field in Jordan.

✧ September 9: BOAC Flight 775 from Bombay to London, a VC-10, is seized while flying over Lebanon. (The British Overseas Airways Corporation is the forerunner to British Airways.) PFLP hijackers say they've seized the plane as ransom for the release of Leila Khaled, the foiled hijacker aboard the El Al plane. The BOAC plane carries 117 passengers and crew. It's allowed to land in Beirut, where it refuels, then flies to Dawson Field in Jordan to join the other two hijacked jets there.[90]

The group then held 445 hostages. Some of the hostages were released, and by September 12 only fifty-four remained captive. As another act of terrorism, the three jets were eventually blown up in Jordan by the hijackers

By September 16, King Hussein announced a military govern-ment to restore order in Jordan, and Yasser Arafat was named head of the Palestine Liberation Army—the military arm of the Palestine Liberation Organization. The following morning the king unleashed the Bedouin Arab Legion in a full-scale operation against the PLO. Tanks demolished every building in Amman from which gunfire erupted. Before Hussein had regained control, an estimated three thousand Palestinian terrorists had been killed. PLO power in Jordan had been broken.

As the king's troops battled the PLO, Syria intervened, sending forces across Jordan's border. The Syrians greatly outnumbered Jordan in both tanks and aircraft, and when the king realized his predicament, he requested that "the United States and Great Britain get involved in the war in Jordan."[91] He asked the United States, in fact, to attack Syria. Some transcripts of diplomatic communiqués show that Hussein actually requested Israeli intervention against Syria: "Please help us in any way possible."[92] The following missive sent from King Hussein pled for assistance:

> Situation deteriorating dangerously following Syrian massive invasion. I request immediate physical interven-tion both land and air . . . to safeguard sovereignty, ter-ritorial integrity and independence of Jordan. Immediate

air strikes on invading forces from any quarter plus air cover are imperative.[93]

Israel and the United States mobilized their forces, giving notice to Syria that if a full-scale invasion were launched Syria would encounter more than Jordanian troops. It worked. Syria held back, and the Jordanians were able to drive the Palestinians out.

From Jordan, the PLO moved to Lebanon, the only Arab nation with a significant Christian (Syrian Orthodox and Catholic) population. When the French pulled out of Syria and Lebanon in 1946, the Christian majority in Lebanon worked out a delicately balanced arrangement with the Muslim minority under a democratic constitution. Beirut became a bustling and prosperous commercial center. At that time, its citizens enjoyed the highest per capita income in the Middle East.

After Israel became a state in 1948, several thousand Palestinian Arabs were admitted to Lebanon—not more, lest the Christian–Muslim balance of population shift disastrously. Disturbing the balance was always a matter of grave concern to the Christians who stood to lose the most.

The Palestinians, however, did disturb the balance in Lebanon—far out of proportion to their actual numbers. PLO agents worked actively in the refugee camps and established bases within them from which to launch terrorist attacks on Israel. The Lebanese government was faced with a serious dilemma: If the PLO were driven out, it would anger the Muslim population; to let them stay would enrage the Christians. The Lebanese prime minister began a delicate tightrope walk—he denied the existence of the PLO in public while covertly negotiating with Arafat to limit raids on Israel. His aim was to not provoke Israel retaliation against the PLO terrorists.

The arrangement worked only briefly. The PLO in Lebanon commandeered an Israeli El Al airliner. Israel responded by dispatching fighter jets to Beirut's airport to destroy Arab aircraft on the ground. While the Lebanese government was knocked off balance, its Muslim neighbors pressed for the right of the PLO to supervise and police refugee camps in southern Lebanon. Additionally, PLO terrorists imprisoned for subversive activities were released from Lebanese prisons. The result: burgeoning terror activities inside Lebanon.

While Lebanon dealt with the PLO problem, Egypt's president Anwar Sadat was busily planning an attack against Israel to gain a foothold and therefore a bargaining chip to retake the lands lost in 1967. On October 24, 1972, he announced his plan to the Egyptian Supreme War Council. He also sought the assistance of Syria and Jordan. Both declined to join Egypt in an attack, as did Lebanon. Authors Simon Dunstan and Kevin Lyles wrote:

Egypt and Syria had both lost territory in 1967 but their aims were now different. Egypt had accepted Resolution 242 and was prepared to recognize Israel while Syria was not. Moreover, Sadat's war aims were directed at the recovery of the Arab territory lost in 1967. In contrast, Syria, in common with the Palestine Liberation Organization (PLO) which it harbored, was bent on Israel's destruction.[94]

Undeterred, Sadat made a diplomatic push to engage support for his plan. By late 1973, he had been joined by approximately one hundred states within Arab countries and had enticed several European nations into joining Arabs on the UN Security Council in unifying for an offensive against Israel.

On October 6, 1973, Yom Kippur, the holiest day of the Jewish year, the Arab coalition struck Israel with a sneak attack in the hope of finally driving the Jews into the Mediterranean. When the war began, Israel was tragically caught off guard. Most of the members of its citizen army were in synagogues, its national radio was off the air, and people were enjoying a restful day of reflection and prayer. Therefore, Israel had no immediate response to the coordinated attacks. Israeli intelligence had not seen the assault coming, and her military was ill prepared to retaliate.

At the outset of hostilities, Egypt attacked across the Suez

Canal. The battle raged for three days, and then the Egyptian army established entrenchments, which resulted in an impasse. On the northern border, Syria launched an offensive on the Golan Heights. The initial assault was successful but quickly lost momentum. By the third day of fighting Israel had lost several thousand soldiers (more Israeli causalities were lost in the first day than in the entire Six-Day War), forty-nine planes, one-third (more than five hundred) of her tank force, and a good chunk of the buffer lands gained in the Six-Day War. The Israelis seemed to again be on the brink of a holocaust.

On the fourth day of the war, in an act of desperation, Prime Minister Golda Meir supposedly opened up three nuclear silos and pointed the missiles toward Egyptian and Syrian military headquarters near Cairo and Damascus. Army chief of staff Moshe Dayan was reported to have said, "This is the end of the Third Temple," in one of the crucial meetings. Later he told the press, "The situation is desperate. Everything is lost. We must withdraw."[95]

At that time Richard Nixon occupied the Oval Office. Earlier in his presidency, "Nixon made it clear he believed warfare was inevitable in the Middle East, a war that could spread and precipitate World War III, with the United States and the Soviet Union squaring off against each other."[96] The president was now staring down the barrel of that war, so he authorized Secretary of State Henry Kissinger to put every American plane that could fly in the air to transport all available conventional arms to Israel. The amount of materiel needed to defend Israel was more than the supplies airlifted to Berlin following World War II; it literally turned the tide of the war, saving Israel from extermination and the world from a possible nuclear conflagration. Nixon carried President Kennedy's agreement to militarily support Israel to the next logical level—a full military alliance.

The IDF (Israel Defense Forces) launched a counteroffensive within the week and drove the Syrians to within twenty-five miles of Damascus. Trying to aid the Syrians, the Egyptian army went on the offensive, but all to no avail. Israeli troops crossed the Suez Canal and encompassed the Egyptian Third Army. When the Soviets realized what was happening, they scrambled to further assist Egypt and Syria. The Soviet threat was so real Nixon feared direct conflict with the USSR and elevated all military personnel worldwide to DefCon III, meaning forces should prepare for the likelihood of war. However, a cease-fire was finally worked out between the United States and Russia, adopted by all parties involved, and the Yom Kippur War was ended.

It was shortly after this, in 1974, that US leaders finally decided to give normal military aid to Israel for the first time. If Israel were attacked again, the United States would do whatever was necessary to protect her as a full ally. If a strong Israel could deter another possible war or even defend herself if necessary, it would save higher direct expenditures in the long run.

Congress voted for the first-aid packages to Israel with part of it earmarked for defense. Before this time most aid to Israel had been in the form of loans, all of which Israel repaid. There were some loans for defense reasons but no grants or gifts. Starting in 1976, however, Israel would become the largest recipient of US foreign assistance. Since 1974, Israel has received several billions in aid, much of that in loans.

After the October 1973 war between Arab countries and Israel, Arafat opted to take a different approach: He decided to become a diplomat! With the use of smoke and mirrors and sleight of hand, the newly-made-over terrorist managed to create the illusion of civility and legitimacy. With dogged determination, he gained acceptance as the leader of the PLO pack.

Arafat's transformation obviously did not deflect his determination to destroy Israel in whatever way he deemed appropriate. He and his Palestine Liberation Organization, as well as other self-styled terrorist groups, failed to bolster the position of the Palestinian people by continuing attacks against the Israelis at home and abroad:

- In 1972, another arm of the PLO, Black September led by Mohammed Oudeh [more commonly known as Abu Daoud], claimed responsibility for the deaths of eleven Israeli athletes during the Munich Olympics in Germany.

- One year later, PLO terrorists murdered Cleo Noel, US Ambassador to the Sudan, and his chargé d'affaires

George Moore. The terrorists were arrested, but for some unknown reason, were not charged with the murders—even though proof pointed directly at Arafat as a party in the crime.

✧ February 1978: A bomb planted on a bus filled to capacity exploded in Jerusalem; two were murdered, forty-six injured.

✧ March 11, 1978: A Fatah terrorist murdered Gail Rubin, niece of U.S. Senator Abraham Ribicoff, on the Tel Aviv beach.

✧ March 11, 1978: PLO terrorists seized a bus on the coastal road, killing thirty-five men, women, and children.

✧ March 17, 1978: PLO terrorists launched Katuysha rockets on the Western Galilee, killing two and wounding two.

✧ June 2, 1978: A PLO terrorist bombed a Jerusalem bus, killing six and wounding nineteen.

✧ August 20, 1978: PLO terrorists attacked El Al members while on a crew bus in London, killing a stewardess and wounding eight.

✧ December 21, 1978: PLO terrorists launched a Katuysha rocket, killing one and wounding ten in Kiryat Shmona.[97]

The killing did not end when the clock struck midnight on January 1, 1979. Arafat's *intifadas* against Israel have produced death and destruction from then until now. Many fail to comprehend what it is like to live in a city so vulnerable to the violence of terror attacks. Journalist David Grossman describes it this way:

> An international TV program once interviewed a young Israeli couple und asked how many children they wanted to have. The beautiful bride said immediately: "Three." And the interviewer asked: "Why three?" And she said with a smile: "So that if one of them is killed in a war or in terror we shall still have two left."
>
> We did not have three children out of this calculation, but I must admit that this thought had crossed my mind when we started having children. The option of personal catastrophe is connected to the special fate of this country.
>
> As I fear for my children, all my life I lived with this fear of what happens if a catastrophe occurs in Israel. The question of whether we shall exist here in the future, whether we will still live here within a few decades time, prevail[s] subconsciously in the mind of most Israelis. We are living with difficult and partly violent neighbors, most of whom don't want us here. Some of them even threaten to eradicate us. I take them very seriously.[98]

Jerusalemites have always lived under the threat of death, where everyday decisions often evolve into crucial situations. Their beloved city has been repeatedly ransacked, captured, or faced a major siege.

With the perils and complexities of Jerusalem's stormy past and continued threats to her security, keep in mind that this is not just a story of kings and soldiers and armies. It is the history of civilians, men like David Grossman and his family, who are the ones to pay the heaviest price for living in this city threatened constantly by turbulence of one kind or another.

Despite Arafat's fingerprints being all over attacks within Israel's borders, his good friend and confidant, President Jimmy Carter continued to provide help. His pro-Arafat and pro-Palestinian leanings are legendary. According to Carter's assessment in his book *Palestine: Peace Not Apartheid* (one, I might add, that is held by the world at large), Israel is the crux of the problem. Never mind that Israel has endured decades of terror attacks from the PA, Lebanon, Syria, and Gaza, worthless peace agreements, and a desire by its Arab neighbors to see it "wiped off the map." None of this moves Mr. Carter. In his world Yasser Arafat was the poor, pitiful, put-upon Palestinian leader sorely abused by the Israelis.

Perhaps it is fitting that both Yasser Arafat (in 1994) and Jimmy Carter (in 2002) received the prestigious Nobel Peace Prize. After all, as historian Douglas Brinkley wrote: "There was no world leader Jimmy Carter was more eager to know than Yasser Arafat, the master logistician and survivor of byzantine Middle East politics. . . . Carter felt certain affinities with the Palestinian."[99]

By 1994, Arafat had risen in notoriety to lead the Palestinian Authority that had emerged as a result of the Oslo Accords. In 1996, he was elected president of the organization by an overwhelming 83 percent. He served three years before his death.

By the time William Jefferson Clinton assumed office as the forty-second president of the United States, Yasser Arafat was a household name and had become a major player in the Middle Eastern version of Russian roulette. One can only wonder how a fanatical terrorist like Arafat could achieve the position of viable "peace partner" with Israel. Perhaps the answer can be found in advice that Arafat received from Romanian dictator Nicolae Ceauşescu:

> In the shadow of your government-in-exile [PLO], you can keep as many operational groups as you want, as long as they are not publicly connected with your name. They could mount endless operations all around the world, while your name and your 'government' would remain pristine and unspoiled, ready for negotiations and further recognition.[100]

Clinton, working with Israel's prime minister Ehud Barak, was determined to put together the same kind of peace agreement that had been set in motion by President Carter and Prime Minister Menachem

Begin in 1978 at Camp David. That attempt had resulted in a treaty between Israel and Egypt. The president was determined to fashion a workable plan even though Arafat had done little since Oslo to convince Israel that he was willing to compromise. Conversely, Arafat seemed resolute in his dream to destroy the Jewish nation. Despite that, Barak was willing to sit down and agree to most of the Palestinian's demands: withdrawal from 97 percent of the West Bank and 100 percent of the Gaza Strip; destruction of many of the settlements; creation of a Palestinian state with East Jerusalem as its capital.

Arafat was required only to acknowledge that Israel was a sovereign state, allow control of the Western Wall, and permit three Israeli-manned early warning stations in the Jordan Valley. Arrogantly, Arafat walked away from the negotiating table and launched yet another intifada against Israel.

Terrorists, emboldened by Arafat's refusal to cooperate, targeted unsuspecting Israelis with suicide bombings, and opening fire on buses, shopping malls, restaurants, and other locations. Victims were murdered or maimed with impunity. Families were torn apart, children orphaned, parents left childless in the wake of terrorism that ravaged the cities of Israel. The more Arafat was warned to cease his terror activities, the more determined he seemed to be to escalate them. And, the ranks of such organizations—Fatah, Hezbollah, Hamas, Islamic Jihad, ISIS, and others—have continued to swell long after the death of their role model.

The despot succumbed to "flu-like" symptoms in 2004, after having been transported to Paris, France, for treatments. An autopsy that could have revealed the cause of death was refused by his widow, Suha. In 2005, medical records were opened, disclosing that the PA leader had died from a possible stroke. After a review of the records, some analysts suggested Arafat may have died from AIDS.

CHAPTER

20

"Thus says the Lord GOD: This is Jerusalem.
I have set her in the center of the nations, with countries all around her."

EZEKIEL 5:5 ESV

O n Tuesday afternoon, September 24, 1996, Jewish worshipers
were evacuated from the Western Wall as angry Palestinians
cried out, *"Allahu akhbar!* (Allah is great!)" From their vantage
point outside the Al-Aqsa Mosque, located directly above the Wall,
men young and old shouted their rage. As the disturbance grew, Israeli
police fired rubber bullets to disperse the rioters that were pelting
Jewish worshipers with stones.

This time the incident didn't end with just a few stones being
thrown. Instead, violence escalated stage by stage until the entire
nation teetered on the brink of civil war. By the next day, the Palestinian authority had called an official strike in the West Bank, Gaza,

and East Jerusalem. This time, as Israeli soldiers tried to break up the renewed rioting, they were fired on by the Palestinian police armed with guns the Israelis had been forced to give them under the Oslo Accords.

From Jerusalem, fighting spread to other towns and villages. The worst fighting broke out in Nablus (biblical Shechem), where Israeli soldiers and settlers had been mobbed at Joseph's Tomb, a Jewish holy site. Palestinians ransacked a nearby *yeshiva* (Orthodox university) and burned thousands of holy books. To prevent a massacre, the Israel Defense Forces moved tanks and attack helicopters into position. Six soldiers were killed in the ensuing skirmish, but the majority of Israelis trapped at the site were rescued.

After four days of fighting, more than seventy people had been killed and hundreds wounded. A state of emergency was declared in the nation of Israel. President Bill Clinton summoned Israeli and Palestinian leaders to Washington for a hastily arranged summit conference. Once again, the world's attention was focused on tiny Israel, and particularly Jerusalem, where the violence had erupted. Reporters, photographers, and television anchors trumpeted the story nonstop to an international audience.

Government leaders around the world weighed in with pronouncements on the situation in Jerusalem. Following its long-standing pattern, the United Nations Security Council, not surprisingly, yet again passed a resolution condemning Israel for provoking the violence.

The pretext for the initial rioting was the opening of a new exit to the Hasmonean Tunnel, an archaeological site that runs along the Western Wall and under a portion of the Old City, a few hundred meters away from the Temple Mount area. The tunnel had been open to tourists for about ten years. With only one opening, visitors had to double back and exit the same way they entered. A newly-opened exit allowed one-way flow of traffic in the tunnel, and at the same time afforded many more tourists the opportunity to visit this important historical site in the heart of Old Jerusalem.

What Washington and most of the world failed to understand was that this most recent outbreak of violence in Israel was not simply another example of the smoldering tensions between Israelis and Palestinians. This battle was not about the Arab–Jewish nationalist conflict. This war was about sovereignty over Jerusalem and specifically who owns the title deed to the forty-five-acre plot in Jerusalem that is home to holy sites for both Jews and Muslims.

Today, the Temple Mount is a landscaped park, home to the Islamic shrine known as the Dome of the Rock and the Al-Aqsa Mosque. All traces of Jewish ownership of the site, including Solomon's and Herod's temple, lie buried beneath the bedrock platform . . . and that is the way the Muslims intend to keep it. NO architectural work is allowed to be done on the site. In fact, over the years archaeological discoveries on the Temple Mount have been purposefully destroyed.

To most students of Bible prophecy it appeared that the "age of the Gentiles" came to an end in 1967, when Israel regained control of the entire city of Jerusalem, including the Temple Mount. Indeed, the reestablishing of Jewish sovereignty over the Holy City during the Six-day War is one of the most significant prophetic events in modern history. In actuality, one need only look at the Temple Mount to be reminded that the Gentiles are still firmly in control of one of Israel's holiest sites.

Within days of the war's end, the Temple Mount area had been restored to Arab supervision. Israel's defense minister, Moshe Dayan, met with leaders of the Jordanian *wakf,* the Muslim religious body with oversight of mosques and Muslim holy sites, and essentially turned control of the Temple Mount back to them.

Many of Israel's secular Jews viewed Dayan's action as a political necessity, believing it would bring an end to the Arab nations' historic conflict with Israel. Religious Jews viewed it as a sin against God, who had miraculously brought about a victory for His people in the short war, resulting in the return of many of the biblical land to Jewish control.

Restoring the Temple Mount area to Muslim control did not bring peace with Israel's neighbors as Dayan had naïvely hoped. Instead, in Arab eyes it was seen as weakness on Israel's part, as appeasement inevitably is. So the *jihad* over Jerusalem, and particularly over this forty-five-acre tinderbox at the heart of the Old City, continues today.

When Israel opened the new exit to the Hasmonean Tunnel Yasser Arafat had complained that it was just one more attempt to "Judaize Jerusalem," which was, in his view, the capital of a de facto Palestinian state. It is difficult for those familiar with the Bible to understand how the Arabs can grumble about making Jerusalem more Jewish, since Jewish association with the city and particularly with the Temple Mount area extends back at least four thousand years. When did Muslims first claim an affinity with Jerusalem? Author Daniel Pipes writes in his *Middle East Forum*:

Where does Jerusalem fit in Islam and Muslim history? It is not the place to which they pray, is not once mentioned by name in prayers, and it is connected to no mundane events in Muhammad's life. The city never served as capital of a sovereign Muslim state, and it never became a cultural or scholarly center. Little of political import by Muslims was initiated there.

One comparison makes this point most clearly: Jerusalem appears in the Jewish Bible 669 times and Zion (which usually means Jerusalem, sometimes the Land of Israel) 154 times, or 823 times in all. The Christian Bible mentions Jerusalem 154 times and Zion 7 times. In contrast, the columnist Moshe Kohn notes, Jerusalem and Zion appear as frequently in the Qur'an "as they do in the Hindu Bhagavad-Gita, the Taoist Tao-Te Ching, the Buddhist Dhamapada and the Zoroastrian Zend Avesta"—which is to say, not once....

Why do Palestinian demonstrators take to the streets shouting "We will sacrifice our blood and souls for you, Jerusalem" and their brethren in Jordan yell "We sacrifice our blood and soul for Al-Aqsa"? ... Why did two surveys of American Muslims find Jerusalem their most pressing foreign policy issue?

Because of politics. An historical survey shows that the stature of the city, and the emotions surrounding it, inevitably rises for Muslims when Jerusalem has political significance. Conversely, when the utility of Jerusalem expires so does its status and the passions about it.[101]

Palestinian youth are educated using textbooks that contain no mention of Israel. Maps of the Middle East used in Arab schools label the area of the nation of Israel as Palestine. Against all historical (not to mention biblical) evidence, Arab youth are taught that Jerusalem has always been an Arab city and that the Jews are illegal occupiers in the region. To bolster their claims on the land, Palestinians boast that they are descended from the Canaanites who occupied the land before the ancient nation of Israel and, therefore, have a prior legal right to the land. Again, the claim defies all historical evidence.

That, however, is not the point, as a report from the *Wall Street Journal* indicated just after the riots over the tunnel opening. Reporter Amy Dockser Marcus wrote:

> Archaeologists and biblical scholars say they are often amazed at the historical liberties taken by political leaders, who disregard or sometimes rewrite ancient stories to suit current needs.[102]

Marcus described an August 1996 ceremony held by the Palestinian Authority in the ancient amphitheater in the village of Sabatsia, near Nablus:

> Young people recreated the pagan legend of Ba'al, the Canaanite god, as a narrator read aloud an ancient text designed to resonate with the modern political troubles of its audience: Warnings about Hebrew tribes led by Joshua that were then starting to conquer Canaan.[103]

After pointing out some of the "scholarly holes" in the ceremony, Marcus indicated that the purpose of the celebration was entirely political, not historical—a fact that didn't bother the Palestinians one bit.

When Yasser Arafat accused the Israeli government of "Judaizing Jerusalem," he was simply rewriting history to suit his political purposes. He would have liked for the world to ignore the Jewish history of Jerusalem, and especially the Jewish connection to the Temple Mount.

The Tabernacle of Moses, for instance, is also associated with Mount Moriah. The tabernacle functioned as a portable temple, used for the Israelites' worship as they traveled out of Egypt and into the Promised Land. After Joshua led the conquest of Canaan, the tabernacle came to rest in Shiloh, where it remained for approximately four hundred years.

Shiloh was destroyed around 1050 BC and the Ark of the Covenant was carried off by the Philistines. Sometime later the tabernacle was moved to Jerusalem and was eventually erected on Mount Moriah. David recovered the Ark of the Covenant and had it taken to Jerusalem. He had purchased the "rock of Abraham," being used as a threshing floor by Araunah the Jebusite, as a location for a permanent house of God.

When Solomon built the First Temple on this sacred site on Mount Moriah, the old tabernacle was dismantled. Many Jews believe the tabernacle was put into storage underneath the Foundation Stone—where it may remain hidden to this day.

Solomon's Temple was completely destroyed by the Babylonians in 586 BC and rebuilt on the same spot seventy years later by the returning Jewish exiles. The Second Temple was enlarged and lavishly restored by Herod the Great beginning in 20 BC. It was this Second Temple that was in existence during the lifetime of Jesus

Christ. Here He was named and circumcised, found in dialogue with the religious teachers when He was twelve years old, preached and taught, and overturned the tables of the money changers who had converted God's "house of prayer" into a "den of thieves" (Matthew 21:23). It was probably here in the outer courts of the temple grounds that Peter, on the day of Pentecost, preached his greatest sermon.

Since being leveled by armies of Rome, the Second Temple has never been rebuilt. For two thousand years Jewish people have been without a temple for worship or sacrifices. For centuries, in fact, the Temple Mount lay in ruins. Pagan temples built on the site by the Romans were destroyed by Byzantine Christians. Christian churches were built in Jerusalem beginning in the early fourth century, but not on the sacred rock of Mount Moriah.

Why would David pay for a place God had promised to give His people? Gershon Salomon offers this answer:

> Three places in the land of Israel were bought by the people of Israel even though the land had been promised by G-d, because, when the nations come and say, 'This land does not belong to you,' the answer to them will be: 'This land was given to us by G-d Who is the owner of all the universe, and we also paid for those three places which symbolize this land.' These three places are the

Temple Mount, the Machpelah cave of the Patriarchs in Hebron, and the tomb of Joseph in Shechem.[104]

All three of those edifices have either been turned over to Muslim control already, or soon will be if Jews are forced to again surrender additional lands in the never-ending attempts to coerce their compliance to Arab demands. The Palestinians told the Israelis, "This land does not belong to you," and backed up their words with bullets. It is time for a voice to be raised in Israel: "Not only did God give us this land; we have also paid for it with our blood and the blood of our children."

While Christian worship was never established on the Temple Mount, it is a very important site historically and spiritually. Many believe that Jewish custodianship of the holy site is mandated in Scripture; in order for prophecy to be fulfilled, there must be a third temple built by the Jews on the same spot as the previous two temples.

In the Old Testament, Daniel spoke of the prince who would make a covenant with the Jewish people and guarantee them freedom to make sacrifices and oblations. These can only be done in the temple. The prophet also predicted that after three and one-half years, the temple would be desecrated by the Antichrist, who would invade the inner sanctum and proclaim himself God. So it seems certain that the temple will ultimately be rebuilt.

The New Testament also describes Jewish worship in a future temple. Jesus quoted the prophecies of Daniel regarding the Antichrist and the temple (see Matthew 24:15). The apostle Paul also referred to Daniel's prophecy:

> Don't let anyone deceive you in any way, for that day [the return of Christ] will not come until the rebellion occurs and the man of lawlessness is revealed, the man doomed to destruction. He will oppose and will exalt himself over everything that is called God or is worshiped, so that he sets himself up in God's temple, proclaiming himself to be God. (2 Thessalonians 2:3–4)

Walk the narrow alleyways of the Jewish Quarter in the Old City. Talk to the people in the shops and yeshivas. You'll find ample evidence of the spiritual longing of the Jews for their ancient temple and the worship associated with it.

Gershon Salomon also said:

> There are three biblical conditions for the complete redemption of the people of Israel and for the coming of Mashiach ben David [Messiah]: the regathering of the Israeli nation from all over the world to the Promised Land; the foundation of the Israeli state in the land which G-d promised to Abraham, Isaac, and Jacob in the eternal

covenant . . . and the rebuilding of the temple, the Third Temple.

The first two conditions have already been met in our time through mighty godly miracles. The third condition, the rebuilding of the temple, is soon going to be fulfilled. This is the right time to do it immediately. So many houses were built during the last fifty years in the land of Israel and only one house, the biggest house and most holy house in the world, the House of G-d, is still in ruins.[105]

To devout Jews, rebuilding the temple is seen as a *mitzvah*, or commandment. Of the 613 commandments codified in Mosaic Law, 202 of them are contingent upon the temple for their fulfillment. Therefore, many in the religious community in Israel have been earnestly preparing to fulfill these *mitzvoth* (commandments).

According to Rabbi Chaim Richman of the Temple Institute in Jerusalem, "the Torah enumerates ninety-three categories of *klei sharet*, sacred vessels, to be used in the *Beit HaMikdash* [Holy Temple]. Of this number, the Temple Institute has already constructed more than half." The Temple Institute maintains a museum displaying temple vessels, including such items as the copper washbasin, the golden crown of the High Priest, the silver trumpets, and the priestly garments.

"These vessels are not models, copies, or replicas," Richman says, "but are actually kosher, functional pieces, made from gold, copper, silver, and the other original source materials. The restoration is so accurate that should the temple be rebuilt immediately, the Divine service could be resumed without delay, utilizing these vessels."[106]

The Temple Institute is only one of several organizations in Jerusalem actively researching and preparing items for use in the future temple.

Every person who has seen a Christmas pageant has heard of frankincense and myrrh, two of the gifts brought by the wise men to the Christ Child. What exactly were frankincense and myrrh? They were two of the eleven holy spices that made up the *Ketoret* (incense), or incense offering, burned every morning and evening on the altar of incense in the ancient Jewish temple.

Beged Ivri was established in 1983 for the purpose of reviving the Levitical ministry. Its promotional literature states: "Behind the tumultuous scenes and out of view of the news media, a dedicated group of people are quietly restoring ancient customs, rebuilding the original vessels and instruments and a number of special schools are training those who will use them."[107]

Researchers have authenticated all eleven of the original

ingredients of the Ketoret: balsam, clove, galbanum, frankincense, myrrh, cassia, spikenard, saffron, costus, aromatic bark, and cinnamon. Because Ketoret was used in every ceremony conducted in the temple, identification and production of these aromatic oils is an important step in the preparation for the Third Temple. Perhaps it will not be long before the fragrance of the Ketoret fills the air from Jerusalem all the way to Jericho.

Preparations for other instruments to be used in the temple are far advanced. All that remains is for the temple to be rebuilt. The question persists: How to rebuild without starting World War III? If just opening a new exit to the Hasmonean Tunnel could spark a civil war in Israel, what would happen if the Jews attempted to build a temple anywhere near the Temple Mount, let alone right on top of it?

According to rabbinical law the only place the Jewish temple can be built is on the exact spot where the first two temples sat. There is one major obstacle to building the temple there; the third holiest place of the Muslim faith, the Dome of the Rock, sits squarely in the center.

It is not inconceivable that God could use an earthquake to settle the question; the Bible records earthquakes said to result from God's judgment. It happens that Jerusalem lies very close to the African Rift Zone, the deepest break in the earth's crust. It runs from Africa through the Red Sea, the Dead Sea, and the Jordan River Valley. Some seismologists say that Israel, like California, is overdue for "the big one."

Although traditional mind-set still holds with the majority of archaeologists and rabbis, two other views have gained a growing number of adherents. Both of these theories conclude that the temple site is adjacent to, but not directly over, the Dome of the Rock. The advantage is that, at least theoretically, the Third Temple could be built on the Temple Mount area without destroying the Muslim holy sites.

About twenty years ago, Dr. Asher Kaufman, a professor of physics at the Hebrew University, proposed a northern location on the Temple Mount as the original Temple site:

> Based on a number of topological and archaeological considerations, research by Dr. Asher Kaufman over the past two decades has resulted in serious consideration being given to a site 330 feet to the north of the Dome of the Rock. The Mt. Moriah bedrock outcrops within the Dome of Rock, as is well known. Although the bedrock elevation drops sharply to the south in the direction of the City of David, the level of the bedrock is just beneath the paving stones for over 100 meters to the North of the Dome of the Rock shrine. One particular level outcropping of this bedrock lies under a small Islamic shrine known as "The Dome of the Tablets" or "The Dome of the Spirits," to the Arabs. Both names suggest an association with the Jewish Temples. It is under this small, unimpressive

canopy supported by pillars that Dr. Kaufman locates the Temple site.[108]

Perhaps the Arabic names convey a sense of the original purpose of the spot: "Tablets" could refer to the tablets of stone on which the Ten Commandments were written. These tablets were stored in the Ark of the Covenant, which was housed in the holy of holies. "Spirits" could refer to the presence of God, which was said to dwell in the holy of holies.

One reason for this belief is the location of the Eastern or Golden Gate, which has long been sealed. It originally led directly to the front entrance of the temple, which sat on an east-west line with the Holy Place and the holy of holies at the western end.

The dome site is roughly one hundred yards south of an east-west line that would bisect the Eastern Gate. Archaeologists have discovered remnants of the ancient Eastern Gate directly beneath the location of the present one.

There is some documentary evidence for Kaufman's theory. *The Mishnah,* a collection of Jewish laws and traditions dating from the time of Herod's temple, and other ancient extra-biblical records provide evidence that the ancient temple stood with its northern wall outside and north of the platform on which the dome now stands; likewise its shorter eastern wall probably stood slightly east of the platform wall that exists today.

A southern location on the Temple Mount has been proposed as the original temple site by Israeli architect Tuvia Sagiv. He places the original foundation on a spot that today is occupied by the El-Kas fountain, about halfway between the Dome of the Rock and the Al-Aqsa Mosque. Sagiv has reconstructed the Temple Mount area using topographical maps of Mount Moriah, comparing them to ancient records recording the relative height of the various buildings known to have been on the Temple Mount. He believes the Antonia Fortress was actually on the spot now occupied by the Dome of the Rock. That, according to Sagiv, would put the original temple site south of the Dome of the Rock, since ancient records agree that the fortress was adjacent to and just north of the temple.

Another critical consideration in Sagiv's theory is the location of the temple in relation to the aqueduct bringing water to the temple site. Rabbinical law required flowing water, not water stored in cisterns, be used both for the *mikvah*, the ritual bath for the temple priests, and for cleansing the area where animal sacrifices were offered. That means water would have to flow from a higher source down to the temple area. Surveys of the ancient aqueduct put the location of the water source about sixty yards below the bedrock on the site of the Dome of the Rock. Therefore, says Sagiv, the temple could not have been located on that site or the flowing water would have to defy the laws of gravity to reach the temple site above. In Sagiv's proposed southern location, the Temple would be positioned well below the water source, as required.

Additional methods used by Sagiv to back his theory include ground-penetration radar and thermal infrared imagery. He says the results of this high-tech testing support his conclusion that the original temple site was lower than, and therefore, to the south of, the Dome of the Rock.[109]

Which of these theories about the precise location of the First and Second Temples might be correct is impossible to prove at the moment, because excavation of the Temple Mount is prohibited. A review of these newer studies gives the impression that careful analysis may have uncovered a long-overlooked truth. If that is valid, the rebuilding of the temple may be closer than we think.

CHAPTER
21

It is not an enemy who taunts me—I could bear that.
It is not my foes who so arrogantly insult me—I could have hidden from them.
Instead, it is you—my equal, my companion and close friend.

PSALM 55:12–13 NLT

Prior to 2017, the United States government had been controlled by the Liberal mind-set, and the majority of career bureaucrats in the State Department fell into the pro-Muslim camp. In spite of press reports about a powerful Jewish lobby in this country, Israel has not had many true friends at the highest levels of government. Perhaps this has been most evident in the State Department. When it comes to the Middle East, many politicians still hold to the alligator-feeding school of thought: If we feed *Israel* to the alligator, then the alligator will leave *us* alone.

The alligator, the antagonism of the Islamic world toward the West, raged for a millennium before Israel was ever added to the mix of Middle East powers. Islamic extremists, terrorist-sponsoring dictators, and oil-rich sheiks do not hate the West because of Israel; they hate Israel because of the West. In their eyes, the United States was the "Great Satan" long before it was declared so by the Ayatollah Ruhollah Khomeini, and long before the modern nation of Israel came into existence. The principles of democracy, firmly rooted in the Judeo-Christian tradition, are an enigma to the Islamic world.

What many in our government fail to realize is that there can be no true peace in the Middle East unless the Arab world recognizes Israel's right to exist and embraces democracy. As Bernard Shapiro, director of the Freeman Center for Strategic Studies, points out, democracies rarely go to war with each other:

> All our major wars of the last two hundred years have been between dictators or between democracies defending themselves from dictators." That's why, in Shapiro's view, "it seems a bit odd that our State Department is pushing democracy and human rights from one end of the globe to the other with the remarkable exception of the Middle East. Why are the Arabs insulated from pressure to democratize their societies?[110]

How effective would be any attempts to democratize Arab countries? The Islamic resurgence sweeping most of the Arab world makes a true democracy in the region virtually impossible—as Egyptians,

Libyans, and other Arab peoples have seen. My experience during the Persian Gulf War make this fact clear. I was part of a group of journalists allowed to accompany General Khalid, Saudi Arabia's commander-in-chief of the multinational forces, on an inspection of troops positioned at the Kuwaiti border. When we returned to Dhahran the next day, it appeared that a major development in the war was looming on the horizon. The king called a meeting and virtually everyone of significance was summoned, including four-star general Norman Schwarzkopf, who commanded coalition forces during the Gulf War, along with other top US brass.

Word spread like wildfire that an invasion of ground troops into Iraqi-held territory was imminent. There were indeed a lot of sweaty palms in the room that day as a momentous decision was made. This top-level meeting, however, had nothing to do with an imminent ground war; this meeting had to do with the breakfast menu. A decision was being made on whether American troops would be allowed to have bacon with their eggs. The Saudis had refused to allow supplies of bacon to be off-loaded from American ships. Officials feared that if our troops ate pork on Saudi soil it could cause the overthrow of their government by Islamic fundamentalists.

That may sound silly to most Americans, but the Saudis had a genuine concern. With a groundswell of fundamentalism advocating a government based on strict Islamic law, there was indeed a threat to the stability of the Saudi kingdom. So the momentous breakfast decision was made: Ship-based troops could have bacon with their eggs, but not US troops on the ground there.

Imagine for a moment that this scene had taken place in Israel. Orthodox Jews keep to a strict kosher diet, and like Muslims, do not eat pork. The idea of Jewish extremists keeping US troops from eating bacon for breakfast is absurd. Israel was birthed from the womb of democratic ideals. There is a healthy debate over the boundaries between religious faith and government in Israel. Even among Jewish extremists it would be hard to find a single person who believes that the sanctity of the nation would be defiled by foreigners eating pork on Israeli soil.

Yet a violation of the Islamic prohibition against pork would cause a political problem of enormous consequence in many Arab countries today. Islamic fundamentalists have risen to power in these countries, causing a backlash against Western culture and values. Fundamentalists have plunged the nation of Sudan into civil war. Algeria's president was assassinated by fundamentalists in 1992 shortly after he attempted to prevent an Islamic takeover of his country.

One key element ties these dissimilar movements together in different countries: The desire to return to the glory days of Islam by forcefully liberating former Muslim lands. At the top of every Islamic fanatic's list is the liberation of one particular city: *al Quds*—Jerusalem.

The impetus for this rising tide of fundamentalism is the Iranian Revolution, which ousted the shah in 1979 and swept Ayatollah

Khomeini to power. The mullahs of Iran visualize a vast Islamic republic under their control. The presence of Israel, a pro-Western democracy occupying a tiny speck of sand in the middle of the vast desert lands of the Arab world—just under 11,000 square miles compared to more than six million square miles—is a perpetual threat to the Islamic ideal.

Because the crown jewel of Israel, Jerusalem, is also the third holiest city of Islam, the ayatollahs are not at all interested in peace agreements between Israelis and Palestinians. Since the Madrid Peace Conference in 1991, Tehran has made every effort to undermine a Washington-brokered comprehensive peace in the Middle East. Intelligence sources say that Tehran spends millions—perhaps billions—annually to fund extremist groups dedicated to destroying peace prospects by attacking Israeli and US targets in the region.

The Iranians' determination to destroy peace and export their revolution can be seen in the creation of a special force within the Islamic Revolutionary Guard Corps—the Quds (Jerusalem) Force—charged with planning and executing all revolutionary activities outside of Iran. The Quds Force's Second Corps, with command headquarters in Damascus, is stationed in the Bekaa Valley, adjacent to the security zone in southern Lebanon where Israeli troops are positioned to defend against Hezbollah incursions into the Upper Galilee.

These questions beg to be answered: Why, in spite of intelligence reports showing a likely outbreak of aggression against Israel, did the

Clinton administration continue to put pressure on Israel, our most stable ally in the Middle East, to give up yet more land in the hope of securing a fragile agreement for peace? Shouldn't we also have put more pressure on the Arab nations to give up land, or something, for the sake of peace? Are Western nations responding out of fear or apathy?

There are two important reasons why presidents Carter and Clinton and later, George W. Bush and Barack Obama played the appeasement card. The first reason is that peace-agreement signings play well to the home audience. Much of the American public has lost patience with protracted negotiations and endless rounds of international shuttle diplomacy. Most do not understand the convoluted politics of the Middle East, and do not realize that it will take far more than signatures on a series of agreements, like the Hebron Agreement, the Oslo Accords, and in more recent years the Road Map Plan and the Annapolis Summit to bring true, lasting peace to the Middle East.

It was during the early days of President Clinton's administration that the United States was rocked by a devastating attack planned by Osama bin Laden's organization: the February 26, 1993, truck bombing of the World Trade Center. While this first World Trade Center attack went relatively ignored, in it were seeds of the eventual September 11, 2001, attacks at the same location. Because at that point President Clinton was more occupied with implementing his economic program than keeping America safe, no one else paid much attention to the bombing either. In his regular radio address the day after the bombing, President Clinton mentioned the "tragedy" (he never once used the words *bomb* or *terrorist* in the address) and never mentioned the incident in public again. Neither did he ever visit the site of the blast. The author of *Losing bin Laden*, Richard Miniter, addressed Clinton's inability to deal with bin Laden throughout his presidency:

> In 1993, bin Laden was a small-time funder of militant Muslim terrorists in Sudan, Yemen, and Afghanistan. By the end of 2000, Clinton's last year in office, bin Laden's network was operating in more than fifty-five countries and already responsible for the deaths of thousands (including fifty-five Americans).
>
> Clinton was tested by historic, global conflict, the first phase of America's war on terror. He was president when bin Laden declared war on America. He had many chances to defeat bin Laden; he simply did not take them. If, in the wake of the 1998 embassy bombings, Clinton had rallied the public and the Congress to fight bin Laden and smash terrorism, he might have been the Winston Churchill of his generation. But, instead, he chose the role of Neville Chamberlain (whose appeasements of Hitler in Munich in 1938 are credited with paving the way to

the Nazi invasion of Poland that began World War II the next year).[111]

In September of that same year, Clinton held a celebration on the White House lawn for what he called "a brave gamble for peace," where he forced—actually standing with his thumb pressed into the prime minister's back—Israeli Prime Minister Yitzhak Rabin to shake hands with PLO Chairman Yasser Arafat over a blank sheet of paper that represented the Declaration of Principles, or Oslo Accords. The paper lay on the same table over which President Jimmy Carter had presided, as Menachem Begin and Anwar Sadat signed the peace treaty between Israel and Egypt in 1979. President Clinton later described it as one of "the highest moments" of his presidency as the two "shook hands for the first time in front of a billion people on television, it was an unbelievable day."[112]

One of Clinton's greatest hopes was to go down in history as the man who finally resolved the Arab–Israeli conflict in the Middle East. In order to do this, he used his tremendous aptitude at image transformation to change terrorist and murderer Yasser Arafat into a diplomat. Arafat became the most-welcomed foreign leader to the White House during the Clinton years. It also seems likely that Arafat got some coaching from Clinton and his advisors on what to say, how to speak, and what to do to help in this metamorphosis.

The late Jewish actor and spokesman Theodore Bikel said of Arafat:

> Arafat turned out to be no partner for peace... he had never intended to be such a partner in the first place. Oslo and the handshake gave him the cachet of peacemaker; it also gave him half of a Nobel Peace Prize, which, if he had had any sense of shame, he would have returned. In truth, for him Oslo was nothing more than an opportunity to obfuscate and spin wheels. In all the summit meetings, he appeared to be pacific, conciliatory, and seemingly accommodating, yet he withdrew as soon as real concessions were required. . . . He never meant for the Oslo Agreement to be implemented.[113]

Bill Clinton and his obsession with going down in history as the author of peace in the Middle East caused an unremitting erosion of Israel's negotiating position with the Arab world in the 1990s. When Israel was forced to fight against terror, he did not give it his full backing. As the Jewish state was the center of it all, it was also the main focus of the president's pressure to force agreements. When driven to the bargaining table in Oslo, Israel would negotiate separate peace accords with Jordan, Syria, and the Palestinians, yet only one of these was ever signed, and that was with Jordan on October 26, 1974. For Syria, Israel's deportation of 415 Hamas members in December 1992 precipitated a crisis in continuing the talks, so that Syria demanded the PLO be part of their negotiations. The PLO was given the power of veto. The fate of the Golan Heights was also a major issue, as these mountains provide a natural protective barrier from which to launch attacks, as Syria had done in the Six-Day War. Prime Minister Yitzhak Rabin, representing Israel, saw no mutual basis upon which Jerusalem could negotiate with Damascus.

In the wake of the signing of the Oslo agreements, however, Clinton formulated a comprehensive peace plan for the Middle East with Syria as the main objective. From 1994–1995, he pushed contacts between Israel and Syria into high gear, and as a result, a peace agreement appeared to be taking shape. The proposed peace settlement, which included a complete Israeli withdrawal from the Golan Heights, awakened tremendous opposition within the Israeli populace. Reportedly, Rabin gave President Clinton what became known as the "deposit," a paper stating that if all of Israel's security needs were addressed and its demands regarding normalization and a withdrawal timetable were met, Israel would be willing to carry out a full retreat from the Golan Heights. The paper was only to serve to inform the president as to what Israel would be willing to do in order to ultimately attain a peace agreement. The paper was made public, and apparently Clinton betrayed Rabin, pinning the failure to reach a peace agreement on the prime minister. Seen as a traitor, Yitzhak Rabin was assassinated by an Israeli extremist on November

5, 1995. What Clinton had called his "brave gamble for peace" failed miserably.

Later, with George W. Bush (43) in office, it seemed the Israelis at last had a peace partner that would put their need for survival ahead of the desire to please the policy makers at OPEC. President Bush began his first term of office with what appeared to be a pro-Israel outlook, and hopes were high for that administration. In April 2004, Mr. Bush assured Prime Minister Ariel Sharon that Palestinians would not have the so-called "right-of-return" to Israel proper. The president also reiterated that "currently existing Israeli population centers" (a.k.a. settlements) in the West Bank would not be placed on the table during negotiations.

All seemed well between Israel and the United States. . . until Annapolis. Mr. Bush's apparent last-ditch efforts to gain his own lasting legacy of peace in the Middle East had overshadowed his commitments to Mr. Sharon. In his 2007 speech at Annapolis, President Bush said:

> The Israelis must do their part. They must show the world that they are ready to begin—to bring an end to the occupation that began in 1967 through a negotiated settlement. This settlement will establish Palestine as a Palestinian homeland, just as Israel is a homeland for the Jewish people. Israel must demonstrate its support for the

creation of a prosperous and successful Palestinian state by removing unauthorized outposts, ending settlement expansion, and finding other ways for the Palestinian Authority to exercise its responsibilities without compromising Israel's security.[114]

This rhetoric was not simply another minor land-for-peace grab; it was a demand that Israel give up land that is its most strategic area to ensure survival for the Jewish people. Add to that the fact that President Bush's demand was not to be the final outcome of any negotiations between Israel and the PA; it was only the first step in any peace talks. Such a concession would have left Israel with no bargaining chips whatsoever.

The Palestinian Authority, which has always made only demands, but with no appreciable steps forward in the negotiating process, would again hold the winning hand. Israel would not be able to demand that the PA acknowledge the Jewish state's right to exist. It would not be in any position to demand security concessions. Would Israel wish to demand technical reciprocity from the PA, whose only claim to fame is the ability to wage jihad against those who disagree with it? Israel would be left with nothing. . . no cards on the table, no chips with which to bargain, and no guarantee of peace and safety from an entity whose ultimate vision continues to be to see Israel wiped off the map.

Should the United States persist in trying to force Israel, our only real ally in the Middle East, to the bargaining table in order to appease rabid Arab regimes, may God have mercy. The United States–Israel alliance in the region has been the key to forestalling yet another all-out onslaught against Israel. If the United States blinks, Israel will suffer the consequences, and the United States could well lose what has been its closest friend for the past sixty years.

In a December 19, 2007, speech at Fredericksburg, Virginia, President Bush said of Iran: "We need to take their threats seriously about what they have said about one of our allies, Israel. And therefore my attitude hasn't changed toward Iran."[115]

President Bush apparently understood the threat that Iran poses to the Jewish state; why did it seem to be so difficult for him to comprehend that the terror organizations behind the PA that are trained, armed, and funded by Iran pose the same dire threat?

Perhaps the most frightening aspect of the current situation in the Middle East is the threat of nuclear war. Both Iran and Pakistan now possess nuclear weapons or nuclear weapons capability. Arab nations all have a simple philosophy of nuclear warfare: the Muslim world, with its six million square miles of land and millions of soldiers, can absorb a massive nuclear attack and still survive; Israel cannot.

The same is true today as it was when the House Task Force on Terrorism and Unconventional Warfare was released in 1996. The report stated:

The nuclear factor is essentially irrelevant. . . for as long as Arab leaders can hold their position in a strategic nuclear brinkmanship. While Tehran and Damascus are willing to gamble on such brinkmanship, Jerusalem cannot afford to be wrong. Israel will not survive as a viable country in the aftermath of a strike with the few tactical nuclear warheads Iran has.[116]

Under recent administrations, it has become more and more apparent that Israel can no longer necessarily rely on the United States to come to her aid in the face of a credible nuclear threat by Iran or Pakistan. Given US involvement in Iraq and Afghanistan, and perhaps in Syria, Washington may be very hesitant to commit more troops to the region. This is especially true if there were a serious risk of exposure to nuclear, biological, or chemical weapons.

The extent of Israel's nuclear capability was completely unknown until 1986, when a disgruntled employee of Israel's top-secret chemical reprocessing plant handed inside information and photographs to the London *Sunday Times*. Fired for his outspoken pro-Palestinian views, Mordechai Vanunu provided extensive details about Israel's nuclear arsenal and estimated that Israel had stockpiled more than two hundred nuclear warheads, almost ten times the number estimated by various intelligence agencies at the time.

In 1991 Seymour Hersh, a Pulitzer Prize–winning journalist published a political history of Israel's nuclear program; it was titled *The Samson Option*. According to Hersh, "Israel has developed low-yield weapons for artillery and land-mines, as well as thermo-nuclear weapons."[117] (That particular nuclear weapon features an enhanced radiation warhead producing a marginal discharge while releasing large amounts of deadly radiation.)

Israel's nuclear reactor at Dimona, in the Negev desert, was built in 1958. For years its existence was one of the best-kept secrets in military intelligence. Proponents of nuclear technology in Israel believed the only way to ensure the nation's survival against its Arab enemies, who were backed by the Soviet Union, would be the deterrence of a bomb or, more accurately, bombs. They were certainly correct in that assessment. After the Six-Day War, the Soviet Union routinely targeted major Israeli cities with nuclear weapons. Israel returned the favor by repositioning and aiming some of its mobile missile launchers at Soviet targets.

In 1991, when Saddam Hussein began launching SCUD missiles at Israel, the United States pledged support, including batteries of patriot missiles, in return for an Israeli pledge not to retaliate. What most people didn't know, according to Hersh, is that in those first few hours after the SCUD attacks, American satellite intelligence showed that Israel "had responded. . . by ordering mobile missile launchers armed with nuclear weapons moved into the open and deployed facing Iraq, ready to launch on command."[118]

That Israel may once again face a barrage of missiles from a hostile Arab nation requires no stretch of the imagination. Whether Israel would show such restraint again is uncertain, depending perhaps on the extent of damage inflicted on Israel and the amount and reliability of support offered by the United States. Some analysts foresee an escalating situation in which it might be conceivable that Israel, isolated by enemies and abandoned by allies, would be forced to use a doomsday weapon of massive destruction.

It is fascinating to me that four decades ago Israel coined the sobriquet "Samson Option" to describe its nuclear warfare option. Anyone familiar with the Old Testament will grasp the connection immediately: Samson was the biblical strongman who destroyed himself in the process of destroying Israel's enemies. Note the name and location of Israel's enemies as described in the Old Testament account of Samson (Judges 16).

Samson was in *Gaza* when he prayed to die with the enemies of Israel, the *Philistines.* Israel's so-called Samson Option was in place decades before Yasser Arafat, who claimed his Palestinian people were descendants of the Philistines, was handed the Gaza Strip on a peace-process platter.

Arafat built a concrete command bunker in Gaza. What was he preparing for, if not war? And why did our government not acknowledge what he was doing? After the Hebron Agreement, President Clinton invited Prime Minister Netanyahu to Washington. I was in the White House for the press conference following their private meeting in mid-February 1997. Reporters threw only softballs to the president. No questions were asked about the military buildup of Israel's neighbors; no questions about the illegal weapons being stockpiled by the Palestinian Authority.

There is little doubt even today that the Arab world is preparing for what it perceives to be a final confrontation with Israel. They will be patient, but they will not let a single "window of opportunity" close. Yet such a positive twist is put on the situation by Washington spinmeisters that the public is left with the impression of the pursuit of peace, not imminent war.

An illusion of peace when the reality is war; that calls to mind a verse of scripture: "While people are saying, 'Peace and safety,' destruction will come on them suddenly." (1Thessalonians 5:3) The possibility of sudden destruction is very real in Israel.

A few days after the 1997 Clinton–Netanyahu meeting, Major General Meir Dagan, head of the prime minister's anti-terrorism task force, told the Israeli newspaper *Yediot Ahronot* (Latest News) that Israel was preparing for the prospect of nuclear or chemical terrorism. Dagan also stated his concern that Iran might be funneling unconventional weapons to terrorists. What was merely conjecture then is certainly still accurate today.

During the Clinton administration, arms-control reports indicated that Iran ranked third, behind China and North Korea, in nuclear weapons and ballistic missile development. It was reported that Iran had stockpiled some two thousand tons of mustard gas, and that China had sold four hundred tons of chemicals to Iran, including the components for nerve gas. It has been well-documented that Iran has continued to accelerate the construction of centrifuges used to process uranium since that time.

Still of great concern to Israel is the possibility of long-range ballistic missiles armed with nuclear or chemical warheads. That does not sound like peace and safety. Yet Israel's leaders continue to pursue peace with her neighbors who are bent only on the annihilation of the Jewish state.

CHAPTER

22

Send out your light and your truth; let them guide me.

PSALM 43:3 NLT

srael has, as stated earlier, two enemies: Islam and humanism. Islam is the more obvious because it comes from without, and we have examined its relentless attacks on the city of Jerusalem through the ages. Humanism, on the other hand, is vastly more subtle because it comes in the guise of sounding reasonable and "tolerant." This satanic projectile of deception was first launched at Jerusalem by Alexander the Great in the form of Hellenism.

It is interesting to note that Alexander, like Muhammed, also reportedly had a demonic encounter that changed his life. Alexander made a sojourn into the remote Libyan Desert to visit the temple and oracle of Zeus-Ammon. The oracle, nothing more than a demon spirit, convinced Alexander that he was the son of the Greek god Zeus and would, as such, conquer the world. Hellenism, the acceptance of Greek culture including humanistic beliefs, became so popular in Jerusalem that it almost destroyed God's people from within.

Hellenism was a test both for the Jews that had been scattered abroad and those who remained in Palestine. Author Norman Bentwich wrote, "The interaction of Judaism and Hellenistic culture is. . . one of the fundamental struggles in the march of civilization . . ."[119]

The nature of the enticement that beset the Jews in the midst of Hellenism may be noted from the writings of the ancient historian Posidonius:

> The people of these cities are relieved by the fertility of their soil from the laborious struggle for existence. Life is a continuous series of social festivities. Their gymnasiums they use as baths where they anoint themselves with costly oils and myrrhs. In the *grammateia* (such is the name given to public eating-halls) they practically live, filling themselves there for the better part of the day with rich foods and wine; much that they cannot eat they carry away home. They feast to the prevailing music of strings. The cities are filled from end to end with the noise of harp-playing.[120]

Many who had remained in Judah were concerned about the impact of Hellenism on the Jewish people. A movement against the Hellenists surfaced and expressed concern about materialism, including nudity in the gymnasiums, and the disregard for Jewish observances. The more pious Jews, the Hasidim, were prepared to stand up for their beliefs. Under Antiochus IV Epiphanes scores died for the faith they were willing to defend.

Today, this same evil spirit has a viselike grip on government leaders throughout the Western world. It is expressed in terms such as "negotiated settlements" and "mediation for a just and lasting peace between Jews and Arabs." The real purpose is to strip ownership of Jerusalem from the Jewish people and give it to the Arabs. Were this to happen, Jerusalem would again be trodden underfoot by the Gentiles. Jesus is not returning to a Jerusalem controlled by Muslims or a tripartite commission!

If Satan could, he would prevent the return of the Messiah by wielding his sword of destruction through the biblical prophecies. Satan has launched the twin darts of Islam and humanism toward the very heart and soul of Jerusalem in order to bring the city back under Arab Gentile rule and thwart the return of Jesus the Messiah.

Islam is the demonic religious order that works in concert with humanism, deceiving and pressuring international leaders to reject biblical prophecy as inconsequential and superstitious and, most important, as causing all the problems boiling in the cauldron that is the Middle East. Some opine that if Israel would just admit that all this prophecy nonsense is "extreme religious intolerance" and give up Jerusalem, "share" her land with the rest of the world, and be assimilated into the world's population as before—or form a Jewish state, say, in the United States—then all the world's troubles would disappear. That is the humanist view. It completely denies that the Bible is the Word of God and the prophecies about Israel are absolute truth and that the God of the Bible will bring them to pass.

In the past almost seven decades, Jerusalem has been brought from the background of prophetic events onto center stage of history's most dramatic conflict. Her bloody and brutal chronicle did not end with the rebirth of the nation on May 14, 1948; quite the contrary, the attacks have only become more diabolical. And the import of the assault has moved from the dusty back roads of an ancient land to the world arena.

In one of my numerous conversations with Prime Minister Begin, I asked him to speak to the controversial subject of what the world calls "the occupied territories." He began by sharing his first meeting with President Jimmy Carter:

> We were in the cabinet room and Mr. Carter asked
> me a question. In that question, however, there was a very
> negative statement. He said the settlements were illegal.
> I had prepared a counter question to propose to him.
> Like Winston Churchill, I was ready with a "prepared

improvisation." I had asked our embassy in Washington, D.C., to ready a list of American cities with biblical names, i.e., Bethlehem, Shiloh, Hebron, and Bethel. I showed my long list to President Carter and asked him if he could imagine the governor of Pennsylvania proclaiming that anyone could live in the city of Bethlehem except Jews. President Carter agreed that if a man did such a thing, he would be guilty of racism.

I pointed out that I was the governor of the state in which the original Bethlehem, and the original Jericho, and the original Shiloh were located. Did he expect me to say that everybody could live in those cities except Jews? Of course, he didn't; it would be absurd. . . This land we occupy is Eretz Yisrael, the land of Israel, since the days of the prophet Samuel 3,000 years ago. We had a downfall later, but even the Romans called us Judea until after the Bar-Kokhba revolt in the second century. Then, because the Jewish resistance had been so fierce and heroic, and because the Emperor Hadrian had suffered such severe casualties, he decided to try to delete all memory of the connection between the people and that land. The Romans had done it in Carthage, why not here? So he renamed the area *Syria et Palestina*, using the name of our ancient enemies, the Philistines.

So the word "Palestine" came into all languages. Thus the preamble to the British Mandate after World War I used these words: "recognition having been given to the historical connection between the Jewish people and Palestine." In spite of Hadrian, nobody forgot that it was our land. Every intelligent person understands that Palestine is a misnomer for the land of Israel. We have a right to live in Judea and Samaria. . . but that does not mean we want to evict even one Arab from his village or town. We never wanted to do that.

The prime minister further stated:

A Palestinian state is a mortal danger to Israel and a great peril to the Free World. We never agreed to a Palestinian state at Camp David. What we agreed to was autonomy as a way to solve the problem of Palestinian Arabs. . . The Camp David agreement calls for security for Israel and autonomy for the Arab inhabitants, the right to elect their own ministers of council to deal with daily problems.[121]

As we have gathered from history, Jimmy Carter never did embrace Prime Minister Begin's wisdom. After President Ronald Reagan took office in 1982, Prime Minister Begin was slated to meet with him. Dr. Reuven Hecht, an adviser to Mr. Begin, called and asked if I could join them in New York City. The prime minister and Reuven were concerned about how the meeting with the president would be conducted. Dr. Hecht told me Reagan thought Begin was a hardheaded Jew whose brain had been baked in the hot sands of the Middle East. He had heard from the attorney general that, in fact, the meeting might not even take place.

Finally Reuven told me about the proposed meeting with the president. He said, "The cabinet members will meet with the prime minister's advisers." Then I asked if the president would even meet privately with the prime minister. Reuven replied that a fifteen-minute session was scheduled.

When the two men prayed together in the Oval Office, good relations between our countries were restored. Through the power of intercessory prayer and the courage of Bible-believing people world-wide, Ronald Reagan's heart was changed. God has a prophetic plan for His people in this day, and will employ them to bring leadership in this nation to honor God and obey His Word.

The strong arm of humanism can be broken by the faith-filled prayers and actions of God's people. Imagine! No longer would the president and his cabinet try to force Israel to the negotiating table to be humiliated by those who only seek her destruction. No longer would the one in the Oval Office seek to appease Arab wrath by offering Israel as the sacrificial lamb. That person would come to believe God's plan as outlined in His Word is for Jerusalem to be under Jewish control.

US leaders often speak with two voices—some of our ancestors called it "speaking with a forked tongue." They often pursue differing policies regarding Jerusalem, saying one thing and meaning something else entirely. Again and again proposals have been submitted—proposals which Israel has accepted and which the Arab leaders have rejected.

So, what is the solution? The United States simply needs to recognize that Israeli lands belong to the Jewish people and that Jerusalem is, indeed, the capital of Israel—and has been ever since God declared it to be so. For at least a century, Jerusalem has boasted a Jewish majority, and the nation of Israel has paid dearly in lives for defense of the Holy City.

The Oslo Accords, which were to be the framework to establish peaceful relations between Israel and the PLO, were signed in Washington on September 13, 1993. The ceremony was attended by PLO chairman Arafat, Israeli prime minister Yitzhak Rabin, and President Bill Clinton. In the years since the documents were signed, the PLO and its sister terrorist groups have initiated attack after attack.

As if contending with her borders lined with enemies isn't enough, Israel has also fallen victim to a current *en vogue* doctrine in the church that was spawned in hell. This doctrine supports the humanist view that biblical prophecy concerning Israel is irrelevant to the times in which we live. This particular canon teaches that the church has replaced Israel in the plan and heart of God. It is known alternately as replacement theology, progressive dispensationalism, or supersessionism.

The early church did not teach this dogma. Its roots date back to AD 160 when Constantine began to bring paganism into the church. He banned all things Jewish from the church and replaced them with pagan traditions. For example, the Feast of Passover and Resurrection Day were replaced with Easter. It was taught that the church has supplanted Israel in God's plan for the ages. Constantine's actions began to wash away the Jewish roots of the church and opened the door for replacement theology, which teaches that the Jews had been rejected, that Israel failed God, crucified Jesus Christ, and as a result was replaced by the church. The church, it teaches, is the spiritual Israel, and Jerusalem is any town in which there is a church. These heretical doctrines have done great harm to the Jewish people. If God has turned His back on them, it legitimizes the actions of Adolf Hitler and then the fanatical Muslim jihadists, who continue to seek to destroy the Jews.

From the earliest centuries the Roman and then the European church failed to realize and honor the tenet that our eternal salvation comes through the aegis of the Jews. The fingers of the physical descendants of Jacob wrote all but a small portion of the world's best-selling book: the Bible. Almost all the prophets in the Bible were

Jewish, as were all of the apostles, the parents of Jesus, and most importantly, the Messiah. How could the church have overlooked such critical factors in supporting the Jewish people?

The insidious doctrine of replacement theology propagates the age-old practice of blaming the Jews for the world's ills, weighing them in the balance and finding them wanting. Acceptance of this doctrine frees the church from any obligation to share the good news of the gospel of Jesus Christ with those whom He came to seek and to save.

When speaking to the Samaritan woman about eternal life, Jesus pointed out that His heavenly Father's free gift of eternal salvation had been brought to the world via the Jews: "You worship what you do not know; we know what we worship, for salvation is of the Jews." (John 4:22 NKJV)

If the most precious gift that Christians will ever possess came by means of the Jewish prophets, leaders, teachers, and in particular Jesus the Messiah, how can our attitude be other than one of deep gratitude toward Jacob's offspring? We who were born Gentiles and became Christians should be extremely thankful that God, in His shining wisdom and gracious mercy, has allowed us as "wild olive branches" to be grafted into the rich tree of Israel, as revealed in Romans 11:17.

In his New Testament letter to the Romans, the apostle Paul went on to point out that the "grafted in" Gentile believers do not tower over the Jewish people, as many have maintained over the centuries and still do today. Rather, regenerated Jews (including Abraham, our father in the faith) were the original covenant people that remain the bedrock "root" that supports every Christian's spiritual life:

> But if some of the branches were broken off, and you, although a wild olive shoot, were grafted in among the others and now share in the nourishing root of the olive tree, do not be arrogant toward the branches. If you are, remember it is not you who support the root, but the root that supports you. (Romans 11:17–18 ESV)

> For I am not ashamed of the gospel of Christ, for it is the power of God to salvation for everyone who believes, for the Jew first and also for the Greek. (Romans 1:16 NKJV)

Many have said, "The reason I don't support Israel is because Jews crucified Christ. They are under judgment because they rejected God's Word." John 10:17–18 tells us that Christ willingly gave His life. No one took it from Him.

> Therefore my Father loves Me, because I lay down My life that I may take it again. No one takes it from Me, but I lay it down of Myself. I have the power to lay it down, and I have the power to take it again. (NKJV)

God Almighty will judge the person or group that embraces a doctrine of judgment, one that is given the Word and then rejects it through disobedience. Nations that reject God will be judged. Luke 12:48 says, "For everyone to whom much is given, from him much will be required." (NKJV)

There are more churches in America than in any other nation in the world. There are more Christian bookstores, Christian radio and television stations, and Bible schools. The world views America, then, as a Christian nation. America has been given much, and judgment will be meted out accordingly. The truth is, God is much more merciful than mankind. Lamentations 3:22 states, "Through the Lord's mercies we are not consumed, Because his compassions fail not." (NKJV)

Nowhere in His Word does God make eternal promises to the United States, yet He continues to show mercy to this nation. Even wicked Sodom was to be the beneficiary of God's mercy. Why? Because Abraham appealed to God to spare that city if only ten righteous men could be found there. Regrettably, ten righteous men did not answer the call to stand in the gap.

Will you stand with Israel today? Will you stand on the truth of God's Word and defy humanism and any false doctrine in the church that supports it? There could not be a more important or appropriate time in Jerusalem's history for Christians to join in prayer and intercession for David's city. I encourage you to pray for Jerusalem. Pray for her children. Pray for her grandchildren. Pray for her neighbors, and pray that anger and hatred will be bound. This is not a matter in which we can afford to be indifferent or apathetic. Why? It matters to God.

Scores of Bible-believing Christians have steadfastly held to the notion that God really meant what He said when He promised the land of Israel, in perpetuity, to the descendants of Abraham, Isaac, and Jacob. Before 1948 many dispensational prophecy teachers were ridiculed for such statements. Since there had not been a nation of Israel for almost two thousand years, how could it play a role in the last days?

Many critics were silenced May 14, 1948, when the modern State of Israel was born. It happened just as the prophet Isaiah had described:

> Who has ever heard of such things? Who has ever
> seen things like this? Can a country be born in a day or
> a nation be brought forth in a moment? Yet no sooner
> is Zion in labor than she gives birth to her children.
> (Isaiah 66:8)

The sovereign Lord of the universe ordained the nation of Israel. He is the One who established her borders. The Bible says that God does not lie or change His mind as Man does. His Word is unchanging and nonnegotiable; His promises are true. He has promised to bless those who bless Israel, and curse those who curse her. The kings and powerbrokers of the world would be well advised to stop trying to manipulate the rooks and pawns on God's Middle East chessboard, or they will wind up in permanent checkmate—on the eternally losing side.

The same is true of the City of God. Those who pursue the Middle East peace process can hold all the "final status" negotiations they wish, but Jerusalem is not a spoil of war to be divided. Almighty God decreed the preeminence of Jerusalem thousands of years ago: it is not on the bargaining table, and He *will* have the final say on the matter. Jerusalem, the city of stones, is God's immovable rock for all time.

The prophet Zechariah described a future (or perhaps present-day) siege of Jerusalem by the nations surrounding Israel. God declared:

> I am going to make Jerusalem a cup that sends all the surrounding peoples reeling. Judah will be besieged as well as Jerusalem. On that day, when all the nations of the earth are gathered against her, I will make Jerusalem an immovable rock for all the nations. All who try to move it will injure themselves. (Zechariah 12:2–3)

God vows to use the leaders of Judah as torches to ignite the other nations like a burning woodpile:

> On that day I will make the clans of Judah like a firepot in a woodpile, like a flaming torch among sheaves. They will consume all the surrounding peoples right and

left, but Jerusalem will remain intact in her place. . . .
On that day I will set out to destroy all the nations that
attack Jerusalem. (Zechariah 12:6, 9)

That will be a divine payday. Nations will be judged by whether
they helped Jerusalem or tried to destroy her, and will be rewarded or
punished accordingly. At that point the nations of the world will finally
quit trying to either occupy or divide Jerusalem. God's "immovable
rock" will only cause pain to the heathen. There are those who believe
that time has already arrived. Look at the abundance of floods, fires,
earthquakes, famine, and anarchism we see occurring worldwide.

CHAPTER
23

And when he had said these things,
he went on ahead, going up to Jerusalem.

LUKE 19:28 ESV

It is impossible to consider Jerusalem—past, present, and future—without a chapter on the One who bridged the gap in history—Jesus Christ, the literal Son of God. As Mary's child, He was also a natural descendant of King David. Jesus, therefore, is called both the Son of God and the Son of Man in the Bible. It is also no accident that He was born in David's hometown, Bethlehem of Judah, as prophesied in Micah 5:2:

> But you, Bethlehem Ephrathah, though you are little among the thousands of Judah, yet out of you shall come forth to Me the One to be Ruler in Israel, whose goings forth are from of old, from everlasting. (NKJV)

As His earthly ministry drew to a close, it was Peter who in Matthew 16:16 made a confession of faith, "You are the Christ, the Son of the living God," when Jesus set His face toward Jerusalem to observe the Passover. First, however, He would perform one of His most noted miracles in Bethany, just outside Jerusalem. This was the miraculous resurrection of Jesus' friend Lazarus, who had been in the grave four days. After this great marvel, the Messiah entered Jerusalem on a lowly donkey, the exuberant welcome of the crowds ringing in His ears. He did not go to win the city; He went to be rejected, die a cruel death, and rise from the dead after three days.

It was imperative that Jesus go to Jerusalem to accomplish the task the Father had given Him—that of becoming the sacrificial Lamb who would take away the sins of the world—the Passover Lamb. Had He stayed in the Galilee, He would have simply been one of many itinerant preachers—remarkable and unusual—but still only a preacher. God had a much bigger plan for Him.

At the dawn of creation, God confronted His creation's rebellion. The first eleven chapters of Genesis relate the story of mankind's unrelenting mutiny—the fall of man, Cain murdering Abel, mankind's descent into depravity, and the flood. Following the Tower of Babel episode, God turned his attention to Abraham. From that one man, He fashioned the nation of Israel as His chosen people. This people would bear witness to the truth about God in the midst of all who had turned their backs on Him, the one true Creator.

Even as Israel's story was marked by cycles of intense worship that regressed to backsliding, apostasy, and idolatry, a fresh shoot sprang forth—Jesus was born. With His life, He purchased the forgiveness of sins and opened the door to the kingdom of God for the Gentiles—the other nations—as well as to the nation of Israel.

In His ultimate humiliation, Jesus revealed the heart of God to a degree never known before:

> For God so loved the world that He gave His only begotten Son, that whoever believes in Him should not perish but have everlasting life. (John 3:16 NKJV)

He also sowed the seeds of the destruction of the kingdom of darkness; Satan's hold on the planet was broken. In Matthew 16:18 Jesus avowed that the very gates of hell would not stand against His kingdom. Since then, His followers have had the glorious task of bombarding the gates of hell to free those held captive.

In Jerusalem, Jesus carried out the unlikely series of tasks by which He unlocked the mystery hidden from all previous generations. The writer of Philippians captured God's purpose and plan perfectly in chapter 2, verses 6–11:

> . . .who, being in the form of God, did not consider it robbery to be equal with God, but made Himself of no reputation, taking the form of a bondservant, and coming

in the likeness of men. And being found in appearance as a man, He humbled Himself and became obedient to the point of death, even the death of the cross. Therefore God also has highly exalted Him and given Him the name which is above every name, that at the name of Jesus every knee should bow, of those in heaven, and of those on earth, and of those under the earth, and that every tongue should confess that Jesus Christ is Lord, to the glory of God the Father. (NKJV)

Jerusalem became the focal point of God's determination to reclaim mankind—despite our continuing efforts to squander our lives in sin and degradation. It is God's city, and though the *salem* in its name refers to peace, there always has been and continues to be strife, contention, and conflict. Why? The answer is simple—Satan is determined to wrest God's creation from His hand.

There are only two instances in the New Testament of Jesus weeping publicly—just before He raised Lazarus from the dead (see John 11:35), and when He rode into Jerusalem on a donkey (see Luke 19:41). As Jesus entered the city, He warned the people of Israel that the time would soon come when their enemies would encircle them, hem them in on every side, and leave not one stone standing atop another. He said this would happen because they had rejected Him as their Messiah: "Truly I tell you, not one stone here will be left on another; every one will be thrown down." (Matthew 24:2)

When the disciples asked when these things would come to pass, Jesus used the opportunity to teach them about future events. He talked of tribulation, of armies surrounding Jerusalem, and of Gentile domination "until the times of the Gentiles are fulfilled" (see Luke 21:24). Forty days after Jesus' resurrection, He ascended back to the Father from the Mount of Olives in Jerusalem. Upon Jesus' command, the disciples tarried in Jerusalem until the day of Pentecost, when the Holy Spirit was poured out upon them in the upper room, and the church was gloriously born in Jerusalem.

When you and I pray for Jerusalem, we are saying *"Maranatha! Come, Messiah!"*

The Messiah is indeed coming back, and He is coming to Jerusalem! That is something on which both Jews and Christians agree. As Christians, we believe we know His identity; He is Jesus of Nazareth. The Jewish people say they do not know who He is. We have been assured, however, that when Messiah comes, everyone will recognize Him.

In 1995, from the top of Megiddo, I looked out over the plain that was prophesied to be the site of the Battle of Armageddon. The Valley of Jezreel spreads from the Mediterranean to the Jordan River. Napoleon is said to have stood on the same hill and, awed by its grandeur, exclaimed, "All the armies of the world could maneuver their forces on this vast plain."[122]

Looking down on what the Old Testament prophet Joel called the "Valley of Jehoshaphat" (see Joel 3:2), I found myself wondering how long it would be before this scenic, tranquil spot would be filled with men and machines of death and war. It seems inevitable. When Israel was reborn on May 14, 1948, she was immediately embroiled in controversy over ownership of the land. The Middle East conflict has become a sore that never heals—a pit of white-hot coals that can burst into roaring flames at any second. It is a black hole of strife and enmity, which could suck in all the nations of the world.

Since my first climb up that prophetic hill, little has changed. As it was then, so it is now. It appears that Israel can do anything or nothing and still be castigated for every problem that springs forth on planet Earth. In early 2010, a housing project was initiated in the Ramat Shlomo neighborhood in northwest Jerusalem. It is a sign of the basic irrationality of the conflict that every point on the Jerusalem compass is referred to erroneously by detractors as "East Jerusalem." This loaded term is cynically used to designate anywhere Arabs live in the city, despite the reality that more Jews than Arabs live in Jerusalem's eastern neighborhoods.

Many of our politicians have failed to remember or take seriously Israel's repeated overtures to the Palestinians. Perhaps each should have reviewed the history of the rejection by Palestinian leaders of Israel's proffered olive branches. Noises from former president Barack Obama's administration sounded suspiciously like the same old rhetoric I heard in 1995 from a Radio Amman broadcast: Israel being boycotted by the Islamic world; Israel should be barred from the United Nations General Assembly meetings; the United States condemned for supporting Israeli aggression in the "occupied territories." A later item in the report quoted a Kuwaiti man as saying, "The main obstacles to a just and comprehensive Middle East peace is Israel's intransigence and refusal to withdraw from the occupied Arab territories, as well as its denial of the Palestinian people's legitimate rights."[123]

A few weeks later a prominent Israeli government official said to me, "In the 1930s the strength and the might of Nazi Germany was its steel and coal. Now we have the Arabs with their oil. Their thrust is anti-Semitic now, just as it was then; and the attitude of the Western democracies is one of appeasement now, as it was then."

How will this end? Many Israelis take comfort in the words of the ancient Hebrew prophets. We have already seen that virtually all the significant historical events in the saga of the Jewish people were foretold before they actually came to pass. If these prophecies proved to be accurate, can we not expect other as yet unrealized prophetic passages to reveal the future of Israel and the world?

The Old Testament is accepted by the Jews as the Word of God. In addition to the Psalms, which deal with prophecy, there are sixteen other prophetic books in the Bible. Christians accept both the Old and New Testament writings, which are rife with prophetic utterances. For hundreds of years, Jewish and Christian Bible scholars have studied these prophecies. Many agree there is one inescapable conclusion: The Middle East crisis will continue to escalate until it threatens world peace and eventually brings the nations to Armageddon.

The warnings of Bible scholars who research prophetic events have been echoed by secular academics. Before his death in 2008, Soviet exile Aleksandr Solzhenitsyn sounded an alert:

There are meaningful warnings that history gives a threatened or perishing society. Such are, for instance, the decadence of art, or a lack of great statesmen. There are open and evident warnings, too. The center of your democracy and of your culture is left without electric power for a few hours only, and all of a sudden crowds. . . start looting and creating havoc. The smooth surface film must be very thin, then; the social system quite unstable and unhealthy.

But the fight for our planet, physical and spiritual, a fight of cosmic proportions, is not a vague matter of the future; it has already started. The forces of Evil have begun their decisive offensive; you can feel their pressure.[124]

To better understand what is happening today, and when the Messiah might return, it is imperative to examine the writings of the prophets. We can begin with Daniel and his first recorded prophecies, which were the result of King Nebuchadnezzar's dream. The late Dr. Harry A. Ironside called Daniel's prophecy "the most complete, and yet the most simple, prophetic picture that we have in all the Word of God."[125]

Nebuchadnezzar's dream was of an image of a man. His head was gold, his breast and arms were silver, his midsection and thighs were brass, his legs were iron, and his feet were part iron and part clay. As the king watched, a great stone crashed down upon the image, smashing it so completely that the wind blew away the pieces. The stone then became a great mountain that filled the whole Earth (Daniel 2:31–35).

When called upon to interpret the king's dream, Daniel's explanation was simple yet profound: The head of gold represented Nebuchadnezzar, whose power in the Babylonian Empire was absolute. Later scholars summarized the dream as follows: The silver portion of the statue represented the Medo-Persian Empire, which came after the fall of Babylon. The belly and thighs of brass represented the Greek Empire of Alexander the Great. The legs of iron were emblematic of the Roman Empire, while the ten toes of iron and clay represented the revival of the Roman Empire in the last days, or ten leaders of a European federation.

The stone is symbolic of an all-powerful divine force, which will ultimately destroy all earthly kingdoms and be recognized as supreme. Many agree this refers to the coming kingdom of the Messiah, which will be established upon His return to Earth. Jesus quotes Psalm 118:22 when He refers to Himself as the "stone which the builders rejected" (first coming) and says He will become the "chief cornerstone" (second coming) (see Mark 9:10).

In Daniel 7:1–7, the prophet recorded another dream, which is thought to reinforce Nebuchadnezzar's earlier dream. Daniel saw a lion with eagle's wings, a bear with three ribs in its mouth, a leopard with four wings and four heads, and a strange, ten-horned beast that was "dreadful and terrible, and strong exceedingly." The lion represented the Babylonian Empire; the bear was the Medo-Persian Empire. The leopard was the empire of Alexander the Great, and the beast with ten horns was figurative of a future Roman Empire or European federation.

Near the end of his life, Daniel began praying about returning to Jerusalem. He confessed his own sins and the sins of his people, crying out to God for forgiveness. During his prayer, the angel Gabriel appeared and revealed a timetable of coming events that would affect Israel. This angelic vision is often referred to as "the vision of seventy weeks." It may very well be the backbone of all prophecy. This mathematical revelation gave the Jews the exact time to expect the coming of their Messiah. It also foretold His death, the destruction of

Jerusalem, the rise of the Antichrist, and the ultimate establishment of the Messiah's kingdom on earth.

The prophecy declared that seventy weeks of trouble would come upon the Jewish people. The weeks were not actually units of days but rather years—490 years that would cover a series of events determining the eternal destiny of the Jewish people. Daniel prophesied that from the time the order was given to rebuild Jerusalem, 483 years would elapse before the coming of the Messiah and His rejection (see Daniel 9:24–27).

It is interesting to note that the Bible gives the exact date when Artaxerxes, king of Persia, would grant the decree that Jerusalem and its temple should be rebuilt: "And it came to pass in the month of Nisan, in the twentieth year of King Artaxerxes." (See Nehemiah 2:1) The king had ascended the throne in 465 BC, and his twentieth year would have been 445 BC. When translating the date given on our calendar, the king's decree to rebuild Jerusalem would have been issued on March 14, 445 BC.

Precisely 483 years after that decree, the Messiah rode into Jerusalem, as had been prophesied in Zechariah 9:9 (NKJV):

> Rejoice greatly, O daughter of Zion! Shout, O daughter
> of Jerusalem! Behold, your King is coming to you; He is
> just and having salvation, lowly and riding on a donkey,
> a colt, the foal of a donkey.

Daniel's extraordinary prophecy further decreed that the Messiah would be "cut off," a euphemism for being killed. After that, an army would march into Jerusalem and destroy it and the rebuilt temple.

We are left to wonder what happened to the last week, the last seven years covered by Daniel's vision. Those events are yet to take place. It seems to the natural man that God has pushed the Pause button. In God's timing, the end of the age will be highlighted by the return of the Messiah, the bodily resurrection of the dead, and the millennium—when Messiah reigns on the earth for one thousand years. Scripture tells us, however, that the last seven years before the Messiah returns to earth will be the most horrific time since the world began. Matthew 24:21 (NKJV) describes it this way: "For then there will be great tribulation, such as has not been since the beginning of the world until this time, no, nor ever shall be."

Daniel recorded in chapter 12, verse 1 (NKJV): "And there shall be a time of trouble, such as never was since there was a nation, even to that time."

As this fearsome week begins, the ten-horned beast Daniel described will arrive on the scene in the form of the revived Roman Empire. Out of the European federation a powerful political leader will emerge whose magnetic charm and personal appeal will win the confidence and loyalty of the world. The Bible identifies this individual as the Antichrist. This individual will offer solutions to the perplexing problems and international crises that threaten the very existence of the world. Immensely powerful, the Antichrist will sign a seven-year peace treaty with Israel (see Daniel 9:27).

In the beginning, everything will go well. The peace treaty imposed by the powerful Antichrist will relieve centuries of armed tension. Israel will be able to turn full attention to development of the country and its resources as never before. Some arrangement will even be made for rebuilding the temple in Jerusalem. There, sacrifices and oblations will be resumed.

After three and one-half years, just when everything seems to be going well for the Jewish people, perhaps for the first time ever, the Antichrist will break the treaty with Israel. He will halt the sacrifices and oblations in the temple and declare himself to be God. This is the "abomination of desolation" spoken of in Daniel 12:11.

Ezekiel picks up the prophetic narrative at this point. His credibility has already been established by his foretelling of the scattering and returning of Israel some twenty centuries before the fact. His vision of the valley of dry bones (see Ezekiel 37:1–10) is one of the most vivid and moving in the Bible.

The Lord showed Ezekiel that the bones represented Israel. Their dry and disconnected condition represented the dispersed Jews around the globe and their despair at ever becoming a nation united again. Ezekiel proclaimed the message God had given him, and his words infused a glimmer of hope into the hearts of the Jewish people across the centuries. In the midst of incredible persecution and suffering, the promise of God offered a lifeline: "For I will take you from among the nations, gather you out of all countries, and bring you into your own land." (Ezekiel 36:24 NKJV)

The words of the prophet were like a brilliant light slicing through the gloom and darkness of the ghettos and death camps that have housed Jews over the centuries.

With the survival of the Jewish people and the rebirth of Israel as a nation, Ezekiel's prophetic track record is totally convincing. He speaks in specific detail about events that will bring the world to the precipice of Armageddon. In chapters 38 and 39, he gives a detailed account of a great military offensive, which will be launched against Israel by Russia (called Magog in Scripture) and a confederation of Arab and European countries. Ezekiel identifies the other participants as Meshech and Tubal (Moscow and Tobolsk), Gomer (Germany and Slovakia), Togarmah (southern Russia and Turkey), Persia (modern-day Iran and possibly Iraq), and Ethiopia and Libya (the black descendants of Cush and the North Africa Arabs).

Led by Russia, this force will arm itself and march against Israel. The assault will be totally unexpected because of Israel's treaty with the Antichrist, and the three and one-half years of peace. Russia's resolve to attack is clearly written in the pages of Holy Writ:

"You will say, 'I will go up against a land of unwalled villages; I will go to a peaceful people, who dwell safely, all of them dwelling without walls, and having neither bars nor gates'—to take plunder and to take booty, to stretch out your hand against the waste places that are again inhabited, and against a people gathered from the nations, who have acquired livestock and goods, who dwell in the midst of the land." (Ezekiel 38:11–12 NKJV)

The concerted attack on Israel will ultimately be one of Russia's most egregious military blunders. The battle will be brief and hideously destructive. Ezekiel's description of the "cloud to cover the land," a great shaking, earth-rending explosions, mountains toppling, and a deadly rain of hail and fire could signify nuclear warfare, but will more likely be the result of divine intervention. The Bible declares that God alone will destroy Israel's enemies in a supernatural way (see Ezekiel 38:22). The defeat of its invaders will make Israel acutely aware that God has protected them.

Only one-sixth of the Russian army will survive. So many will have died that it will take Israel seven months to bury the bodies and seven years to burn the weapons left on the battlefield. The devastation wrought by this battle will empower the Antichrist to make his move to establish his seat of government in Jerusalem under the pretext of protecting the Holy City.

With only forty-two months remaining in the prophetic week, the Antichrist will, according to Daniel 11:44 assert his power, break his treaty with Israel, and face his first challenge—a massive Asian army marching toward the Middle East. When that clash occurs, casualties will total one-third of the remaining world's population, according to this passage in Revelation 9:16–18 (NKJV):

> Now the number of the army of the horsemen was two hundred million; I heard the number of them. And thus I saw the horses in the vision: those who sat on them had breastplates of fiery red, hyacinth blue, and sulfur yellow; and the heads of the horses were like the heads of lions; and out of their mouths came fire, smoke, and brimstone. By these three plagues a third of mankind was killed—by the fire and the smoke and the brimstone which came out of their mouths.

Following this conflagration, the Antichrist will assume total economic control, forcing the population to take his mark on the hand or forehead in order to transact business. The penalty for opposing him will be death. The Antichrist will then implement his foolhardy plan to defeat the Messiah.

So here it is: the last great conflict. The battle lines will be drawn with the vortex in the Valley of Megiddo. Indescribable slaughter will be the result. It will be so terrible that Revelation 14:20 tells us blood will rise to the bridle of a horse for a distance of two hundred miles north and south of Jerusalem. As the battle reaches its climax, the Messiah will return. Jesus prophesied in Matthew 24:22, 30 (NKJV):

> And unless those days were shortened, no flesh would be saved; but for the elect's sake those days will be shortened. Then the sign of the Son of Man will appear in heaven, and then all the tribes of the earth will mourn, and they will see the Son of Man coming on the clouds of heaven with power and great glory.

CHAPTER
24

This vision is for a future time. It describes the end, and it will be fulfilled.
If it seems slow in coming, wait patiently, for it will surely take place.
It will not be delayed.

HABAKKUK 2:3 NLT

In light of all the blood that has been shed over this ancient soil, it is important to understand that biblical prophecy has been or will surely soon be fulfilled regarding Jerusalem. This city is the centerpiece of Bible prophecy, and it is to this place that the Messiah will return. Jesus will not return to a Muslim city. Not because He is prejudiced against them, but because He promised to do so two thousand years ago. Through the centuries this prophecy has stood as a permanent benchmark by which we can gauge the often-confusing events of Jewish history.

On July 30, 1980, the Israeli Knesset passed the "Basic Law," which states (in part):

Jerusalem, Capital of Israel:

1. Jerusalem, complete and united, is the capital of Israel.

2. Jerusalem is the seat of the President of the State, the Knesset, the Government and the Supreme Court.[126]

Sadly, in world opinion, Jerusalem remains only the *unofficial* capital of Israel, prevented from taking her rightful place alongside other international capitals. What right could any other nation possibly have to step in and designate an Israeli capital of its choice?! The city's recapture by the Jews is one of the single most prophetic events in history. The time of the Gentiles is now past and there has been a changing of the guard. Men may argue and pontificate, but something irrevocable has happened: Jerusalem is no longer trodden down by non-Jews. History has turned a corner.

No one can deny that Jerusalem occupies a central and critical role in history. The city of David has always had a special God-ordained destiny and a unique purpose. The prophet Daniel called Jerusalem God's "holy mountain." As the site of the temple in Israel, and as the city to which Messiah will return to usher in his earthly kingdom, Jerusalem is known by believers throughout the earth as the Holy City or City of God.

New Testament writers spoke of Jerusalem. John provides more information than other authors of the Gospel, detailing the visits of Jesus during His brief but dramatic ministry. It is Luke, the Gentile, who pays greatest attention to the prophetic nature of the city. All of Jesus' appearances following His resurrection as recorded by Luke took place in Jerusalem, and the disciples are told by Jesus to wait there until Pentecost. At that time, He said, the Holy Spirit would come upon them. This event would introduce a new spiritual age during which the truth of God's relationship with mankind would no longer be experienced through ritual and sacrifice but through the Word of God indwelling the hearts of Believers. After the experience of Pentecost, Jerusalem suddenly became the heart of the church and the center of evangelism that would extend to the ends of the earth.

Jerusalem also figures prominently in John's vision of the end times. As recorded in the Bible's final book, the earthly Jerusalem emerges for the last time following the thousand-year reign of Christ. It is there that forces of the Antichrist will be marshaled and the ultimate battle will take place. It is there Satan will be finally defeated and the forces of evil destroyed by fire from heaven.

John then describes the luminous vision of New Jerusalem descending from heaven. This beautiful new city of gold and silver and precious stones will be the home of the faithful; those who have sought the kingdom of God and His righteousness. Saints who have fought the good fight, who have resisted unto death, and who have loved the Lord their God with all their heart, mind, soul, and strength will be welcomed inside. Clearly, in this sense, Jerusalem is the ultimate home and the goal of Believers. It will be, after all, our eternal home.

Today, nations wage a war of words against the City of God. Washington demands that the peace process continue, and a chorus of world power brokers sounds the "amen." From every side we hear, "Peace, peace!" But as an American Jew bitingly observed, "If this is *peace*, then what is *war?*" God's Word shows there will come a time when national leaders will seek to calm the people with claims of peace. But peace will not come: "They dress the wound of my people as though it were not serious. 'Peace, peace,' they say when there is no peace." (Jeremiah 6:14)

Ezekiel prophesied:

> "'Because they lead my people astray, saying, "Peace," when there is no peace, and because, when a flimsy wall is built, they cover it with whitewash, therefore tell those who cover it with whitewash that it is going to fall. Rain will come in torrents, and I will send hailstones hurtling down, and violent winds will burst forth. When the wall collapses, will people not ask you, "Where is the whitewash you covered it with?"
>
> "'Therefore this is what the Sovereign LORD says: In my wrath I will unleash a violent wind, and in my anger

hailstones and torrents of rain will fall with destructive fury. I will tear down the wall you have covered with whitewash and will level it to the ground . . . So I will pour out my wrath against the wall and against those who covered it with whitewash. I will say to you, "The wall is gone and so are those who whitewashed it, those prophets of Israel who prophesied to Jerusalem and saw visions of peace for her when there was no peace, declares the Sovereign LORD.'" (Ezekiel 13:10–16)

Jesus gave an indication of how we would be able to identify the time.

The disciples came to Him privately, saying, "Tell us, when will these things happen, and what will be the sign of Your coming, and of the end of the age?" (Matthew 24:3 NASB)

Those born as the fig tree blossomed on May 15, 1948, are those who have seen its branches become tender and shoot forth leaves. While some have called the generation that fought in World War II "the Greatest Generation"[127] the world has yet known, it is not difficult to see that the generation living since the rebirth of Israel has seen the greatest acceleration of change and quality of life in human history.

Because of the incredible advances in technology and the proliferation of communication since 1948, this generation has faced unprecedented mile markers. This has been the first generation for which

✧ world citizenship is conceivable;

✧ the entire planet could be destroyed in war (now several times over!);

✧ the world population has doubled and then tripled (from around 2.4 billion to 7 billion people);

✧ the average life expectancy of human beings has increased by more than twenty percent;

✧ families have gone from one rotary-dial phone tethered to the wall to nearly every member having his/her own cell phone, from which they can call almost anywhere in the world from almost anywhere else in the world;

✧ people can travel from one continent to another in hours instead of weeks.

When a vision of the end times was given to Daniel in the last three chapters of his book, he was told to seal it up for the generation in which "many will go back and forth, and knowledge will increase" (see Daniel 12:4 NASB). No generation in the history of the world has traveled so much or seen knowledge increase so quickly as has ours.

From the birth of Jesus Christ to the invention of the steam engine, people largely traveled in the same way—it was virtually the same for Charles Dickens as it had been for William Shakespeare or Julius Caesar. Today, we can be anywhere in the world in hours and have even stepped from Earth to the moon within days, and are preparing for even longer celestial voyages.

What humanity has knowledge of, is inventing, or is discovering is increasing at an exponential rate. Computers have gone from machines that fill entire rooms to "smart phones" you can hold in your hand, or even smaller devices that can be worn on the wrist. Topics that took months of research, traveling between libraries and paging through tomes of books, can now be exhausted in a few hours of surfing the Internet. Literally anything you want to know in the world is accessible through a few keystrokes or clicks of a mouse.

It is interesting to note that in the 1890s, William Blackstone quoted Daniel 12:4 and spoke of how scripture was being fulfilled in his time. If he could see the fulfillment of the signs of Daniel 12 and Matthew 24 in his generation, how much more applicable are they to our time? Moreover, in Blackstone's time returning to the land of their fathers was little more than a pipe dream for the Jews. Even as sure as he was that Israel would be reborn, little could Blackstone have fathomed that it would come into existence half a century later.

Today the fig tree has come to life, and the signs Jesus spoke of are occurring all around us. As another decade has dawned in the twenty-first century, it is worth reviewing these signs to see just how much more prominent they now are than they have ever been before.

In watching for His return, Jesus told us to learn a lesson from the fig tree: "As soon as its twigs get tender and its leaves come out, you know that summer is near. Even so, when you see all these things, you know that it is near, right at the door." (Matthew 24:32–33)

> Then He added a startling comment: "Truly I tell you, this generation will certainly not pass away until all these things have happened." (Matthew 24:34)

How are we supposed to understand that? We first have to decide what He meant by the phrase "this generation." There has been a lot of disagreement on how to interpret this phrase. Did that mean the generation of people of which Jesus himself was a part? Surely not! The context of the verse helps us interpret it as it talks about a fig tree. "This generation" of which it speaks is the generation of people who will see the fig tree putting forth leaves from tender twigs.

What is the significance of the fig tree? We must resort to symbolism at this point to help unlock the mystery, but the symbolism Christ intended here is not difficult or obscure. The fig tree stands for restored Israel. If you've ever been to Israel, you've noticed that the leaves of the fig tree are a common ornament on government buildings. I challenge you to order breakfast anywhere in Israel without its being served with some figs. In the Bible, references to the fig tree are generally symbolic of the nation of Israel. Jesus uses the fig tree to talk about the end of the Age because He meant that Israel itself would be the key sign to His return.

The generation of people who see the blossoming of the fig tree (Israel's rebirth and establishment in the family of nations) is the generation that will see the completion of "all these things" (the signs of the end recorded in Matthew 24). The generation of people that saw this "blossoming" of modern Israel was born between 1925 and 1935. Their expected life-span is seventy years according to the Bible and actuarial tables. Some of them will live much longer, but I believe the Lord will have returned before their entire generation has passed away.

The Bible tells us no one will know the day or the hour of Christ's return, but we are exhorted to recognize the season. The rebirth of Israel, then, is a sign that His return will occur within the lifetimes of some of those now living.

Nothing stands in the way of its happening tonight or tomorrow. If ever a generation of people had a reason to believe they were living in the days immediately prior to the Lord's return, it is our generation. So, where are we now in the countdown to the beginning of the last chapter in the history of mankind? What events must yet take place to trigger the ticking of God's prophetic clock?

Bible scholars say there is nothing to delay the return of Messiah for those who serve Him. It could take place at any moment, and no one can say for sure when it will be. Jesus said, "But about that day or hour no one knows, not even the angels in heaven, nor the Son, but only the Father." (Matthew 24:36)

He also warned: "You also must be ready, because the Son of Man will come at an hour when you do not expect him." (Luke 12:40)

CHAPTER
25

*Yet to his son I will give one tribe, that David
my servant may always have a lamp before me in Jerusalem,
the city where I have chosen to put my name.*

1 KINGS 11:36 ESV

In the past three thousand years, Jerusalem has experienced more sorrow than any city in the world. In the midst of ongoing pogroms and holocausts, Jews have never ceased to cry out, "Next year in Jerusalem!" They utter the words at the Seder on the eve of Passover. In the *Amidah*, the silent part of the prayer, they pray, "May our eyes behold thy return to Zion in mercy." Traditional Jews face the east to fast and pray for the return of the Jews to the Holy City. In saying grace after meals, traditional Jews plead that "the Almighty might rebuild Jerusalem speedily in our days." Everything in the life of a Jew, the very scarlet thread of Judaism and the Jewish people, has run through the heart of Jerusalem, the holiest of cities for both Christians and Jews.

Jerusalem has been desecrated, broken, and abused, but one day she will be completely renewed. In the New Testament, John the Revelator declares in his mighty vision of the end times, "Then I, John, saw the holy city, New Jerusalem, coming down out of heaven from God, prepared as a bride adorned for her husband." (Revelation 21:2 NKJV) For all of the stress and strain of the last sixty-plus years, a new day is coming, when Jerusalem will experience true and everlasting peace!

As the center of Israel's worship, Jerusalem was preceded by Shiloh, where Joshua placed the tabernacle and the Ark of the Covenant, around the thirteenth century BC. Some three thousand years later King David made Jerusalem his capital. After David's son Solomon built the magnificent temple there, every aspect of Jewish life became focused on Jerusalem. It was the center of commerce and religion. Jews came to Jerusalem for the feasts of Passover, Pentecost, and Tabernacles. They thronged to Jerusalem to bring their sacrifices, to study the Torah, and to rejoice.

Even Jesus of Nazareth went to Jerusalem each year, foresaw the sorrows and tragedies that would come upon the Holy City, and He wept. Indeed, for Him it was a city of tears.

Down through the centuries even greater indignities have been heaped upon the ancient capital and, all too often in contemporary times, America has led the international pack with ruthless and odious demands. How terrible that so much of the world's injustice has been focused there, on that city and on those, her people.

Contrary to what you may hear, when the Old City was under Jordanian sovereignty between 1948 and 1967, Muslims the world over did not bother to make pilgrimages to the Al-Aqsa Mosque in Jerusalem. Today, the power-brokers say the site of the Muslim mosque is of great importance to Arabs, yet after the Six-Day War in 1967, the traffic was one-way. Israeli Arabs flocked to Egypt by the thousands, while not even a trickle of Egyptians trekked to Jerusalem. The fifteen million Egyptian Muslims felt no urge to make the pilgrimage to Jerusalem to pray at the Al-Aqsa Mosque. They did not long to see the Dome of the Rock, as some have claimed, in spite of the fact that the bus fare was a mere forty dollars and the Israeli army assured their safety.

The prophetic history of Jerusalem has been ignored or conveniently forgotten by those determined to rape her yet again. The ancient city is treated with supreme disrespect. For example, American embassies are never located in any city except the accredited capital of the host nation. Jerusalem is the heart and soul of Israel and its true capital, but America has only consular offices there, a second-level presence. For politically correct reasons, the US Embassy has been located at Tel Aviv. Despite the Jerusalem Embassy Relocation

Act (US Senate Bill S. 1332, Public Law 104–45 of the 104th Congress) legislation to force the White House to move the embassy, the answer is still a resounding no. Perhaps President Donald Trump will be the leader who stands his ground, makes good on his campaign promise, and moves the embassy to Jerusalem.

America's foreign-affairs specialists have an overriding desire to placate the Arab world, assuring that the status of Jerusalem remains open to negotiation. I was in Dhahran when America spent billions of dollars to defend Saudi Arabia, a dictatorship, and American blood was being shed to restore another dictatorship in Kuwait. The United States gave the country back to the Kuwaitis and paid billions to the Arab world for its show of force. Our secretary of state paid homage to one of the most notorious aggressor-nations on earth—Syria—and its late president, Hafez al-Assad.

Who could have imagined that the money we were paying them would be used to buy missiles from North Korea for one purpose only: to mobilize for war against Israel. Syria continues to threaten the safety and security of Israel at this writing.

For thousands of years, more blood has been shed over the stones of Jerusalem than any spot on earth. Attempts throughout history to desecrate this holy place are not coincidental; they are not mere chance events. I am convinced they are demonic acts, birthed from the bowels of hell itself. They are events that will one day be consummated by the wrath of God Almighty against those who dare to lift their hand against Jerusalem and God's chosen people, the Jews. The Bible assures us that the worst battle in all of history, the Battle of Armageddon, will be waged for control of this city; but He who holds title deed to the land will have the final word.

If claims are true that Muslim countries have treated Jews in their midst fairly and in democratic fashion, then why have the Jews in those Arab nations been forced to flee for safety to Israel? Why have Jews been driven to return to their homeland throughout the centuries? Quite simply, it is because of the unspeakable persecution they have endured. Under Islamic law, Jews and Christians are granted slight protection because of a policy called *Dhimmi*. Discriminatory practices against Christians and Jews are listed in the covenant *Shurut*, attributed to the Caliph Omar AD 634–644. Consider the implications of just these historic restrictions:

> This is a writing to Umar from the Christians of such and such a city. When You [Muslims] marched against us [Christians],: we asked of you protection for ourselves, our posterity, our possessions, and our co-religionists; and we made this stipulation with you, that we will not erect in our city or the suburbs any new monastery, church, cell or hermitage; that we will not repair any of such buildings that may fall into ruins, or renew those that may be situated in the Muslim quarters of the town; that

we will not refuse the Muslims entry into our churches either by night or by day; that we will open the gates wide to passengers and travellers; that we will receive any Muslim traveller into our houses and give him food and lodging for three nights; that we will not harbor any spy in our churches or houses, or conceal any enemy of the Muslims....That we will honor the Muslims and rise up in our assemblies when they wish to take their seats; that we will not imitate them in our dress, either in the cap, turban, sandals, or parting of the hair; that we will not make use of their expressions of speech, nor adopt their surnames....That we will not display the cross upon our churches or display our crosses or our sacred books in the streets of the Muslims, or in their market-places; that we will strike the clappers in our churches lightly...[128]

So much for tolerance! Are these just archaic Islamic policies from centuries past? Hardly. A Christian who has that illusion should try making his residence in any one of the twenty Arab dictatorships in the Middle East. What happens to a Christian who practices his faith with enthusiasm in one of these Muslim countries? His life will be short on this earth, for he will be imprisoned and most likely beheaded. Islam is not just a religion; it is a way of life. It impacts every aspect of society in a Muslim nation, and it is making inroads and having an impact in other nations worldwide, certainly including the United States.

In December 2016, ISIS claimed responsibility for a bomb that detonated inside a Coptic Church in Cairo, Egypt. The subsequent blast killed twenty-seven men, women, and children during a Sunday worship service. The bigotry that is endemic in Egypt—and other Muslim countries—leaves Christians isolated and their lives subject to the whims of various Islamic regimes. *New York Times* journalist Mona Eltahawy wrote:

> Egyptian churches have been bombed before, but this was the first time a bomb had been taken inside a church to directly target worshipers; and it was the first time that Islamic State affiliates in Egypt targeted civilians after months of attacking the police and, in the Sinai province, the military.
>
> Coptic Christians are the largest Christian community in the Middle East, numbering about 10 percent of Egypt's 90 million people. The cruel reality for Egyptian Christians is that only the Egyptian military has killed more Christians in recent times than did the Dec. 11 bombing.[129]

This is only one instance of Christians in predominately Muslim countries having been targeted for their beliefs. Many have witnessed the desecration of the Holy City, including some who profess no love for God or His commandments. Karl Marx, father of Communism, admitted in an article in the *New York Daily Tribune* published on April 15, 1854:

> . . .the sedentary population of Jerusalem numbers about 15,500 souls, of whom 4000 are Mussulmans [Muslims] and 8000 Jews. The Mussulmans, forming about a fourth part of the whole, and consisting of Turks, Arabs and Moors, are, of course, the masters in every respect, as they are in no way affected by the weakness of their government at Constantinople. Nothing equals the misery and the sufferings of the Jews at Jerusalem, inhabiting the most filthy quarter of the town, called *hareth-el-yahoud*, in the quarter of dirt between the Zion and the Moriah, where their synagogues are situated—the constant objects of Mussulman oppression and intolerance . . .[130]

The oppression and intolerance has never stopped. Neglect and abuse of Jewish holy places have continued for decades. Between 1948 and 1967, conditions were considered deplorable, even by medieval standards. Jewish residents were expelled from the Jordanian-controlled area, and Jordan transformed part of its territory into an armed camp ruled by guns, snipers, and landmines.

Under Jordanian oversight, Jews were not permitted to live in

Jordan. The country's Civil Law # 6 was very specific: "Any man will be a Jordanian subject if he is not Jewish."[131] Jews were barred from worshiping at the Western Wall. The Jewish Quarter in the Old City was destroyed, and fifty-eight synagogues demolished. Zion's Karaite Synagogue was destroyed; the Kurdish and Warsaw Synagogues were leveled. These are just a few of the places of worship turned into cowsheds, stables, or public lavatories. Others were razed.

Still, the world cries to the Jews in Israel, "Let the peace process continue! Give up your land for peace!" Until 1967 the Jews did not have the land, and they certainly did not have peace. They won back the land God had given them by wresting it from those whose aim was to decimate them, and today the land provides a buffer by which Israel can defend herself. How, then, can we or anyone ask the Jews to relinquish what they have suffered for so long and paid so great a price to win back from their enemies?

In Exodus 23:25 the Lord God declared, "And I will take sickness away from the midst of you." Many believe the time will come when the misery will depart, but there seems to be a sinister force that works to destroy the ancient city and its people. Some call it a death angel, and others say it is a demon; but they feel some sinister force hovering over the city of Jerusalem, a demonic entity that holds the wounded soul of Israel in distress. It is a brutal form of terrorism that never ends, with moments of joy followed by days of deep heartache and despair.

When will it end? What strange mysteries are yet to be uncovered on this soil? How can anyone explain the injustices that take place on a daily basis? Columnist Richard Cohen defined the consummate problem: "How the Arab world will ever come to terms with Israel when Israelis are portrayed as the devil incarnate is hard to figure out."[132] It will never end until Arab schoolchildren are no longer subjected to anti-Semitic tirades disguised as education.

Kindergarteners are taught to hate Jews. King Ibn Saud of Saudi Arabia was quoted as saying, "For a Muslim to kill a Jew, or for him to be killed by a Jew, ensures him an immediate entry into Heaven and into the august presence of God Almighty."[133] According to Syrian minister of education (1968) Suleyman Al-Khash, "The hatred which we indoctrinate into the minds of our children from their birth is sacred."[134]

In 1977 the Hashemite Kingdom of Jordan provided a guide for instructors of children in the first grade. It was used to educate West Bank teachers. It reads in part: "Implant in the soul of the pupil the rule of Islam that if the enemies occupy even one inch of the Islamic lands, jihad (holy war) becomes imperative for every Muslim."[135]

I will never forget the words Israeli prime minister Yitzhak Rabin spoke at the White House peace ceremony in 1993: "We have come to you from Jerusalem, ancient and eternal capital of the Jewish people."

Chairman Arafat never mentioned Jerusalem during his visit at the White House, but in his speech that same evening, his voice was beamed via satellite to the Arab world, "By God's will, we shall raise our flag over the walls of Jerusalem, capital of the Palestinian State, over all minarets and churches in the city." We should not be ignorant of what Arafat had planned for the churches and synagogues in Jerusalem. Thousands of jubilant Arabs draped Palestinian flags over the city walls upon hearing the chairman's words. That plan has not changed. His successor, Mahmoud Abbas, hoisted the banner of Israel's demise high and carries it still. We must never forget that as chief financial officer of Arafat's organization, this leader who today demands unilateral statehood was one of those responsible for the Munich massacre during the 1972 Summer Olympics. At that time, Abbas was known as Abu Mazen.

Prime Minister Yitzhak Rabin shared with me his hopes for the restoration of his people, an end to hostilities, and the beginning of peace in the land. He dreamed of his grandchildren never having to go through what he and his generation experienced. He was a great general and a fine prime minister, and was keenly aware of the enormous economic pressure on his nation—and perhaps a little too willing to compromise because of it. He loved Jerusalem with all his heart, and he was willing to give his life for her if it came to that. In the end, he did.

This pinpoints another significant reason why Christians should rejoice in Israel's physical restoration and strongly support her continued existence in the Middle East: Jerusalem is the prophesied capital of our Messiah Jesus when He returns. Holy Scripture reveals that Zion is to be the seat of the Messiah's earthly reign. The nations on earth will come to worship Him in Jerusalem. From there He will rule as King of kings and Lord of lords! This is revealed in several scriptures:

> Many people shall come and say, "Come, and let us go up to the mountain of the LORD, to the house of the God of Jacob; He will teach us His ways, and we shall walk in His paths." For out of Zion shall go forth the law, and the word of the LORD from Jerusalem. (Isaiah 2:3 NKJV)

> Look upon Zion, the city of our appointed feasts; your eyes will see Jerusalem, a quiet home, a tabernacle that will not be taken down; not one of its stakes will ever be removed, nor will any of its cords be broken. (Isaiah 33:20 NKJV)

> "Thus says the LORD: 'I will return to Zion, and dwell in the midst of Jerusalem. Jerusalem shall be called the City of Truth, the Mountain of the LORD of hosts, the Holy Mountain.'" (Zechariah 8:3 NKJV)

> "I will not give sleep to my eyes or slumber to my eyelids, until I find a place for the LORD, a dwelling place for the Mighty One of Jacob." For Your servant David's

sake, do not turn away the face of Your Anointed. For the LORD has chosen Zion; He has desired it for His dwelling place: "This is My resting place forever; here I will dwell, for I have desired it." (Psalm 132:4–5, 10, 13–14 NKJV)

"Moreover I will appoint a place for My people Israel, and will plant them, that they may dwell in a place of their own, and **move no more**; nor shall the sons of wickedness oppress them anymore, as previously." (2 Samuel 7:10 NKJV, emphasis mine)

So, it is clearly evident from Scripture that the Sovereign Lord of Creation chose Jerusalem as His earthly capital. This decision was made by the very same God who promised to restore His covenant, and the Jewish people to the sacred city and surrounding land in the last days before the second coming of the Messiah. How can Christians look for and welcome Jesus' prophesied return and not rejoice in and actively support the Jewish return to their homeland?

God described the details and boundaries of the land in Genesis 15:18: "On the same day the LORD made a covenant with Abram, saying, 'To your descendants I have given this land, from the river of Egypt to the great river, the River Euphrates.'" (NKJV) This was a royal land grant, perpetual and unconditional:

> Also I give to you and your descendants after you the land in which you are a stranger, all the land of Canaan, as an everlasting possession; and I will be their God. (Genesis 17:8 NKJV

> I am the LORD God of Abraham your father and the God of Isaac; the land on which you lie I will give to you and your descendants. (Genesis 28:13 NKJV)

God has never revoked Abraham's title deed to the land, nor has He given it to anyone else.

The spot where God confirmed His covenant is an area north of Jerusalem between Bethel and Ai. It is in the heart of what is called the West Bank, or Judea and Samaria. (The United Nations refers to this as "occupied territory" and demands that Israel relinquish it.) An inalienable right is one that cannot be given away. The Bible declares this to be so in Leviticus 25:23. The people were forbidden to sell the land: "The land shall not be sold permanently, for the land is Mine; for you are strangers and sojourners with Me." (NKJV)

Jerusalem, often called the City of God and the Holy City, is the only city God claims as His own. He declared to Solomon in 2 Chronicles 33:7, "In this house and in Jerusalem, which I have chosen out of all the tribes of Israel, I will put My name forever." (NKJV)

I have mentioned that the United States has refused to recognize Jerusalem as Israel's capital; this is a grave mistake. By declaring East

Jerusalem as "occupied territory," the United States is effectively call-ing for the division of the city. I have shouted former Prime Minister Begin's words to world leaders from the White House in Washington to the Royal Palace in Madrid with the words, "God does not recognize America's non-recognition of Jerusalem!"

The late Dr. Jerry Falwell observed:

> God deals with nations in accord with how those nations deal with Israel. . . Down through the centuries, those nations, those potentates, those emperors, who dared to malign the apple of God's eye, the Jewish people, paid severely. . . I think I can take pride in saying that outside the Jewish community itself, the best friends the Jews and the State of Israel have in the world are among Bible-believing Christians here in America. We believe that God honors His Word. God blesses His people, and God honors those who honor His Word.[136]

For sixty-five years Israel has been America's one true friend and strategic ally in the Middle East, yet today Dr. Falwell's words continue to fall on deaf ears. The actions of President Obama and his administration further clouded the relationship between the two nations. Israel's Prime Minister Benjamin Netanyahu was stiff-armed during his trip to the White House like "some third-world, tin-pot dictator" and even denied the customary state dinner.

President Barack Obama and his administration, including sec-retaries of state Hillary Clinton and John Kerry, openly resorted to public censure of Israel. The condemnation surfaced in regard to poli-cies surrounding the easing of sanctions against Iran—Israel's avowed enemy. It continued with Prime Minister Netanyahu's handling of attacks against his country from Gaza and plans to erect additional housing in Jerusalem.

One of the more surreptitious attacks was in regard to the Euro-pean Union's demand that Israeli products manufactured in the West Bank be labeled as having been made in "occupied territories." Lest you thought the days of forcing Jews to wear a badge of division ended with Hitler's death, think again! The Obama administration's reasoning behind that move was explained by John Kirby, a State Department spokesperson:

> Well, as you know, our longstanding position on settlements is clear. We view Israeli settlement activity as illegitimate and counterproductive to the cause of peace. We remain deeply concerned about Israel's current policy on settlements, including construction, planning, and retroactive legalizations. The U.S. Government has never defended or supported Israeli settlements, because administrations from both parties have long recognized that settlement activity beyond the 1967 lines and efforts

to change the facts on the ground undermine prospects for a two-state solution. We are no different.[137]

Such comments are blatantly hostile toward Israel and reek of open anti-Semitism, especially when paired with John Kerry's hints that the United States could not prevent boycotts aimed at curtailing Israeli businesses if concessions were not made to the Palestinians. *Washington Post* blogger Jennifer Rubin wrote:

> Only the worst apologists for the administration can ignore the pattern of consistent antagonism toward our ally. The Obama-Clinton-Kerry foreign policy has been a nightmare for the U.S.-Israel relationship, but moreover, has signaled to friends and foes alike that the United States is a disloyal, unhelpful ally. After all, if this is how the United States treats its closest Middle East ally, Israel, what country can expect anything better?[138]

It was no secret that the relationship between Barack Obama and Benjamin Netanyahu began on a frosty note and advanced to frozen before Obama's term in office ended. White House special envoy Martin Indyk posed this reasoning for the cause of what he indicated as Obama's original faux pas:

> He [Obama] reached out to the Arab and Muslim world and then he didn't go to Israel. That was the

original miscalculation. He lost them there and he never got them back. It sent a message that he didn't like them that much, that he wanted to put some distance between the United States and Israel.[139]

During the Obama administration, the president's arrogant and cavalier treatment of Prime Minister Netanyahu endangered the long-standing alliance between Israel and the United States—one that dates back to the presidency of Harry S Truman. A year or so after the Jewish state came into being its chief rabbi paid an official call on Truman. The Israeli dignitary blessed the president with the words: "God put you in your mother's womb so you would be the instrument to bring about Israel's rebirth after two thousand years."[140] Truman's eyes filled with tears.

Since Truman, all US presidents through George W. Bush have considered the support of Israel a moral imperative, with the exception of Clinton and Obama, believing that a secure and strong Israel is in America's self-interest. It appeared that America then had a forty-fourth president who was not going to celebrate the birthday of the nation and even further disputed that birth certificate, even as some questioned his.

When Donald Trump took office in January 2017, the tide seemed to again swing in Israel's favor. Prime Minister Netanyahu's relationship with Barack Obama was strained due partly to the Iran nuclear deal brokered in 2015 and the president's support of a two-state resolution that seemed to favor the Palestinians. During his presidency, Obama traveled to Israel only twice—once in 2013 and again in 2016 for the funeral of former Israel leader Shimon Peres.

Although Trump had not made a state visit to Israel at this writing, Netanyahu and he have met at the White House. Trump appointed David Friedman, an Orthodox Jew, as ambassador to Israel. According to the *American Conservative:*

> "Friedman not only thinks the [West Bank] settlements are legal but has called the two-state solution an 'illusion' and has promised. . . Trump will do nothing to pressure Israel into negotiations. [Friedman] is an active supporter of and donor to the conservative Beit El settlement in the West Bank.[141]

Trump never kept his aversion to the Iran deal quiet. Only time will tell whether or not he took steps to negate the agreement and impose new sanctions. The question is only: Is it too late now that the genie is out of the bottle? Have the battle lines been drawn that will launch the cataclysmic event ushering in the return of the Messiah to Jerusalem? Scripture gives evidence that a "man of sin" will step forth with a plan for world peace. In light of some of the strange things happening today, it is imperative that the church be alert to developments that could signal further fulfillment of prophecy. In

Luke 12:40, Jesus warned, "Therefore you also be ready, for the Son of Man is coming at an hour you do not expect." (NKJV)

I believe Israel is the key to America's survival, and the future is certain. Although no person knows God's timetable or when the prophetic clock will chime the midnight hour, we can be sure of one thing: Jerusalem is God's city, and one day soon Jesus *will* reign from there.

CHAPTER
26

Behold, how good and how pleasant it is for brethren to dwell together in unity!
It is like the precious oil upon the head, running down on the beard,
the beard of Aaron, running down on the edge of his garments.
It is like the dew of Hermon, descending upon the mountains of Zion;
for there the Lord commanded the blessing—life forevermore.

PSALM 133 NKJV

Following Israel's rebirth, organizations in support of the return of the Jewish people to the Holy Land began to spring up—many comprised of Bible-believing Christians. By the late twentieth century, Evangelicals had been infused with ever-growing numbers of those God-fearing people who bless Israel in daily prayer and intercession as well as with monetary support. Many are members of groups whose focus is on biblical promises made by God to Abraham and his descendants. Among them is the Jerusalem Prayer Team.

The members of these organizations have great respect for the Jewish people and for Judaism. They believe this is the very foundation upon which Christianity is based—after all, Jesus was a Jew who kept the entire Mosaic law.

A Jerusalem Prayer Team–sponsored petition to President Bush in 2003 read in part:

> We support Israel's right to their land spiritually and legally. History records that God deals with nations in accord with how these nations deal with Israel. We rejoice that here in America, for 228 years, we have been committed to the Jewish people. The Jewish people have found refuge here; they have found a people who love them; and we can take pride in saying that Israel is not an exclusively Jewish issue.
>
> Bible-believing Evangelicals consider the support of Israel a biblical mandate. Regardless of contrary opinion, we do not believe Israel has to offer an excuse for its existence. Israel lives today as a right! A right that has been hallowed by the Bible, by history, by sacrifice, by prayer, and by the yearning for peace![142]

Multitudes believe God's promise to Abraham: Those who bless His descendants will be blessed of God.

In 1982, I sponsored the first National Prayer Breakfast in honor of Israel. A "Proclamation of Blessing" was introduced in support of the Jewish nation, and read in part:

As Bible-believing Americans, we believe there exists an iron-clad bond between the State of Israel and the United States. We believe that bond to be a moral imperative.

Representing the vast majority of evangelicals in the United States, we have gathered together at this National Prayer Breakfast to reaffirm our support and prayers, that this bond not be weakened or diminished.

But it was in East Texas that I had perhaps the encounter that dramatically changed my life. I was in Texarkana, a town on the Texas–Arkansas border, when I met an elderly lady carrying her suitcase into a Holiday Inn. As I hurried to open the door for her, I asked if I might carry her bag. She smiled her thanks, and as she did, her eyes lit up. Suddenly I realized I was standing in the presence of one of my heroines: Corrie ten Boom. We enjoyed a bowl of soup together and shared our love for the Jewish people. It was Corrie's vision that her home and the clock shop in Haarlem, Holland, be restored.

Later, after her death, I thought of Corrie's dream, and by faith flew to the Netherlands to visit the clock shop and follow God's leading. As I walked around the shop, I asked about seeing the upstairs, where a total of eight hundred Jews had been hidden and saved during the Holocaust. The owner advised me that the door was kept locked, as the area was only used for storage. My heart broke. I felt that the ten

Boom clock shop should be open as a testimony to the world of the love of a Christian family for the Jewish people. I prayed, "Lord, I want to buy this house and restore it. Help me."

The next day I returned and asked the owner if he would sell the shop to me. Just as he refused my offer, the clocks in the shop began to toll the noon hour. He turned to me and asked if I knew what day it was. I mentioned the day of the week. "No," he said. "That is not what I meant—today is April 15, Corrie's birthday. And, yes, I will sell the shop to you."

When the sale was complete, I vowed that no one would ever pay a cent to visit the ten Boom home; that the story of God's love would be available to all. Since its restoration was completed, the shop has been open, free of charge, to thousands of visitors. Many leave with tears of remembrance and grateful hearts for the family that gave their lives to help Jewish people escape Hitler's plan from hell. Some who have come were relatives of the people whose lives were saved by the courageous ten Boom family. All the work there is done on a volunteer basis. No one, including the board of directors, of which I am chairman, has ever received any compensation for our work, and we have paid all our own expenses.

In 2002, I founded the Jerusalem Prayer Team (JPT) and Churches United with Israel (CUI). Then mayor of Jerusalem, Ehud Olmert, flew to Dallas, Texas, to join me in launching JPT, an outreach of the Corrie ten Boom Fellowship. In 1844, a ten Boom family patriarch had begun a weekly meeting to pray for the Jewish people, after a moving worship service in the Dutch Reformed Church of Reverend Witteveen. The first and second Great Awakenings that had swept Protestant Europe and North America played an important role in the yearning to pray for the Jewish people. Casper ten Boom felt the need to continue the weekly meetings, where his family and others who stopped by specifically prayed for the peace of Jerusalem (Psalm 122:6). These meetings took place for one hundred years, until February 28, 1944, when Nazi soldiers raided the house and arrested members of the family for aiding local Jews. Following the tradition of the ten Boom family, the Jerusalem Prayer Team was founded to encourage people to continue to pray for the peace of Jerusalem and to help the Jewish people—God's chosen ones.

Through the years JPT has grown from that large rally in Dallas to several million people worldwide who receive weekly email updates. Churches United with Israel was formed to encourage churches to stand alongside the Jerusalem Prayer Team and encourage their members to actively pray for the Jewish people. It was the first organization of its kind and has some 300 top church leaders on its board of governors.

Evangelicals are not engaged in terrorist attacks against their enemies; they are not intent upon doing God's work on earth *for* Him. They are, instead, advocates for the State of Israel; they are defenders of God's Word and His children. Many evangelical groups support programs to provide food, clothing, housing, and more for Jews who have returned to Israel, especially those from Russia. They employ whatever political clout has been amassed in order to stand in strong support of Israel. With over sixty million Christians in the world, their presence will remain a force with which to be reckoned.

Those who support the Jewish people have expended billions of dollars in assistance to orphanages, and by providing medical supplies and sponsoring social-assistance programs for the poor and needy in Israel. Information is dispensed through conferences in support of Israel, through promoting better understanding between Christians and Jews, by denouncing anti-Semitism, and through prayer. Various groups have sponsored marches through Jerusalem in support of the nation and the right of the Jewish people to live in Israel. Still others have aided Jews from Russia and other countries to immigrate to Israel. The Jerusalem Prayer Team has been at the forefront of these efforts to provide assistance to the Jewish people.

JPT has raised funds and invested millions of humanitarian dollars in Israel by providing food for the hungry, warm hats and coats for thousands of elderly Jews, basic necessities for Russian Jewish refugees, backpacks for schoolchildren, medical equipment for terror victims, and the reconstruction of a bomb shelter/community center in Jerusalem to be used as a safe place during terrorist strikes. It contains a kitchen, televisions, telephones, and much more. The Jerusalem Prayer Team is also helping to fund bomb shelters near schools for children to seek safety during attacks. It continues to invest in the lives and safety of the Jewish people in Israel, and prayers for Israel can be posted on an interactive prayer wall website open not just to JPT members but to people worldwide.

The stated purpose of the Jerusalem Prayer Team: to guard, defend, and protect the Jewish people and *Eretz Yisrael* until she is secure; to see Christians and Jews standing together to gain a better understanding of each other; to establish a strong and secure Bible Land; and to benevolently meet the needs of those whom Jesus describes in Matthew, chapter 25:

> "For I was hungry and you gave Me food; I was thirsty and you gave Me drink; I was a stranger and you took Me in; I was naked and you clothed Me; I was sick and you visited Me; I was in prison and you came to Me....
>
> "And the King will answer and say to them, 'Assuredly, I say to you, inasmuch as you did it to one of the least of these My brethren, you did it to Me.'" (Matthew 25:35–36, 40 NKJV)

Perhaps the most important edict for Christians is to "pray for the peace of Jerusalem" (Psalm 122:6). God calls the land of Israel "My land" (Ezekiel 38:16) and gave it to Israel by a blood covenant that is irrevocable. As we have seen, Christians are called to bless Israel. The chief way we can do that is through prayer. Nothing is more important than prayer, for God will do nothing without it. The fuel that moves the heart of God is prayer. God has a purpose and a plan for our nation and the nation of Israel, but it is dependent on our prayers. His will and His blessings are bound up in what we declare on this earth. His purposes and plans are more important than anything we can do. Abraham was a striking example of the power of prayer. Wherever Abraham pitched his tent and camped for a season with his household, he erected an altar of sacrifice and prayer. God heard Abraham's prayers, and He hears ours as we pray for the peace of Jerusalem.

Another focus is the dire threat Iran poses to Israel and the entire world, as its leaders strive to secure nuclear weapons. Evangelical Christian organizations are closing ranks to stand behind the nation of Israel during this time of danger. As I wrote in *Cursed*:

> Although no people group has been targeted more than the Jewish people, God has not allowed them to be exterminated. Many horrific attempts have been made to annihilate them, but such attempts have ended in utter failure, defeat, and humiliation for the perpetrators. From Pharaoh to Haman to Hitler, their efforts to destroy the Jewish people have ended ignominiously. Haman was hanged on the very gallows he had built for Queen Esther's uncle, Mordecai (Esther 7:10). Pharaoh "commanded all his people, saying, 'Every son who is

born you shall cast into the river, and every daughter you shall save alive'" (Exodus 1:22 NKJV). This ruler, who ordered every Hebrew male child to be thrown into the river, was drowned with his own army in the Red Sea!

In 2012, I traveled to Jerusalem to seek a location for a Christian Zionism Museum. Through the museum, the accounts of Christians who played crucial roles in helping to promote, defend, support, and establish the modern State of Israel would be told, as well as the stories of those men and women who fulfilled the moral duty to rescue Jewish people from the Holocaust. I believed the museum should offer interactive displays, areas for research, and also provide a bond between those Christians who have aided Israel through the years. My vision was to have a place where their achievements could be shared with thousands of visitors yearly.

The Friends of Zion Heritage Center is now a reality and stands in the heart of Jerusalem at 20 Yosef Rivlin Street in a prominent location overlooking Independence Park and within walking distance to the Old City. It is one more building block in the plan and purpose God has surely had for my life. The Friends of Zion Heritage Center (FOZ), a $100 million project in Jerusalem gained ten million members in its first year of operation. FOZ, just 600 meters from the Temple Mount, is ground zero for the global Jerusalem Prayer Team prayer movement. With over one billion Christian Zionists worldwide, the goal is to unite them to stand with Israel and the Jewish people. FOZ now has a vast social network platform to mobilize Israel's greatest friends. The organization already has more than one million members in Indonesia alone, and is presently growing by a staggering two million members monthly. A massive communication hub will be linked to the thousands of Christian television and radio outlets, as well as to churches and universities globally.

For decades, sympathetic Gentiles from around the world have joined Jewish people in the trenches. With each succeeding battle for existence, new Bible-believing Christians have sprung up to stand with the children of Israel in their struggle to survive. These are the men and women who are spotlighted in the new Museum of Christian Zionism in Jerusalem—those who have staunchly supported the Jewish people before, during, and after the formation of the State of Israel.

Today my heart is overflowing with gratitude to God as the dream He placed in my spirit more than thirty years ago has become a reality. When the contract for the purchase of the building that houses the Friends of Zion Heritage was signed, I was reminded once again that every promise from God is certain and sure, no matter how long we have to wait for it.

Abraham waited for the promised birth of Isaac for some twenty-five years, but in God's perfect timing, the son of promise was born. When I first met with Prime Minister Menachem Begin more than thirty years ago and we agreed to work together to build a bridge between Christians and Jews, part of that dream was to have a permanent presence in the Holy City. Now we proudly point to this beautiful facility that ministers to the Jewish people and to Christians worldwide.

There is a God-given, biblical—and intimate—connection between Christians and Jews. Based on love and truth, and surrounded by prayer, it can never be broken. The Jewish Messiah and our Lord and Savior sprang from the root of Jesse and will occupy the throne of King David in Jerusalem, Mount Zion, when He returns.

ENDNOTES

1. "The Temple Mount in Jerusalem," Midrash Tanchuma is the name given to three different collections of Pentateuch aggadot; two are extant, while the third is known only through citations. http://templemount.org/; accessed March 2013.

2. Teddy Kollek and Moshe Pearlman, *Jerusalem, Sacred City of Mankind* (Israel: Steimatzky Group, 1987).

3. Daniel 4.

4. Jewish Encylopedia—The Babylonian Captivity, http://www.bible-history.com/map_babylonian_captivity/map_of_the_deportation_of_judah_jewish_encyclopedia.html; accessed February 2013.

5. Alan Redpath, *Victorious Christian Service* (Westwood, New Jersey: Fleming H. Revell Co., 1963), 44–45.

6. Jewish antiquities 11.317–345, as related in "Alexander the Great visits Jerusalem," http://www.livius.org/aj-al/alexander/alexander_t35.html; accessed February 2013.

7. Al Maxey, "The Silent Centuries—The Maccabean Revolt (168–135 BC)," http://www.zianet.com/maxey/Inter3.htm; accessed February 2013.

8. Stewart Henry Perowne, "Herod: King of Judaea," *Encyclopædia Britannica*: Facts Matter, http://www.britannica.com/EBchecked/topic/263437/Herod; accessed February 2013.

9. Ehud Netzer, *The Palaces of the Hasmoneans and Herod the Great.* Jerusalem: Yed Ben-Zvi Press and The Israel Exploration Society, 2001; as quoted on http://en.wikipedia.org/wiki/Masada#cite_ref-Ehud_16-0; accessed February 2013.

10. David van Biema, "Jerusalem at the Time of Jesus," *Time Magazine*, April 16, 2001, http://www.time.com/time/magazine/article/0,9171,999673,00.html#ixzz2KtEHejoP; accessed February 2013.

11. "The Roman Scourge," http://www.bible-history.com/past/flagrum.html; accessed February 2013.

12. Darlene Zschech, "Worthy is the Lamb," http://www.lyricsmode.com/lyrics/d/darlene_zschech/worthy_is_the_lamb.html; accessed February 2013.

13. Isaiah 53:3 KJV.

14. Kur'an, Sura 17:1, https://en.wikisource.org/wiki/The_Holy_Qur%27an_(Maulana_Muhammad_Ali)/17._The_Israelites, accessed January 2017.

15. Isra and Mi'raj, http://en.wikipedia.org/wiki/Isra_and_Mi%27raj; accessed January 2016.

16. "The Arabic Islamic Inscriptions On The Dome Of The Rock In Jerusalem, 72 AH/692 CE," http://www.islamic-awareness.org/History/Islam/Inscriptions/DoTR.html; accessed March 2013.

17. "Version of Raymond d'Aguiliers" from the work of C. Krey August, *The First Crusade: The Accounts of Eyewitnesses and Participants*, (Princeton: 1921), 250–56, http://www.bu.edu/mzank/Jerusalem/tx/Raymondsiege.htm; accessed January 2013.

18. Simon Sebag Montefiore, *Jerusalem* (New York, NY: Alfred A. Knoff, Borzoi Books, 2011), 222.

19. "Godfrey of Bouillon," http://en.wikipedia.org/wiki/Godfrey_de_Bouillon; accessed December 2016.

20. "Ayyubid dynasty," http://en.wikipedia.org/wiki/Ayyubid_dynasty; accessed October 2016.

21. Kerry McQueeney, "Was Columbus secretly Jewish? Historians argue explorer's epic voyage was to establish new homeland for his people as they escaped the Spanish Inquisition," *Daily Mail*, May 21, 2012, http://www.dailymail.co.uk/news/article-2147558/Christopher-Columbus-Jewish-looking-new-homeland-discovered-America-historians-say.html#ixzz2JalM7Oa8; accessed June 2017.

22. Raja Shehadeh, *Palestinian Walks: Forays into a Vanishing Landscape* (New York: Scribner, 2007), 46.

23. Alexander Scholch, "Britain in Palestine, 1838–1882: The Roots of the Balfour Policy," *Journal of Palestine Studies*, Vol. 22, No. 1, Autumn 1992, (Berkley: University of California Press, 1992), 47; accessed July 2011.

24. Aristotle, "Meteorology (1.15)," eBooks.adelaide.edu.au, 25 August 2010; accessed April 2017.

25. Nir Hassan, "Jerusalem's Iconic Windmill to Resume Its Daily Grind," *Haaretz*, July 26, 2012, http://www.haaretz.com/news/national/jerusalem-s-iconic-windmill-to-resume-its-daily-grind-1.453655; accessed May 2016.

26. "PM Netanyahu Dedicates Restored Windmill in Mishkenot Sha'ananim," August 28, 2012, http://www.pmo.gov.il/English/MediaCenter/Events/Pages/eventtachana280812.aspx; accessed August 2016.

27. Mark Twain, a.k.a. Samuel L. Clemens, *The Innocents Abroad*, http://classiclit.about.com/library/bl-etexts/mtwain/bl-mtwain-innocents-56.htm; accessed February 2017.

28. *The Cosmopolitan*, Volume 26, Schlict and Field 1900, 376. http://books.google.com/books?id=56nNAAAAMAAJ&pg=PA376&lpg=PA376&dq=From+Jerusalem+a+light+has+arisen+upon+the+world+%E2%80%93+the+blessed+light+in+whose+splendor+our+German+people+have+become+great+and+glorious.&source=bl&ots=a9Q-Wo4nxL&sig=B3wxdZCd_b1Sr_aWCXeVFCgN7pU&hl=en&ei=U5UbTJujHaPknQfq6fi0Cw&sa=X&oi=book_result&ct=result&resnum=4&ved=0CBsQ6AEwAw#; accessed June 2017.

29. http://www.pef.org.uk/Pages/WildZin.htm; accessed June 2017.

30. "Sykes–Picot Agreement," http://en.wikipedia.org/wiki/Sykes-Picot_Agreement; accessed June 2017.

31. M. E. Yapp, *The Making of the Modern Near East 1792–1923* (Harlow, England: Longman, 1987), 290.

32. "Anti-Semitism: Montagu Memo on the Anti-Semitism of the British Government (August 23, 1917)," *Jewish Virtual Library*, http://www.jewishvirtuallibrary.org/jsource/History/Montagumemo.html; accessed June 2017.

33. Ben Halpern, *A Clash of Heroes: Brandeis, Weizmann, and American Zionism* (New York: Oxford University Press, 1987), 169.

34. Balfour Declaration, https://en.wikipedia.org/wiki/Balfour_Declaration; accessed June 2017.

35. "Bible Prophecy," *Christian Assemblies International*; http://www.cai.org/bible-studies/bible-prophecy-0; accessed May 2017.

36. Colonel C. G. Powles, "The History of the Canterbury Mounted Rifles 1914–1919," New Zealand Electronic Text Collection, http://www.nzetc.org/tm/scholarly/tei-WH1CMRi-t1-body-d14.html; accessed June 2017.

37. "Chaim Weizmann of Israel Is Dead," Obituary, *The New York Times*, November 9, 1952; www.nytimes.com/learning/general/onthisday/bday/1127.html; accessed August 2011.

38. Lawrence Davidson, *America's Palestine: Popular and Official Perceptions from Balfour to Israeli Statehood* (Gainesville, FL: University Press of Florida, 2001), 14.

39. Central Zionist Archives, J1/8783, Minutes of the Eighth Assembly of the Temporary Committee of Palestine Jewry, Jaffa, October 22, 1919; 15, 24.

40. Melvin I. Urofsky, *A Voice That Spoke for Justice: The Life and Times of Stephen S. Wise* (Albany, NY: SUNY Press, 1982), 147.

41. "Balfour Declaration: Test of the Declaration," http://www.jewishvirtuallibrary.org/text-of-the-balfour-declaration; accessed February 2017.

42. Shmuel Katz, *The Aaronsohn Saga* (Jerusalem: Gefen Publishing House, 2007), 194.

43. Michael J. Pragai, *Faith and Fulfillment*, (Edgeware, GB: Vallentine Mitchell, 1985), 80.

44. "John Henry Patterson," *Zionism and Israel—Biographies*; http://www.zionism-israel.com/bio/John_Henry_Patterson_biography.htm; accessed January 2017.

45. Ibid.

46. J. H. Patterson, *With the Judeans in the Palestine Campaign* (London: Hutchinson and Co., 1922), 18.

47. Ibid., 155.

48. Michael Makovsky, *Churchill's Promised Land: Zionism and Statecraft* (Yale University, 2007), 93.

49. Chuck Morse, *Jewish Magazine*, "The Nazi connection to Islamic Terrorism"; http://www.jewishmag.com/116mag/chuckmorse/chuckmorse.htm; accessed June 2010.

50. Nabi Musa was a pilgrimage holiday that flooded Jerusalem with Muslims. It had been instituted by Salah a Din to counter the large number of Christian pilgrims who swelled the city at Easter. http://www.zionism-israel.com/dic/Nebi_musa.htm.

51. Paul Johnson, *Paul Johnson Quotes—Modern Times (The World From the Twenties to the Nineties)*, Chapter 3, "Waiting for Hitler," http://homepage.eircom.net/~odyssey/Politics/Quotes/Modern_Times.html; accessed February 2017.

52. http://thinkexist.com/quotes/with/keyword/names/2.html; accessed April 2017.

53. William Shirer, *The Rise and Fall of the Third Reich* (New York: Simon Schuster, 1960), 10–11.

54. "Lloyd George and Hitler. . . Comments on His Visit to Germany and Meeting With Hitler in 1936," *Daily Express*, September 17, 1936; http://www.worldfuturefund.org/wffmaster/Reading/Germany/LloydGeorge.htm; accessed August 2016.

55. John Toland, *Adolf Hitler: The Definitive Biography* (London: Book Club Associates, 1977), 116.

56. Robert S. Wistrich, *Who's Who in Nazi Germany* (Hove, East Sussex, UK: Psychology Press, 2002), 118.

57. Houston-Stewart Chamberlain, *Letters* (1882–1924 and correspondence with Emperor Wilhelm II) (Munich: F. Bruckmann, 1928), 124. (Translated from the German by Alexander Jacob.)

58. "Adolf Hitler," *Deutsche Presse*, April 20–21, 1944, 1.

59. Deborah E. Lipstadt, *Beyond Belief: The American Press and the Coming of the Holocaust 1933–1945* (New York: Simon and Schuster, 1993), 79–80.

60. "Peel Commission," https://en.wikipedia.org/wiki/Peel_Commission; accessed May 2017.

61. "Wannsee Conference," *Jewish Virtual Library*, http://www.jewishvirtuallibrary.org/the-wannsee-conference; accessed March 2017.

62. Laurel Leff, "How the NYT Missed the Story of the Holocaust While It Was Happening," *History News Network*, April 4, 2005; http://hnn.us/articles/10903.html; accessed March 2017.

63. Walter Laqueur, *A History of Zionism* (London: L.P. Tauris & Co. Ltd, 2003), 557.

64. "Menachem Begin Administration: Speech to Knesset Following Historic Speech by Anwar Sadat," http://www.jewishvirtuallibrary.org/jsource/History/begintoknessetsadat.html; accessed May 2017.

65. "President Harry S. Truman and US Support for Israeli Statehood," *MidEast Web*, http://www.mideastweb.org/us_supportforstate.htm; accessed June 2017.

66. Ibid.

67. Larry Collins and Dominique Lapierre, *O Jerusalem!* (New York: Simon and Shuster, 1972), 411.

68. Ibid.

69. Yehuda Avner, *The Prime Ministers: An Intimate Narrative of Israeli Leadership* (New Milford, CT: The Toby Press, LLC, 2010), 121

70. Frank Adler, *Roots in a Moving Stream* (Overland Park, KS: The Temple, Congregation B'nai Jehudah, 1972), 198.

71. James McDonald to B'nai B'rith's Frank Goldman, March 3, 1950, cited in Adler, *Roots in a Moving Stream*, 224.

72. Michael T. Benson, *Harry S. Truman and the Founding of Israel* (Westport, CT: Greenwood Publishing Group, 1997), 20.

73. David McCullough, *Truman*, (New York, NY: Touchstone, 1992), 336–337.

74. Paul C. Merkley, *The Politics of Christian Zionism, 1891–1948* (London: Frank Cass Publishers, 1998), 167.

75. Walter Isaacson and Evan Thomas, *The Wise Men: Six Friends and the World They Made* (New York: Simon & Schuster, 1986), 452; quoted in A. F. K. Organski, *The $36 Billion Bargain: Strategy and Politics in U.S. Assistance to Israel* (New York: Columbia University Press, 1990), 26.

76. Michael Beschloss, *The Conquerors: Roosevelt, Truman and the Destruction of Hitler's Germany, 1941–1945* (New York: Simon & Schuster, 2002), 24

77. Paul Johnson, *Modern Times* (New York, NY: HarperCollins Publishers, Inc., 1983), 485.

78. "Law of Return," *Jewish Virtual Library*, http://www.jewishvirtuallibrary.org/jsource/ Immigration/Text_of_Law_of_Return.html; accessed February 2017.

79. "Ethiopia Virtual Jewish Tour," *Jewish Virtual Library,* http://www.jewishvirtuallibrary.org/ jsource/Judaism/ejhist.html; accessed February 2013.

80. "Immigration to Israel: Introduction and Overview," *Jewish Virtual Library,* http://www. jewishvirtuallibrary.org/jsource/Immigration/immigration.html; accessed January 2017.

81. "Jerusalem," http://en.wikipedia.org/wiki/Jerusalem; accessed March 2013.

82. Montefiore, *Jerusalem*, 481–482.

83. Personal Interview with Mordechai Gur, 1995.

84. Ibid.

85. Personal interview with Chief Rabbi Shlomo Goren, 1995.

86. Ibid.

87. Teddy Kollek, *Foreign Affairs*, Vol. 55, No. 4 (Council on Foreign Relations: July 1977), 701.

88. *U.S. News and World Report*, November 7, 1994, 7.

89. Abraham Rabinovich, *The Yom Kippur War* (New York: Schocken Books, 2004), 21.

90. "The 1970 Palestinian Hijackings of Three Jets to Jordan: Jets Are Blown Up in the Jordanian Desert," *ThoughtCo.*, http://middleeast.about.com/od/terrorism/a/dawson-field-hijackings.htm; accessed January 2017.

91. "Jordan asked Nixon to attack Syria, declassified papers show," November 28, 2007. http://www.cnn.com/2007/POLITICS/11/28/nixon.papers/; accessed May 2017.

92. Ibid.

93. Ibid.

94. Simon Dunstan and Kevin Lyles, *The Yom Kippur War 1973: The Sinai* (Westminster, MD: Random House, 2003), 17.

95. Seymour M. Hersh, *The Samson Option: Israel's Nuclear Arsenal and American Foreign Policy* (New York: Vintage Books, 1991), 223.

96. Seymour M. Hersh, *The Price of Power: Kissinger in the Nixon White House* (New York: Summit Books, 1983), 234.

97. Tamar Sternthal, *"International Herald Tribune* Op-Ed Erases 20-Plus Years of Terror," http://www.camera.org/index.asp?x_context=2&x_outlet=139&x_article=751; accessed February 2017.

98. "SPIEGEL Interview with Author David Grossman: 'Foreigners Cannot Understand the Israelis' Vulnerability,'" August 10, 2009, http://www.spiegel.de/international/world/spiegel-interview-with-author-david-grossman-foreigners-cannot-understand-the-israelis-vulnerability-a-641437.html; accessed January 2017.

99. Douglas Brinkley, *The Unfinished Presidency: Jimmy Carter's Journey Beyond the White House* (New York: Viking, 1998), 324.

100. Cited by William F. Jasper in "PLO: Protected Lethal Organization; Despite their terrorist track record, Yasser Arafat the PLO are not only protected from punishment, but are warmly welcomed at the UN," February 11, 2002; https://www.thefreelibrary.com/PLO%3a+Protected+Lethal+Organization%3b+Despite+their+terrorist+track...-a082777454; accessed June 2017.

101. Daniel Pipes, "The Muslim Claim to Jerusalem," *Middle East Forum*, September 2001, http://www.danielpipes.org/84/the-muslim-claim-to-jerusalem; accessed April 2017.

102. "Who Owns Jerusalem? A Biblical Perspective," http://ldolphin.org/psalm2.html; accessed January 2017.

103. Ibid.

104. Ibid. (Jews consider the name of God to be so holy that they refuse to write the entire word, using only G-d.)

105. Ibid.

106. Rabbi Chaim Richman, "Does Anybody Out There Care About The Holy Temple," July 4, 1999, http://www.lttn.org/99-07-14-email.html; accessed March 2017.

107. "Ketoret," http://www.begedivri.com/ketoret.htm; accessed February 2017.

108. Dr. Asher Selig Kaufman, Biblical Archaeological Review, March/April 1983; *Tractate Middot*, Har Yearieh Press, Jerusalem, 1991, http://templemount.org/theories.html#anchor408725; accessed March 2017.

109. Tuvia Sagiv, "Where is the Temple?" http://www.templemount.org/sagiv00.html; accessed March 2017.

110. Bernard J. Shapiro, "Will There Ever Be True Peace Between Israel And The Arab States?" A lecture as part of the Torah Learning College, Congregation Beth Yeshurun, Houston, June 23, 1993. Shapiro is the executive director of the Freeman Center For Strategic Studies and editor of, *THE MACCABEAN ONLINE*. http://www.freeman.org/MOL/pages/oct-nov-2005/will-there-ever-be-true-peace0D0Awill-there-ever-be-true-peace-between-israel-and-the-arab-states.php; accessed March 2017.

111. Richard Miniter, *Losing bin Laden: How Bill Clinton's Failures Unleashed Global Terror* (Washington, DC: Regnery Publishing, Inc., 2003), xvi, xix. (Insert added.)

112. "White House Report, Friday, August 11, 2000 (Clinton on life, career, decisions)," http://wfile.ait.org.tw/wf-archive/2000/000811/epf501.htm; accessed November 2016.

113. Alan Dershowitz, *What Israel Means to Me* (Hoboken, New Jersey: John Wiley & Sons, Inc., 2006), 53.

114. Jeff Emanuel, "Israel, Palestine, and Obama: Is the President Already Walking Back his Demands on Israel?" May 23, 2011, http://www.redstate.com/jeff_emanuel/2011/05/20/israel-palestine-and-obama-is-the-president-already-walking-back-his-demands-on-israel/; accessed August 2017.

115. "George W. Bush, Economic Update: Address in Virginia, Fredericksburg, Virginia, December 17, 2007," http://www.presidentialrhetoric.com/speeches/12.17.07.html; accessed December 2016.

116. Murray Kahl, "Preface to Document," US House of Representatives: Task Force on Terrorism, December 10, 1996, http://www.eretzyisroel.org/~jkatz/taskforce.html; accessed March 2017.

117. Nuclear Files.org, http://nuclearfiles.org/menu/key-issues/nuclear-weapons/basics/nuclear-stockpiles.htm accessed March 2017.

118. "How Israel Gained Eyes for Its Nuclear Weapons," http://articles.latimes.com/1991-11-10/opinion/op-2198_1_nuclear-weapons; accessed August 2017.

119. Norman Bentwich, *Hellenism* (Philadelphia: The Jewish Publication Society of America, 1919), 11.

120. E. R. Bevan, *Jerusalem Under the Hig- Priests* (London: Edward Arnold, 1904), 41.

121. Personal interview with Menachem Begin, 1995.

122. Philologos Bible Prophecy Research, "Armageddon," Submitted by: research-bpn@philologos.org. November 20, 1998. Undated: April 6, 2001. philologos.org/bpr/files/a005.htm; accessed April 2010.

123. Mike Evans, *Save Jerusalem* (Euless, TX: Bedford Books, 1995), 270.

124. Aleksandr I. Solzhenitsyn, "A World Split Apart—Commencement Address Delivered At Harvard University, June 8, 1978," http://www.orthodoxytoday.org/articles/SolzhenitsynHarvard.php; accessed April 2017.

125. H. A. Ironside, *Daniel: An Ironside Expository Commentary* (Grand Rapids, MI: Kregel Publications, Reprint 2005), 9.

126. "Jerusalem Law," http://en.wikipedia.org/wiki/Jerusalem_Law; accessed December 2016.

127. For example, see Tom Brokaw's book, *The Greatest Generation*.

128. http://www.bu.edu/mzank/Jerusalem/tx/pactofumar.htm; accessed April 2017.

129. Mona Eltahawy, "Egypt's Cruelty to Christians," *New York Times*, December 2016, https://www.nytimes.com/2016/12/22/opinion/egypts-cruelty-to-christians.html?action=click&contentCollection=Middle%20East&module=RelatedCoverage&region=EndOfArticle&pgtype=article; accessed March 2017.

130. Originally published in New York *Tribune*, 15 April 1854, http://www.marxists.org/archive/marx/works/subject/russia/crimean-war.htm; accessed March 2017.

131. Jordanian Nationality Law, *Official Gazette* No. 1171, Article 3 of Law No. 6 (February 1954), 105.

132. Richard Cohen, "Where Bigotry Gets a Hearing," *Washington Post*, A21. October 30, 2001; https://www.washingtonpost.com/archive/opinions/2001/10/30/where-bigotry-gets-a-hearing/86a93f4e-10c9-4ec8-a897-1f5881e819ee/?utm_term=.f178ee8e48e6 archives; accessed May 2017.

133. Elie Kedourie, *Islam in the Modern World* (London: Mansell, 1980), 69–72.

134. Suleiman Al-Khash in *Al-Thaura*, the Ba'ath party newspaper, May 3, 1968.

135. David K. Shipler, *Arab and Jew: Wounded Spirits in a Promised Land* (NY: Times Books, 1986), 167–170.

136. Mike Evans, *Save Jerusalem,* 274–275.

137. *Times of Israel* staff, "US backs European move to distinguish Israel from West Bank," http://www.timesofisrael.com/us-backs-european-move-to-distinguish-israel-from-west-bank/; accessed May 2017.

138. Jennifer Rubin, "Why it's correct to label the Obama administration 'anti-Israel,'" *Washington Post,* https://www.washingtonpost.com/blogs/right-turn/wp/2016/01/20/why-its-correct-to-label-the-obama-administration-anti-israel/?utm_term=.4e697f34f572; accessed March 2017.

139. Ron Kampeas, "Where the Obama–Netanyahu relationship went wrong," *The Times of Israel,* http://www.timesofisrael.com/where-the-obama-netanyahu-relationship-went-wrong/; accessed May 2017.

140. Paul C. Merkley, *The Politics of Christian Zionism 1891–1948*, 191.

141. Kelley Beaucar Vlahos, "Trump and Israel," *The American Conservative,* January 18, 2017, http://www.theamericanconservative.com/articles/trump-and-israel/; accessed April 2017.

142. Jerusalem Prayer Team Petition to President George W. Bush, JPT archives, used by permission.

BOOKS BY: MIKE EVANS

Israel: America's Key to Survival

Save Jerusalem

The Return

Jerusalem D.C.

Purity and Peace of Mind

Who Cries for the Hurting?

Living Fear Free

I Shall Not Want

Let My People Go

Jerusalem Betrayed

Seven Years of Shaking: A Vision

The Nuclear Bomb of Islam

Jerusalem Prophecies

Pray For Peace of Jerusalem

America's War:
  The Beginning of the End

The Jerusalem Scroll

The Prayer of David

The Unanswered Prayers of Jesus

God Wrestling

The American Prophecies

Beyond Iraq: The Next Move

The Final Move beyond Iraq

Showdown with Nuclear Iran

Jimmy Carter: The Liberal Left
  and World Chaos

Atomic Iran

Cursed

Betrayed

The Light

Corrie's Reflections & Meditations

The Revolution

The Final Generation

Seven Days

The Locket

Persia: The Final Jihad

GAMECHANGER SERIES:

  GameChanger

  Samson Option

  The Four Horsemen

THE PROTOCOLS SERIES:

  The Protocols

  The Candidate

Jerusalem

The History of Christian Zionism

Countdown

Ten Boom: Betsie, Promise of God

Commanded Blessing

Born Again: 1948

Born Again: 1967

Presidents in Prophecy

Stand with Israel

Prayer, Power and Purpose

Turning Your Pain Into Gain

Christopher Columbus, Secret Jew

Living in the F.O.G.

Finding Favor with God

Finding Favor with Man

Unleashing God's Favor

The Jewish State: The Volunteers

See You in New York

Friends of Zion:
  Patterson & Wingate

The Columbus Code

The Temple

Satan, You Can't Have
  My Country!

Satan, You Can't Have Israel!

Lights in the Darkness

The Seven Feasts of Israel

Netanyahu

Jew-Hatred and the Church

The Visionaries

Why Was I Born?

Son, I Love You

Jerusalem DC (David's Capital)

COMING SOON:

Israel Reborn

TO PURCHASE, CONTACT: orders@timeworthybooks.com
P. O. BOX 30000, PHOENIX, AZ 85046

MICHAEL DAVID EVANS, the #1 *New York Times* bestselling author, is an award-winning journalist/Middle East analyst. Dr. Evans has appeared on hundreds of network television and radio shows including *Good Morning America, Crossfire* and *Nightline*, and *The Rush Limbaugh Show*, and on Fox Network, *CNN World News*, NBC, ABC, and CBS. His articles have been published in the *Wall Street Journal, USA Today, Washington Times, Jerusalem Post* and newspapers worldwide. More than twenty-five million copies of his books are in print, and he is the award-winning producer of nine documentaries based on his books.

Dr. Evans is considered one of the world's leading experts on Israel and the Middle East, and is one of the most sought-after speakers on that subject. He is the chairman of the board of the ten Boom Holocaust Museum in Haarlem, Holland, and is the founder of Israel's first Christian museum located in the Friends of Zion Heritage Center in Jerusalem.

Dr. Evans has authored a number of books including: *History of Christian Zionism, Showdown with Nuclear Iran, Atomic Iran, The Next Move Beyond Iraq, The Final Move Beyond Iraq*, and *Countdown*. His body of work also includes the novels *Seven Days, GameChanger, The Samson Option, The Four Horsemen, The Locket, Born Again: 1967*, and *The Columbus Code*.

✦ ✦ ✦

Michael David Evans is available to speak or for interviews.
Contact: EVENTS@drmichaeldevans.com.